W9-BIW-364

BILLBOARD'S COMPLETE BOOK OF

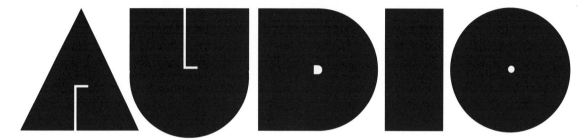

BILLBOARD'S COMPLETE BOOK OF

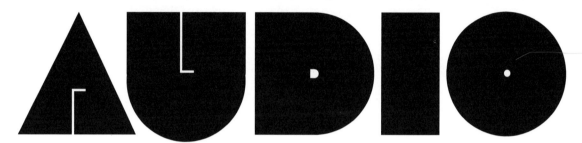

DAVID DRUCKER

BillboardBooks
AN IMPRINT OF WATSON-GUPTILL PUBLICATIONS
NEW YORK

First published 1991 by Billboard Books, an imprint of Watson-Guptill Publications, a division of BPI Communications, Inc. 1515 Broadway, New York, NY 10036.

Technical art: Vantage Art
Cover design: Jay Anning
Book design and composition: Circa 86

Library of Congress Cataloging-in-Publication Data

Drucker, David.
    Billboard's complete book of audio / David Drucker.
        p. cm.
    Includes index.
    ISBN 0-8230-7554-0 (pbk.)
    1. Stereophonic sound systems. I. Title. II. Title: Complete book of audio.
TK7881.8.D78 1991
621.389'33—dc20   90-28913
                                                                            CIP

Manufactured in the United States of America
First Printing, 1991

1 2 3 4 5 6 7 8 9 / 96 95 94 93 92 91

ACKNOWLEDGMENTS

Thanks are owed to Ed Brown who, many years ago, responded to a letter-to-the-editor with the challenge, "Let's see you do better," and gave me my first shot at writing about hi-fi. Somewhat later — and in an indirect sort of way — he taught me the value of leaving bridges unburned.

Another debt is owed to Edward Schneider. I am always inspired (and often disheartened to the point of looking for honest work) by the quality of his writing.

And finally, of course, there's the good old Grateful Dead.

TABLE OF CONTENTS

	Introduction	1
1	The Elements of High-Fidelity Sound	3
2	Tape Decks	11
3	Record Players	31
4	Compact Disc (CD) Players	45
5	Tuners	51
6	Amplifiers	61
7	Speakers	75
8	Signal Processors	126
9	The Purchasing Strategy	138
10	Setting Up the System	145
11	Troubleshooting	151
	Glossary	162
	Recommended Recordings	184
	List of Manufacturers	195
	Index	199

INTRODUCTION

The primary purpose of this book is to provide the understanding you need to buy the best possible high-fidelity audio system for a given amount of money. Its approach is based on the assumption that acquiring some ground-level technical knowledge of sound reproduction will help you make wise purchasing decisions and get the most out of a system. Toward that end, much of the book focuses on the ways individual components work.

Initial chapters explain the workings of sound sources, that is, tape decks, record players, CD players, and tuners. These are followed by a chapter on amplifiers — the component that translates the signal of the sound source into a signal that is usable by speakers, and that ultimately becomes music to your ears.

Among the topics discussed in these sections are specifications: those numbers, formulas, and bits of technical data that describe the performance of a given component. We can make a sweeping statement about most specifications: With certain exceptions (and when they come up we point them out) you shouldn't rely entirely on specs when deciding whether to purchase a particular component. Once an acceptable level of performance is achieved, improvements implied by slightly better specifications usually have little or no effect on perceived sound quality. If, for example, you decide to add $100 to your amplifier budget, it's far more sensible to choose one with more power rather than one whose distortion spec has an extra zero to the right of the decimal point.

Because speakers have the greatest impact on the overall sound you hear, the greatest amount of space is devoted to them. In addition to covering the acoustic aspects of the speakers themselves, this section touches on practical matters like placement (which, even if you have an ideal listening room, should strongly influence what speakers to buy).

Technically inclined readers will find material explaining how different types of speakers work. While knowledge in this area is not essential to the purchasing process, it can certainly add some depth to your involvement in quality audio, and will help to short-circuit the verbal razzle-dazzle used by some salespeople to establish control on the showroom floor.

After you have delved into the technology, you'll find sections on purchasing a system, with advice on budgeting for various components and the pros and cons of different types of vendor.

Once you've chosen and purchased your system, the fun begins: setting it up and listening to it. The latter is strictly your business, but you will find a section dealing with setup beginning on page 146. And if, over the course of time, problems develop, you'll want to give some attention to the troubleshooting section on page 151.

Over the course of your research you will probably encounter hi-fi extremists who make recommendations that appear to contradict good sense. Sometimes these experts have a great deal to offer; sometimes they don't. We will show you where they are right and where their recommendations might lead you astray.

As is true of every technical subject, hi-fi has its own vocabulary. That being the case, it's likely that in the course of your reading you'll come across unfamiliar words. Most, if not all, of these words are defined in the Glossary, which begins on page 162. If you're unfamiliar with the technical nomenclature of audio components, prepare yourself by skimming this section first. In any event, it's there whenever you need it.

1 THE ELEMENTS OF HIGH-FIDELITY SOUND

This is a book about high-fidelity audio, and how you can attain the best sound quality in your listening room.

Audio equipment is better now than ever. A given amount of money will buy far better performance than it would have a few years ago, and, conversely, equipment with a given level of performance can be had for far less money than it would have cost the same few years ago.

Beyond that, today's high-fidelity components can do things that were simply out of the question before the advent of the computer chips that now populate their innards. The digital compact disc (CD), which has both revolutionized and revitalized the audio industry, calls for a level of computing power that in the 1950s would have been unthinkable outside of, say, U.S. Defense Department facilities. The same holds true for the microprocessors that allow the user to simulate the acoustics of a large concert hall or nightclub within his own listening room. The net result can be amazingly life-like sound. A listener with well-chosen audio equipment and a clear-ly recorded and well-manufactured disc or cassette may have the eerie sense that the recording artists are performing live in the home listening room.

But despite — or, perhaps, because of — the wonderful things today's audio components can do, it's important at the outset to get something straight about listening to recorded music on a home hi-fi system: It will never, ever be able to *completely* re-create the expe-rience of being at a live performance. In most instances the total experience includes far more than the music itself. On a purely audi-tory level the acoustics of the room, be it a small club or vast arena, might be well simulated by a home hi-fi system, but even the best equipment can't re-create the live environment. Pants-flapping bass, that combination of low frequency and volume that is felt as much as heard, is largely beyond the capabilities of most conventional home systems, as (perhaps to the good) is the ability to provide the peak levels that, at some rock concerts, set your ears to ringing and turn your bones to Jell-O.

Beyond the sonic considerations are those that make hearing live music an event. Under ideal circumstances there's a synergy between audience and performer that allows you, the listener, to become in some small way a part of the performance itself. Face it: no aggregation of transistors is going to replace live music at the experience level.

But then, listening to live music and listening to music on a home stereo are two distinctly different experiences, each with its own pleasures. On a purely sonic level there can be some significant advantages to listening at home. Assuming one has a well-produced recording, it's conceivable that the sound at home will be even *better* than you'll hear at a live performance. Depending upon the venue and your seating location therein, live music can be pretty disappointing. The quality of the PA system, the skill of the soundboard operator, and the vagaries of room all affect the sound. At a rock concert, for instance, it's not unusual for the voices to be completely overpowered by the instruments, which themselves can be both distorted and out-of-balance. And how many times have you found yourself seated way off to the side at a live concert, listening to a heavy dose of drums and bass, while instruments on the far side of the stage are all but inaudible? Even if the music is *unamplified*, as at most classical concerts, instrumental balances will vary in different parts of the room. At home you have a much better shot at hearing a balanced performance since you have the ability to control the delivery of the reproduction.

And sonic factors aside, when you listen to music at home you have access to the comforts of home. Face it: trying to reach a snack bar at a stadium concert during intermission is no picnic. And when the music is over and you find yourself exhausted and, depending upon the quality of the concert, anywhere from elated to cranky, you still have to make your way home. But if you're listening to your hi-fi system you're already home, and if you find yourself getting cranky midway through the music, it's a simple matter to change the program to something more in tune with your current mood.

So while there's no denying that attending a live music concert is a different experience than listening to a home hi-fi system, and that certain very worthwhile aspects of the former cannot be duplicated

Assuming one has a well-produced recording, it's conceivable that the sound at home will be even better than you'll hear at a live performance.

by the latter, audio systems have become an accepted — if not *required* — part of the home environment, so much so that the industry sells well over a billion dollars' worth of equipment each year.

The purpose of this book is to allow you to make sure that your share of that billion-plus dollars buys the best equipment for your purposes, and to allow you to get the best use out of it: to get sound that is as close to "live" as possible.

We'll start by having a look at what a reasonable high-fidelity system consists of. But before we examine good audio, let's look at the elements of a live performance. Just what is it that we are trying to reproduce?

WHAT IS SOUND?

To better understand the job of a high-fidelity system and the factors that determine its level of realism or accuracy, let's take a moment to examine the basic physics of sound and sound reproduction. We might begin by defining sound as variations in air pressure, which cause rapid motions of the internal parts of the human ear (where those motions are converted into nerve impulses and sent to the brain, to be "decoded" and ultimately perceived as sounds). These changes in air pressure are cyclical, and consist of brief instants of higher-than-normal pressure followed by brief instants of lower-than-normal pressure. The number of times in a second that these changes occur, called the *frequency* of the sound, determines the pitch of that sound, while the degree of variation in pressure determines its *loudness*.

Ripples in a Pool of Air

To illustrate this concept, let's look at a large drum. When the drummer strikes the drum head he sets it into motion, causing it to vibrate back and forth at the rate of, say, 100 in-and-out motions per second. The motion of the drum head causes variations in the pressure of the air next to the drum, which spread out — at the speed of sound — into the room almost like ripples spreading outward when a stone is dropped into still water. When these pressure variations reach the listener's ear, they vibrate the ear's internal mechanism and pass on to the brain.

The ear, of course, does not know how the air-pressure changes it hears have been caused. It is therefore possible to simulate these variations using a diaphragm of some sort that moves back and forth at the same frequency, and with the same relative loudness, as the original sound-producing surface. Our drum head can thus be mimicked by a loudspeaker cone, the success of the imitation being determined by — for the most part — the quality of the loudspeaker system and its associated equipment. Any imperfection will result in an alteration in the sound and will act as a subtle yet annoying reminder that the sound we are hearing is "canned" — artificially reproduced, and not real.

The objective of high-fidelity audio, of course, is to reduce the impact of these small differences between real sound and reproduced sound to an inconsequential level.

THE ELEMENTS OF A MUSICAL PERFORMANCE

Good audio equipment must clearly reveal the full character of the music which it is reproducing, given a recording that has captured the full range of a musical performance's characteristics.

Good audio equipment must clearly reveal the full character of the music which it is reproducing, given a recording that has captured the full range of a musical performance's characteristics (after all, it is the recording, not the live music, that we are reproducing).

Music itself is made up of several elements. They are *frequency* (pitch), *timbre* (tone color), *dynamics* (loudness and softness), and *ambience*. (Music is also made up of some other elements, such as rhythm and duration, but they aren't altered by a sound system, so we're not going to deal with them here.)

Musical notes sound high or low depending upon their *frequency* of vibration. The faster the frequency, the higher the pitch; the slower the frequency, the lower the pitch. A piccolo will produce notes with very high frequencies. A bass will yield slowly vibrating sound waves: very low notes. Rates of vibration can be expressed in numbers. The musical note called "middle C," for example, stands for a vibration rate of 261.6 Hz. (*Hz* is the abbreviation for *Hertz*, which stands for cycles-per-second.) The E string of an electric bass vibrates at about 42 Hz, while a trumpet's high C is a piercing 1,046.5 Hz. A quality stereo sound system must be able to reproduce the highest and lowest ends of the audio spectrum (figure 1-1).

But these numbers refer only to what is called the *fundamental* vibration. In addition, every instrument has its own series of *overtones* (or harmonics), which are multiples of the fundamental tone. When the string on that electric bass vibrates at 42 Hz, it is also vibrating — to a lesser degree — at 84 Hz, 168 Hz, and so forth. It is the relative distribution of these overtones which gives an instrument its characteristic *timbre*, and which allows the ear to distinguish between, for example, a flute and a clarinet when they are playing

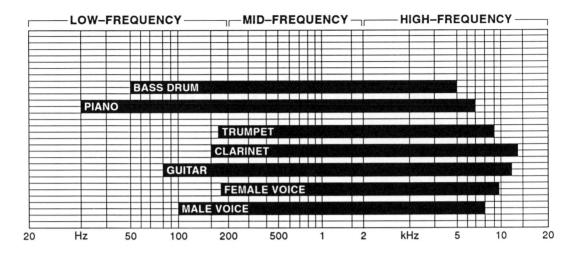

FIGURE 1-1. Music encompasses a ten-octave range of frequencies extending from 20 Hz (cycles per second) to 20,000 Hz (20 kHz). A basic requirement of any high-fidelity system is to reproduce as much of this range as possible.

the same note. These overtones extend in pitch up to, and beyond, the range of human hearing. A quality sound system must be able to faithfully reproduce the distinctive characteristics of different instruments.

The third element of music is dynamics, or loudness. The *dynamic range* of music is the difference between the softest sounds and the loudest. Live music, especially orchestral music, can demonstrate an enormous dynamic range, varying from soft and soothing to powerful and uplifting, and much of the impact of any performance is due to this aspect. It's important to note that the dynamic range of live music is dependent upon several factors, an important one being the background-noise level in the listening room. In order to be heard at all, the softest notes must be louder than such sounds as the rumble of the ventilation system, the rustling of the audience, and the whoosh of traffic on the adjoining street. Your home sound-reproduction system must likewise be able to offer a wide range of loudness/softness levels with a minimum of background noise, or *distortion.*

The final element we're going to look at is *ambience*: the sense of the space in which the music is being heard. If you close your eyes while listening to live music, you will still have a strong sense of the size and character of the room in which you're sitting. If it's large, and the performers are far away, you'll know it because the room sounds that way. By the same token, a room can be bright (if it has hard, reflective surfaces, like a shower stall) or dry (if it tends to absorb sound quickly, like a plush living room). The reproduction of music in your home also involves the simulation of the ambience of a recording.

THE ELEMENTS OF A HIGH-FIDELITY SYSTEM

Sound systems vary in complexity. The simplest type is *monophonic*. This system uses a single loudspeaker, and while it may offer wide dynamics and very accurate frequency response — the reproduction of the highest and lowest ends of the audio spectrum described earlier — it doesn't provide any spatial information. To achieve this sense of depth, we must turn to a second type of system, called *stereophonic*. The literal meaning of the word stereo is solid, three dimensional.

When we listen to live music, the location of the instruments dictates that certain sounds reach one ear sooner than the other. Our brain interprets this difference and provides us with a sense of space: the size of the room, the position of the performers, their distance from us. A stereo sound system presents the same information by using two channels of music, played through two speaker systems. This allows the brain to reasonably recreate the space in which the music was recorded. (The recording engineer, for his part, can simulate the sensation of space on tape, even if the recording was made in a "dead" studio.)

Stereo is not high-fidelity, but high-fidelity is almost always stereo. While stereophonic reproduction plays an important role in allowing a system to provide high-fidelity, it isn't enough. Stereo is a *quantitative* term: it refers to the presence of the hardware needed to provide two separate audio signals. High-fidelity is a *qualitative* term, the implication being that said hardware allows those audio signals to fill the listening room with sounds that meet certain standards of performance.

High-fidelity is a qualitative term, the implication being that said hardware allows those audio signals to fill the listening room with sounds that meet certain standards of performance.

Now, you can buy a stereo for $49.95 at the corner drugstore, but it will provide only a pale imitation of real music. The sound will lack impact; it will have no life. The instruments won't sound right. The audio equipment fails to deliver high-quality reproduction. It's not high-fidelity.

This book is about *high-fidelity* systems, and in the main that requires a component system, where each element is designed for the express purpose of the accurate reproduction of music. Components are like links in a chain (indeed, the French for "system," as in hi-fi system, is *chaine*). In its basic form the chain is a short one, with but three links between you and the music: source, amplifier, and reproducer. There are presently five major *sources*: tuner, analog record player, compact disc player, tape deck, and the audio track of video components. Every system needs at least one source. The final link — the one that is actually heard — is the *reproducer*. It takes electrical energy and changes it into acoustical energy — sound that we can hear. The two reproducers are speakers and headphones.

But our sources don't generate enough electrical energy to be of any use to the reproducers. Thus the need for a connecting link: the *amplifier*. The amplifier operates between the source (a turntable, for example) and the reproducer (the speakers), and increases the signal from the source until it can be used by the reproducer to create sound. A good amplifier will do its job without altering the signal from the source in any way but by degree. By this we mean that it will amplify but it won't add any sound of its own. However, it might be asked to do so: the amplifier is also the logical place to put the various controls and switching functions required by a component system.

A fourth type of component, called a *signal processor*, is optional for it isn't, strictly speaking, an essential link in the chain. Included in this category are equalizers, image enhancers, surround-sound units, and anything else that alters the nature of the signal or affects the sense of musical ambience. Signal-processing circuitry is often incorporated into an amplifier. In fact, bass and treble tone controls are simple signal processors.

There are various ways of configuring these components. The $49.95 horror puts them all, such as they are, into one wood-grained plastic box. Other more viable packages, known as compacts if they are restricted to house current, and boom boxes if they can operate on batteries, also combine several components in one. They usually consist of a control center plus two loudspeakers (which can often be attached to the central unit). The control module incorporates an amplifier and at least one source, such as a tuner, a cassette deck, or a compact disc player. The problem is that, although a few of the hundreds of compacts and boom boxes on the market do actually approach high-fidelity, all too many are just overblown versions of the $49.95 cheapie from Acme Shopping Heaven.

At the other end of the size scale is the console. Consoles are not as common as they once were, but they still tend to be big, heavy pieces of furniture stuffed with shoddy electronics and poor speakers, and some even include color televisions. But we are still not talking about high-fidelity (usually), even if we are talking about big bucks.

So let's begin to explore actual hi-fi components, the only kind that will give us the quality of sonic reproduction we must have if we are

A good amplifier will do its job without altering the signal from the source in any way but by degree. By this we mean that it will amplify but it won't add any sound of its own.

to even begin approaching the sound of live music — or at least accurately reproducing the sound stored on your recording.

Interior-design specialists suggest that you should arrange an entire room around one predetermined item of commanding presence. With hi-fi systems, the notion of a central item is particularly true. There is one single link that determines what you will hear: the speakers. Choose your speakers first, then choose an amplifier with sufficient power to drive them to satisfactory listening levels, and, finally, choose your source or sources. Neither amplifier nor sources, unless they introduce really objectionable noise or distortion, will have anything like the effect on sound that speakers have.

For all our talk about separate components, the most popular kind of stereo component combines two links into one. The *receiver* is a hybrid, containing both an amplifier and a tuner. Plug a pair of headphones into a receiver and you have a hi-fi system, even if only one person at a time can listen to it. Other sources and, of course, speakers can be added at any time.

You can also begin with an amplifier (*sans* tuner), a source (in the form of turntable, tape deck, or CD player), and speakers or headphones.

A particularly popular component system consists of a receiver, a source (cassette deck, turntable, and/or CD player), and a pair of speakers.

To recap, the essential function of an audio source is to produce an electronic signal, which is then amplified and finally converted into audible sound by speakers or headphones. Since the production of the signal is the initial stage in the home system's music reproduction process, our discussion will first focus on the components that fill that function.

A few words of encouragement before we continue: While it's true that, in the final analysis, the megabuck audio systems so beloved by some hard-core audiophiles can at rare times sound better than the ones you and I can reasonably expect to own, the difference is certainly not significant enough to justify the expense, much less the almost constant vigilance required to keep such a system performing properly. And given the electronic sleight-of-hand that much of today's mainstream equipment is capable of — allowing you to compensate for flawed recordings, for example — your system could conceivably outperform that of even the most ardent audiophile in several respects. So if, after choosing a terrific system, you still have a dollar or two left, resist the temptation to "upgrade" part of it to "audiophile" standards. After all, you might want a new tape, or CD, or even a concert ticket or two.

Choose your speakers first, then choose an amplifier with sufficient power to drive them to satisfactory listening levels, and, finally, choose your source or sources.

2 TAPE DECKS

One of the principal signal sources used in a stereo hi-fi system is the tape deck. An audio tape deck is a device for storing (recording) musical information on magnetic tape, and then retrieving it — playing it back — at some later time.

The tape itself is plastic film which has been coated with particles of either metal or an oxide of metal. The method used to store and then retrieve the information is electromagnetism. In the storing process, blank tape is inserted in the deck and drawn past a small electromagnet — the tape "record" head. An incoming musical signal continuously changes the magnetic field of the tape head. The variations in this magnetic field magnetize the metal particles on the tape in a specific way. Later, this recording can be retrieved: when the same tape is drawn across the "playback" head, its configuration of particles changes the head's magnetic field so that it is analagous to the one created in the original recording. The magnetic field yields an electronic signal which is ultimately converted to sound through speakers.

The single most important concept to grasp about magnetic tape and tape deck performance is this: The more tape area exposed to the head per unit of time, the better the sound will be (all other things being equal). A tape which moves at great speed, and which is recorded over its entire width, will sound better than a tape which moves slowly, and is recorded over only a small portion of its width. This principle explains why half-inch and one-inch tape recorded at 30 ips (inches per second) is used by professional studios: a wide band of recorded information passes rapidly over the playback head. It also makes it apparent that a cassette tape, which moves at the snail's pace of $1\frac{7}{8}$ ips, and which is divided into four tracks, is a less-

Cassette tape, which moves at the snail's pace of 1⅞ ips, and which is divided into four tracks, is a less-than-ideal medium for hi-fi reproduction.

than-ideal medium for high-fidelity reproduction. That cassettes work as well as they do (and a good cassette deck can make an all-but-perfect copy of most source programs) is due to the combined efforts of the tape manufacturers (who developed, and continue to develop, better tape formulations) and the deck manufacturers (who are responsible for high-performance hardware — the stable transports, low-noise electronics, and precision tape heads — and who have adopted the noise-reduction systems that further improve the quality of a recording).

THE TAPE HEAD

The devices which erase, record, and play the tape are called heads. These are small electromagnets whose pole pieces (the parts which do the actual magnetic attracting and repelling) make contact with the tape.

The gap between these pole pieces is critical to the accurate recording and playback of music. The gap used in the record head should be roughly equal to the thickness of the coating of the tape: about 175 millionths of an inch in the case of a cassette tape. This enables the head to place a strong signal on the tape. The gap used in the playback head, on the other hand, should be somewhat narrower. The high-frequency response of the deck depends in part upon this factor, for there is a direct correlation between the gap of the playback head and the highest note it will be able to reproduce. A gap of about 50 millionths of an inch corresponds to the highest frequency likely to be encountered, and is therefore ideal.

Ideally, then, a deck should have three distinct heads: one to record, one to play back, and one to erase. Several factors make this ideal difficult to achieve in the cassette medium.

Ideally, then, a deck should have three distinct heads: one to record, one to play back, and one to erase. Several factors make this ideal difficult to achieve in the cassette medium. Among them are the size of the access holes in the cassette shell, and the tendency of the tape itself to follow a less-than-perfectly straight path (to "skew"). If there is any misalignment between the playback and record heads, there could be a loss in high-frequency response (unless the heads were aligned for each individual cassette; possible, but costly and time-consuming). This problem is often solved (when a three-head system is used) by combining the record and playback heads in a single housing, while retaining their separate gaps and magnetic structures. The short distance between the record and playback gaps eliminate tape skew as a problem, and the use of a single housing makes the difficult access academic.

In recent years effective dual-gap combination heads have been developed, and the majority of decks advertised as three-head machines use them. At the same time, though, very fine dual-purpose heads have been designed. These use a single gap for record and playback, and while less than ideal from a theoretical standpoint, they can work very well in practice. A deck with such a combination head can be adequate for all-but-critical recording, and will cost less than an otherwise equivalent three-head machine.

Ultimate performance aside, there is one more significant advantage to a deck with three heads. In a three-head machine the tape first encounters the erase head, which prepares it for recording. It then passes the record head, and finally the playback head (figure 2-1). This means that it is possible to hear the actual recording a fraction of a second after it has been made. The ability to compare the recording with the source — called *monitoring* — can be very comforting to the recordist, for it facilitates the comparison of record-level meter readings with the actual sound being recorded.

It should be pointed out, of course, that it doesn't take very long to become familiar with the characteristics of a two-head machine's

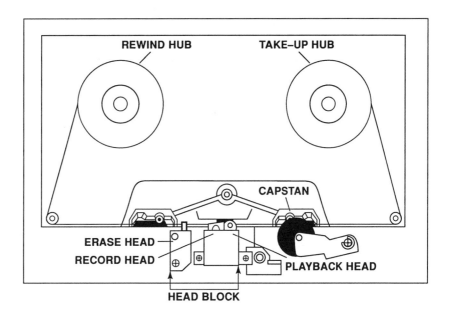

FIGURE 2-1. A cassette deck transport. Notice the relative position of the erase, record, and playback heads. A three–head deck makes it possible to listen to a recording a fraction of a second after it has been made.

record-level meters, and that fine results can certainly be achieved without a monitor head.

BIAS

The nature of magnetic tape is such that it does not respond as well to some frequencies as to others. High notes, in particular, are very difficult to record. So attempting to record a broad sonic spectrum on tape without some sort of electronic doctoring would result in inaccurate response and high distortion.

The universal means of obtaining extended high frequency response along with low distortion, is called *bias*. Bias is an ultrasonic current (ultrasonic means above the threshold of hearing; in this case, about 100 kHz) that is fed to the record head along with the audio signal. Its effect is to reduce distortion and extraneous noise in the audible range. Without record bias the distortion would render the music unlistenable, and — up to a point — the more bias, the less distortion and noise.

Without record bias the distortion would render the music unlistenable, and — up to a point — the more bias, the less distortion and noise.

From a technical standpoint it would be nice if bias requirements were constant. Unfortunately, the amount of bias current required for optimum performance varies with each type of tape used. Indeed, cassette tapes are often described by the amount of bias they require. Standard ferric tapes (Type I) are so called because their coating consists, in the main, of iron oxide particles. They are referred to as "normal"; those which require somewhat more bias (Type II) are called "high." Tapes whose coating is made up of metal particles, rather than an oxide thereof, are named for that fact (Type IV). Metal tapes require even higher bias than "high" bias tapes; for the purpose of simplicity, rather than call their bias needs "higher" they are referred to as "metal bias" tapes.

Bias requirements vary from brand to brand within types, and even from batch to batch within brand. The wrong amount of bias current can result in inferior sound: too much results in a severe loss of high frequencies, too little and the highs can be distorted. Further, improper bias can prevent noise-reduction systems from operating properly. Ideally, then, there should be a way to match the bias level with the tape being used.

The most basic tape matching is a simple selector system on the deck which sets the bias at a predetermined level for each type of tape. This level will be exactly right for the reference tape that was used by the manufacturer to establish a level at each setting, and will be reasonably close for most other standard brands. A better system permits the amount of bias to be varied continuously for each tape type, allowing just the right amount of bias to be applied.

To facilitate this, many decks provide a continuously variable bias control. The effectiveness of such a control will vary, however, depending upon whether the deck also provides some means of calibration beyond trial-and-error. A two-head deck which requires that you make several test recordings at various bias levels, and compare them with the original to find the best setting, can ultimately achieve excellent results. However, the inconvenience of such a system makes it unlikely to be used on a regular basis. A three-head deck allows the source and recording to be monitored, as the bias is adjusted, by switching back and forth between source and tape, but this system is still less than ideal. For one thing, it introduces the system's speaker as a variable, coloring the sound.

A better system uses the cassette deck's record-level indicators as a guide to setting the correct bias. During the setting process a reference tone is recorded on the tape, and the bias control is adjusted until the meter is at the level specified by the deck's maker. This type of system is quick and very accurate. Some high-end cassette decks go a step further and automate the procedure: pressing a single button initiates the process, and within a few seconds the bias has been properly set, and the tape rewound to the point at which the procedure began. Some decks even provide a computer-style memory that permits the optimum bias for a few brands of tape within a given type to be stored, and recalled each time that brand is used.

Dolby HX Pro

An increasing number of cassette decks also incorporate a system called Dolby HX Pro. HX stands for *headroom extension*, and that's the purpose of the circuit: to allow a higher recording level to be used without resulting in high-frequency distortion.

High frequencies are difficult to record: they tend to saturate the tape. The frequency and level at which this saturation occurs depends upon the type of tape used.

We've already said that high frequencies are difficult to record: they tend to saturate the tape. The frequency and level at which this saturation occurs depends upon the type of tape used. Metal tape has terrific high-frequency headroom; standard tape less terrific. HX Pro creates high-frequency headroom by monitoring the signal and varying the amount of bias current from one moment to the next, depending upon the nature and level of the musical signal. Because HX Pro is a one-way process, requiring no decoding, recordings made using this system sound better when played back on all decks — even car players and portables.

TAPE EQUALIZATION

Another means used to compensate for the fact that tape doesn't respond to all musical frequencies with equal intensity is called equalization.

Equalization is the process by which the frequency response of the deck is modified internally so that the overall record/playback response is smooth and flat, and thus able to accurately recreate the overall balance of the source material. (It is similar in principle and purpose to the RIAA curve used on phonograph records — see page 62.) The recording process itself has inherent high-frequency losses (even after the proper bias current is applied), and the slower the tape moves the greater these losses are. Because cassette tapes move so slowly, proper equalization is critical for wide frequency response (figure 2-2).

Two types of equalization are used in all high-fidelity recorders: record and playback. Record equalization deals with the problem of high-frequency losses by boosting those frequencies before they are sent to the tape head. The nature and amount of record equalization varies from manufacturer to manufacturer and model to model, and is preset at the factory.

Unlike record equalization, playback equalization is standardized, enabling tapes recorded on one machine to be played back on anoth-

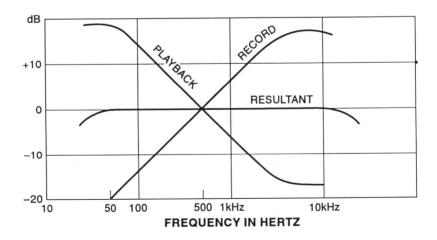

FIGURE 2-2. Equalization is used to compensate for high-frequency loss in the recording process. High frequencies are boosted in recording and cut during playback. The result is flat frequency response.

er with good results. The normal interaction between playback head and the various tape types results in a predictable boost in treble frequencies, at the rate of 6 dB (*decibels*) per octave. Playback equalization applies an equivalent amount of attenuation (reduction) in order to achieve musically flat response. The musical frequency at which this attenuation begins varies according to tape type. For technical reasons having to do with the nature of the circuitry used to achieve this result, the frequency at which the equalization is commenced is often referred to in terms of microseconds. A playback equalization of 120 microseconds (which is standard for Type I ferric tapes) simply means that the treble cut begins at 1,326 Hz; the 70 microsecond equalization used by Type II and IV tapes commences the attenuation at 2,274 Hz. Proper playback equalization is automatically selected when you set the tape type on the deck's control panel. Indeed, many decks make use of identifying cutouts on the cassette itself to automatically select the tape type.

Proper playback equalization is automatically selected when you set the tape type on the deck's control panel.

Of course, record equalization boosts not only the musical highs; it emphasizes tape hiss as well, because that's where tape hiss is — in the highs. So, for a given quality of tape you will always get a better signal-to-noise ratio with 70 microsecond tape than 120 microsecond tape. Fortunately, tape hiss — whether resulting from the tape itself, or from the deck's electronics — is much less a problem than it was a few years ago. Thus, quiet recordings are readily achieved with both types of tape.

TAPE DECK SPECIFICATIONS

The audible significance of performance specifications varies depending upon the component being considered and upon the individual specification being examined. The closer a component class is to achieving ideal performance, the less concerned one needs to be about specs. (In the case of power amplifiers, for example, distortion is often measured in thousandths of a percent, and the difference between six thousandths and a few tenths of a percent is totally inaudible.) In the case of cassette decks, published specifications can be of real value because they correspond to audible, rather than merely theoretical, performance.

In the case of cassette decks, published specifications can be of real value because they correspond to audible, rather than theoretical, performance.

Signal-to-Noise Ratio

Stated in simple terms, a tape deck's signal-to-noise ratio (S/N) specification tells you the difference between the residual noise of the deck (which is generated by the unit's internal electronics) and the maximum signal it can put on a tape before serious distortion occurs — i.e., the amount of hiss that will be present along with the music. A 60 dB S/N ratio indicates that the hiss will be 60 dB softer than the loudest music. Since the noise level is a constant, the S/N ratio is directly dependent upon the recording level (and, of course, the nature of the music, once we get beyond the theoretical). If the music is too soft — that is, recorded at too low a level — the hiss will not be masked. If the music is recorded at too high a level, it will be distorted.

There are several means by which a manufacturer can achieve a good S/N ratio. Among these is the use of electronics with inherently low noise, and this is being done increasingly as technology improves. But the classic means of improving S/N ratio — using more tape in less time — is not available to the cassette deck manufacturer who wants to remain within the licensing agreements established by Philips, the inventor of the format. So, while running the tape at a higher speed, or recording a wider path, would yield better performance, it would result in a tape that couldn't be played on the majority of tape decks on the market.

Fortunately, the combination of low-noise electronics, better tape, and — perhaps of the greatest significance — noise-reduction circuitry (see next page) has made it possible to achieve acceptable results even at the lower end of the price spectrum, and spectacular results at the high end. An S/N ratio of 60 dB is satisfactory; models exceeding 70 dB are not uncommon.

Wow and Flutter

Wow and flutter are lumped together in the specifications column, for they both refer to cyclical speed variations in the tape. They do, however, sound different from one another, and are often caused by different things.

Wow refers to a speed variation occurring between 0.4 and 10 times per second. It is most noticeable during slow musical passages, where notes are held for a long time. Wow causes the pitch of music to vary in a "warbling" manner, and is particularly annoying because it is right up front, as part of the music.

Flutter, on the other hand, is less obtrusive at first. The speed variations defined as flutter occur more quickly: up to 250 times per second. Rather than imparting a specifically definable character to the music, these variations simply detract from its general clarity, or definition.

The ear is more sensitive to wow than flutter, so the weighting system used when measuring them gives more importance to wow. The wow and flutter spec is given as a percentage, with the weighting scale called "WRMS." The lower the number, the better. A good wow and flutter spec will have one zero to the right of the decimal place. A great wow and flutter spec will be better than 0.06 percent.

The good news about wow and flutter is that for the most part they both ceased to be an audible problem on cassette decks (at least from reputable manufacturers) several years ago.

The good news about wow and flutter is that for the most part they both ceased to be an audible problem on cassette decks (at least from reputable manufacturers) several years ago. Transport design has progressed to the point where the tape's motion is just about as smooth as it needs to be.

NOISE REDUCTION

Probably no single development has contributed more to the success of the cassette as a hi-fi medium than has the Dolby B noise-reduction system. Introduced in the late '60s, Dolby B has been incorporated into virtually every cassette tape deck claiming high-fidelity quality ever since, for it achieves an 8-to-10 dB reduction in audible tape hiss, eliminating the greatest drawback to the cassette format (figure 2-3).

Dolby noise reduction takes advantage of a phenomenon known as the masking effect. When loud music is playing the listener tends

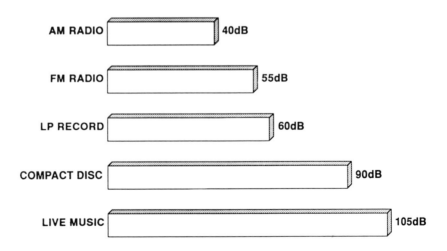

FIGURE 2-3. The relative dynamic range of musical sources. A noise-reduction system increases the dynamic range of a cassette deck so that it is able to reproduce the wider dynamic range of live music.

not to hear the small amount of background noise inherent in the tape. Furthermore, most of that background noise tends to be high frequency in nature. During the *recording* process the Dolby noise-reduction system does nothing when there is loud music present. It relies on the masking effect to cover up the hiss. But during soft musical passages, the high-frequency portion of the spectrum is boosted: the highs being recorded are made louder. The opposite occurs during *playback*. Loud passages are played unaltered, but during soft passages the high frequencies are reduced by exactly the same amount they were boosted during recording. Here's the good part: when the previously boosted highs are reduced in level, the high-frequency noise is reduced by the same amount. The net result is a reduction in hiss of about 10 dB.

The noise-reduction system just described is called Dolby B, and it's been in use for more than two decades. But improvements in source material and other audio components, and competition from other noise-reduction systems, prompted Dolby Laboratories to introduce a second system, called Dolby C. Dolby C provides 20 dB of noise reduction at high frequencies and, because it commences operation at a lower frequency than Dolby B does, 15 dB of noise reduction in the midrange. While there are other noise-reduction systems that can provide equal (or even better) signal/noise improvements, the Dolby systems have some very significant advantages.

The first advantage is, at this stage, acceptance. Dolby B and C are, for all practical purposes, the industry standards. Thus, a tape recorded with Dolby B noise reduction, like most pre-recorded tapes, may be successfully played back on any Dolby-equipped deck. Further, it will sound OK — just a bit bright — when played back on any deck which does not have Dolby B. A tape recorded with Dolby C encoding will sound fine when decoded properly, and acceptable if it's necessary to play it back on a deck with only Dolby B decoding.

In addition to Dolby B and C, a very few cassette decks are equipped with a noise-reduction system called dbx. This system achieves its excellent results in that area (up to 30 dB, in fact) as a side benefit of its original function, which was dynamic-range expansion. Unlike Dolby, whose encode/decode action varies with the frequency of the music, dbx operates uniformly over the entire range, compressing on a 2:1 basis in record, and expanding by an equivalent amount in playback. The end result is that the cassette can contain a much more dynamic signal than would otherwise be possible, and tape hiss is completely eliminated (figure 2-4).

Unfortunately, the dbx process has a couple of disadvantages. First, recordings made with the dbx process *must* be played back with the process. Without decoding, a dbx-encoded tape is virtually unlistenable: strident and lacking both dynamics and extended frequency response. And second, with some types of music the effects of dbx's compression/expansion can be audible as a sort of "breathing" of the ambient noise/space behind solo instruments. But when used with appropriate source material, dbx can provide exceptional results.

Now that there can be three noise-reduction systems from which to choose, the issue of which one to use for various applications becomes important. Generally speaking, Dolby B should be used (in making recordings) when compatibility is a key factor. While most home decks are now Dolby C-equipped, that's not the case with portables and car decks, and their usual environments don't call for

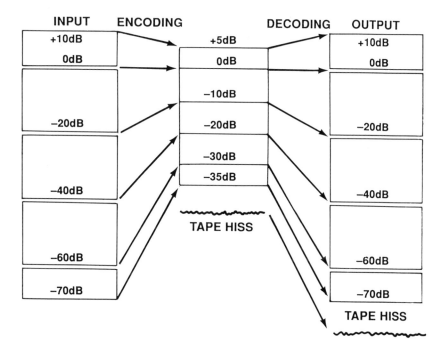

FIGURE 2-4. The dbx encoding–decoding process. During recording, the incoming signal is compressed, while the tape hiss remains constant. In playback, the signal and residual tape hiss are treated as a single entity, and the expansion process drops the hiss below the level of audibility.

the extended dynamic range afforded by the more sophisticated NR systems. On the other hand, the superior dynamics offered by Dolby C make it ideal for home use, where the probable lower background noise level will be a factor. And if compatibility is not a factor at all, and the music to be recorded is broad-band and highly dynamic, dbx can handle source material whose dynamic range is even greater than the 80 dB of the Dolby C process.

TRANSPORT DESIGN

The term "transport" is generally used to refer to those parts of the deck that move the tape and, by extension, to the electronic circuitry used to control them, if any.

The main points to consider when examining a transport are the number and type of motors, and whether or not it has two capstans. This is not to imply that two motors are better than one, or three than two; or that a dual-capstan design is necessarily better than a single capstan system. As is true of every component (and, indeed, of most things), the quality of the design and the care of the execution count for far more than the nature of the design. Still, all else being equal, two aspects of a tape deck transport's design can have an impact on performance: the type and number of motors used, and whether it has one or two capstans.

As is true of every component (and, indeed, of most things), the quality of the design and the care of the execution count for far more than the nature of the design.

The job of the motor(s) is to move the tape, and no matter how many are used it's necessary for that motion to be smooth and constant. In essence, a cassette deck's transport is a miniature version of an open-reel system. There's a supply hub, a take-up hub, and one or two capstans. The job of moving the tape past the heads goes to the capstan — a finely polished shaft of metal which turns at a precisely determined speed. A rubber wheel presses the tape against the capstan, and assures that sufficient contact is made to keep the tape from spilling. In a single-motor design a series of pulleys is used to keep everything turning at the right speed, and to maintain the proper amounts of tension.

The most sophisticated transports available utilize two or more motors. In a two-motor deck, one motor is used to drive the capstan (or capstans), the other the tape hubs. A three-motor deck usually provides a separate motor for each tape hub, and — using electronic regulation to prevent the tape from spilling out of the cassette shell — can often provide very impressive fast forward and rewind speed.

Some manufacturers use the third motor for another purpose: to gently and firmly position the head block against the tape. This prevents the jolting that some electromagnetic (i.e., solenoid) systems subject the block to.

TRANSPORT CONTROLS

The transport controls are used to initiate the various tape motor functions and to initiate the playback or record process. The basic controls are Play, Record, Fast Forward, Rewind, Stop, and Pause. The Pause function is similar to Stop in that tape motion ceases, but differs in that rather than retract the head block from the tape and shut off the record or playback electronics, the system is kept in a "standby" mode in order to allow a smooth transition when motion is resumed.

There are basically two types of transport control in widespread use today: mechanically assisted soft-touch and fully electronic.

Mechanically assisted soft-touch controls operate in a manner that is similar to that of an electric (as opposed to electronic) typewriter. The same motions take place as in a manual machine, but they are aided by a motorized system which reduces the effort required and the distance the control must be pushed before the desired result is achieved. In addition to providing a luxurious feel to the deck, this type of control system yields a consistency of operating forces that extends the useful life of the transport.

The various soft-touch control systems which have no mechanical connection between the controls and the transport use solenoids or other electronic controls (including microprocessors) to actuate the various transport modes.

A term that is often associated with soft-touch controls is "full logic." This refers to the ability to switch from one transport mode to any other (e.g., from Rewind to Play) without having to first press the Stop button. The reference to logic refers to a series of "decisions" that the deck makes when a control is pressed. If, for example, one were to press Rewind while in the Play mode, some decks would automatically insert a Stop command before rewind in order to prevent a tape spill. The nature of the logic used, and the means by which it is achieved, may vary from machine to machine, but the purpose is always to protect both the tape and the transport.

METERING SYSTEMS

In order to achieve the best combination of high signal-to-noise ratio and low distortion, it's important that the record level be properly set. In order to enable you to do so, meters of one type or other are provided. Each type has its pros and cons, but good results are possible with any of them.

Up until a few years ago, the most common type of level meter was an actual meter: a needle which moved along a scale to indicate the strength of the recorded signal. These meters, often erroneously called VU (for Volume Unit) meters, can be designed to read either average signals, or near-instantaneous peak signals. Since an averaging meter responds more slowly than a peak meter, and generally doesn't reveal the presence of short-duration high-frequency bursts (which can overload the tape), lower indicated record levels should be used to achieve good results.

Over the past few years this mechanical metering system has been all but superseded by another type. This uses light (light-emitting diodes [LEDs], plasma discharge arrays, or fluorescent bars) to indicate level (figure 2-5). The theoretical advantage of such a display is a total lack of inertia: it can respond to a signal with no delay at all. That being the case, it's easier to provide true peak indication, and most manufacturers calibrate their displays in that fashion. Some

The theoretical advantage of an LED display is a total lack of inertia: it can respond to a signal with no delay at all. That being the case, it's easier to see true peak indication.

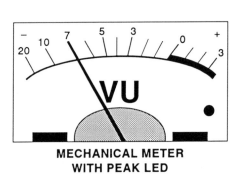

**MECHANICAL METER
WITH PEAK LED**

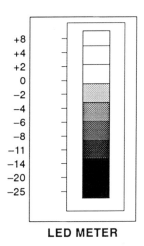

LED METER

FIGURE 2-5. The inertia inherent in a mechanical meter (left) makes it potentially less accurate than a purely electronic meter (right). This is especially true when the meter is used to indicate instantaneous peaks.

even make a provision for the highest level encountered during a recording to be "stored" and displayed for a period of time. This is called *peak hold*. A nice feature of some of these displays is their use of a different color (usually red) to indicate too high a level. Sometimes yellow is used in the near-danger range. It's important to note that while some meters appear to provide a wide range of operation, they often lack fine resolution. The more able a meter is to display the difference between levels of, say, +3 and +6, the more precisely you'll be able to determine where the level controls should be set for a given recording. This is more important than having a full-scale range from -100 to +10, for example.

In sum, knowing the characteristics of your deck's metering system is a key factor in making good recordings.

CONVENIENCE FEATURES

Some features make recording easier and/or more fun. Some facilitate finding a specific location on the tape, or optimize the interface between the deck and the rest of the system. Others provide a greater level of control over the record and playback process. While these features aren't necessary for the performance of the deck's basic functions, some of them can greatly enhance your enjoyment of it. Here, briefly, are some of the features to look for.

The Tape Counter

The ability to find a song in the middle of a tape is facilitated by a tape counter. If a tape is begun at Zero, and a note is made of what number comes up when the desired selections begin, it's easy to find them again. Tape-counter displays may be mechanical or electronic, but for the most part they provide the same type of information: how many revolutions the takeup spool has made.

Real-Time Counters

Much more useful, but only found on costlier decks, are those displays which indicate time, rather than arbitrary numbers. Some real-time counters require that the tape be rewound to the beginning, and then set to Zero in order to operate properly. A more advanced system uses a sensor to detect the difference in rotational speed between the supply and takeup hubs. It then calculates how much tape is wrapped around each, and converts those figures into elapsed and remaining time, either of which can be chosen for display.

Knowing how much time remains on a tape makes it easy to "program" a recording so that there is neither wasted tape nor interrupted songs.

Memory Functions

One or more types of memory are often keyed to the tape counter. The simplest kind of memory stops the tape (from the rewind mode) when Zero is reached. An obvious use of this feature is during recording, to quickly find the beginning of the selection just recorded. It's also useful to repeat a favorite song. You set the counter to Zero at the beginning of the song and press Rewind when it ends. With the memory function engaged, the tape will stop when the counter reaches Zero. Some decks allow you to set a pair of memory locations, and repeatedly play the section that they bracket. This is called *block repeat*.

Another type of memory puts the transport into the play mode at the end of the wind cycle. This feature lets you start the rewind process and then walk away from the deck, rather than have to wait for the tape to stop, and then press Play.

Timer Operation

A hi-fi system can be pressed into service as an elaborate alarm clock, with one's favorite tape used as a wakeup call.

The ability to set a timer to turn a cassette deck on means, among other things, that an FM broadcast needn't be missed just because it occurs at an inconvenient time. The cassette will automatically record it at the designated time. It also means that a hi-fi system can be pressed into service as an elaborate alarm clock, with one's favorite tape used as a wakeup call. It's important that when set up for timer operation the deck isn't left with the pinch roller against the capstan: this would cause a flat spot on the rubber roller and, eventually, result in audible wow. A proper timer mode leaves the deck in "neutral" until power is turned on by the timer. Then the deck is automatically placed in the record or play mode (depending upon how it was set up).

Output-Level Controls

The output-level control is used to match the perceived volume of the tape deck with that of other sources, such as record players. It prevents any unpleasant surprises when switching between sources.

Music-Search Systems

Finding individual selections on a tape is simplified by music-search systems. These systems vary in their implementation, but they all operate by sensing the blank space between songs. Some systems simply fast wind (in either direction) to the beginning of a song and begin playback. Others allow you to select a specific song or series of songs (in any order) by number. Another option operates in a manner similar to a tuner's scan mode, automatically playing the first few seconds of each song on the tape.

Auto Space

Because music-search systems work by sensing the blank space between songs, some decks incorporate a circuit that automatically inserts such a space between recorded selections. When the appropriate control is pressed, several seconds of silence are recorded, and then the deck is placed in the record/pause mode.

AUTO-REVERSE DECKS

Auto-reverse has always been a useful feature; up until recently it was usually accompanied by sacrifice in performance.

Auto-reverse decks can automatically play (and record) both sides of a cassette. Generally, such decks allow you to choose between one-time and continuous play of both sides, and to disable the feature completely.

Auto-reverse has always been a useful feature; up until recently it was usually accompanied by significant sacrifice in performance. That's because of the difficulty in maintaining the required head-to-tape alignment (which is crucial for extended high-frequency response) in both directions (figure 2-6). There are two possible solutions to this problem. One of them is to devise a mechanism that physically removes the cassette from the machine, flips it over, and reinserts it. The obvious drawbacks to this type of system are cost and complexity. A secondary consideration is the inevitable time lag which occurs while the cassette is physically removed from the transport, turned around, and put back in position. The development of a working example of such a mechanism is clearly a technological achievement, but not terribly practical. The other method achieves similar results in a more reliable and cost effective package. In order to provide acceptable performances in both directions, the head block is physically rotated 180 degrees. Some manufacturers provide a

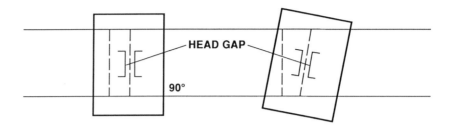

FIGURE 2-6. Auto-reverse decks have an especially difficult time in maintaining the proper tape-to-head angle (azimuth). When the optimum angle of 90 degrees is not maintained, as on the right, the result is significant high-frequency loss.

means to adjust the *azimuth* (head-to-tape angle) alignment for each side of the tape.

Once satisfactory record and playback performance have been assured, other factors come into play. In order for an auto-reverse deck to realize its potential for convenience, it's necessary to equip it with a means of changing direction virtually instantaneously. Any delay during recording will result in that portion of the music being omitted from the tape. In order to provide a seamless transition between sides, a deck must be able to compensate for the five-to-seven seconds of unrecordable "leader" tape at the beginning (and end) of every cassette. Thus, a deck that waits until the tape physically runs out before changing direction will, of necessity, "edit out" music of a duration that is twice the length of the leader during an auto-reverse recording session. During playback, there will be an equivalent amount of silence.

To eliminate this problem, many manufacturers employ a non-mechanical means to trigger the auto-reverse process. Because the tape leader is transparent, a photocell can be used to sense its presence and immediately reverse the tape's direction. This eliminates the delay inherent in mechanical systems, and results in a nearly seamless transition between sides.

Some auto-reverse models also offer a "blank skip" feature that eliminates the wait between sides when you haven't completely filled a side of the cassette with music. This feature monitors the playback, and when it "hears" more than 10 seconds of silence, it infers that the music is finished. At this point, the tape is fast-wound to the end, and playback of the other side commences.

The Best Blank Cassettes

....

Has a friend ever asked you to tape something for him and then groused when you delivered an impeccable recording on your favorite brand of high-grade tape, the tape you literally swear by? Well, brand loyalty is a powerful thing, but it is not always based purely on caprice. You may have experimented carefully with different brands of tape before falling in love with Brand A, but then your friend probably did the same before falling in love with Brand C. Fact is, some tapes sound better on one machine, some on others. This is especially true in the case of machines whose characteristics — specifically, bias level and Dolby tracking — cannot be optimized for an individual tape. So the notion of "best brand" is somewhat dependent on factors outside the tape itself. However, the big-name brands have consistently done best in technical tests conducted by the hobby magazines.

  Apart from the question of what brand to buy there is the question of what type of tape you will want to use. Three types are recommended for musical recording. Regular ferric oxide is known as Type I, and it is just fine for pop music. It works at standard bias and equalization settings and is not as quiet as the other quality types, which is why it is okay for most kinds of pop: the generally loud volume of the music effectively masks the excess hiss. Some special ferric oxide formulations share the Type II nomenclature with chromium dioxide (aka chrome) tapes. These require a higher recording bias and a different playback equalization than Type I tapes. Although Type II tape can be a trifle more sensitive to overloading than regular ferric oxide, it is lower in noise and is therefore better for any music, such as classical, with a wide dynamic range (i.e., plenty of quiet passages as well as healthy loud ones). The Type III designation denotes the FerriChrome formulation, which is no longer made and therefore does not figure in this survey. Type IV uses metal particles, rather than oxides, as the recording medium, and requires the highest bias. If you make recordings for "archival" purposes, you might try metal tape; there are times when it sounds best of all.

DUBBING DECKS

You simply place a recorded tape in the left transport, and a blank in the right, and by pressing a single button make a copy of the original recording.

Dubbing decks, which consist of two tape transports and their associated electronics in a single chassis, have grown enormously in popularity in recent years, and it's no wonder. You simply place a recorded tape in the left transport, and a blank in the right, and by pressing a single button make a copy of the original. In general, dubbing decks are capable of copying a tape at twice normal speed, although if you're not in a hurry better results will be obtained by choosing the normal speed. Beyond their ability to conveniently make copies, dubbing decks often provide such features as sequential recording, which, when associated with auto-reverse, records both sides of a cassette in transport A and continues the recording by switching to transport B. This allows, using C90 cassettes, programs of up to three hours in length to be recorded.

3 RECORD PLAYERS

The venerable phonograph has been the centerpiece of most home audio systems for well over a century, and although it will eventually become obsolete, as of this writing it is still with us. This is no surprise, for no matter how impressive compact discs are, and no matter how firmly a digital convert swears never to spin a conventional platter again, many music lovers who own large LP collections are neither willing nor able to replace each large black disc with its small silver equivalent. A further consideration is the fact that while the list of back titles available on CD continues to grow at an impressive rate, a vast number of records has yet to be transferred to the new medium.

So the market for record players still exists, which in today's competitive environment means that there is a good selection from which to choose.

So the market for record players still exists, which in today's competitive environment means that there is a good selection from which to choose. That in turn means — both in theory and, luckily, in practice — that everyone's needs are well served. Whether you want to spend $90 or $900, there will be something on your dealer's shelf that will play your LPs with acceptable accuracy without ruining them in the process.

THE PARTS OF A RECORD PLAYER

What we usually refer to as a turntable is actually three distinct components: the turntable, the tonearm, and the base.

The job of the *turntable* is easy to define. It must rotate the record at a precise speed — usually 33.33 or 45 rpm (revolutions per minute) — without wavering or adding any noise of its own to the playback system.

The *tonearm*'s task is to hold the phono cartridge in position over the record, and to allow the stylus to track the groove. The cartridge must be held as close to perfectly tangent to the groove as possible. In an ideal world, the tonearm should apply force in a single direction: straight down, so that the stylus stays in the groove. In actuality, though, another, sideways force must be applied as well, to compensate for *skating* (about which more, further along in this chapter). In addition, the cartridge/tonearm assembly's natural tendency to resonate must be kept in check. The frequency and amplitude (e.g., level) of the resonance must not result in audible problems.

The final portion of the record player is one which is too often taken for granted. Not only must the *base* support the tonearm and turntable, it must isolate them from external vibration and, in doing so, prevent the audible and inaudible effects of air- and surface-borne feedback.

The phono cartridge is obviously a vital portion of the record player, but is usually considered a separate unit. Therefore, the details of its operation will be explained somewhat later in this chapter.

Rumble; Wow and Flutter

We'll go into more detail about all three parts of the record player, but first let's take a look at its two most frequently discussed specifications: *wow and flutter* and *rumble*.

Rumble. It is something which, if your turntable has it, will make your listening room sound like a third-class compartment on the Trans-Siberian Express. Similarly, you might think that excessive wow and flutter would give the impression of a $15 walkabout cassette player running with its batteries on Low.

Neither fault is quite so gross, which makes them all the more insidious and even dangerous. Rumble, in particular, can pose a problem. It is a very low-frequency sound generated by the drive motor. Often it cannot be heard at all, but your amplifier knows it is there, and does its best to amplify it, sapping power and muddying the sound of the music. Rumble is specified as a given number of dB below a fixed reference point. So that this abstract number can be correlated more closely with the way our hearing works, a "weighting curve" (called DIN B — DIN for Deutsche Industrie Norm [German Industry Standard], and B for the specific curve used) is used to give more importance to the more audible frequencies. It would be nice to be able to say that lower is better when talking about rumble. Unfortunately, things aren't that simple. Different

Rumble, in particular, can pose a problem. Your amplifier knows it is there, and does its best to amplify it, sapping power and muddying the sound of the music.

types of record players produce rumble differently, and direct-drive models in particular do so in a way that wasn't a factor when the DIN B spec was promulgated. (This is not, mind you, to imply that direct-drive technology is flawed — only that it is different.) This makes direct comparison of different types difficult, for on paper a *superb* record player might look worse than a so-so model. Still, it's better than nothing: look for a unit with a DIN B rumble rating of 65 dB or better — unless you're considering a belt-drive model, in which case a somewhat lower number is quite acceptable.

Wow and flutter are lumped together in the specifications column, for they both refer to cyclical-speed variations in the platter. They do, however, sound different from one another, and are often caused by different things, as discussed in the cassette chapter. Wow imparts a warbly, unsteady sound to the music, while flutter detracts from its clarity without necessarily having a distinctive character of its own. The wow and flutter specification is more straightforward than the one for rumble: the two are simply expressed as a combined percentage figure, and any thing less than 0.1 percent is acceptable.

PLATTER DRIVE SYSTEMS

While the quality of execution is more important than the type of design used, it is worthwhile to know the various attributes and drawbacks of the different methods used by manufacturers to spin the turntable's platter.

Belt-Drive Turntables

The combination of a synchronous motor with belt drive of the platter is one of the two basic systems in widespread use today (figure 3-1). Unlike more conventional motors, whose speed is controlled by the amount of voltage applied, synchronous motors lock onto the 60 cycles-per-second frequency of the AC current. Because synchronous motors don't vary their speed with line voltage they are used in applications where accuracy is of paramount importance, such as clocks.

An elastic belt is used to transmit the rotation of the motor shaft to the platter. This has a desirable secondary result: The elasticity of the belt tends to damp the vibration of the motor, keeping rumble from being introduced into the system via the platter, the LP, or the cartridge.

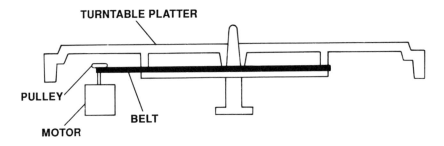

FIGURE 3-1. A belt-driven turntable uses an elastic pulley to transmit the rotation of the motor shaft to the platter.

Ideally, there should be some way of making sure that the turntable turns at the proper speed, and in fact, there is: servo control.

Controlling Variations in Speed. While the long-term speed accuracy of a synchronous-motor/belt-drive turntable might be superb, there is still the potential for short-term variations — which result in wow and flutter. Ideally, there should be some way of making sure that the turntable turns at the proper speed, and in fact, there is: *servo control.* Momentary speed errors are detected (and corrected) by comparing the motor's speed with an ideal reference stored in the servo contoller's circuitry. Differences are compensated for by sending a signal to the motor, telling it to correct itself. Naturally, the correcting mechanism must be precisely calibrated. Too much correction and the platter would be constantly alternating between too fast and too slow. Too little would be the same as having no correction mechanism at all.

A problem inherent in a belt-driven servo-controlled turntable stems from one of the factors that makes belt drive desirable in the first place: the belt's ability to isolate the motor from the platter. A speed correction applied to the motor might, if small enough, be absorbed by the elasticity of the belt. A second drive system eliminates this problem: *direct drive.*

Direct-Drive Turntables

In a direct-drive system, the platter is an extension of the motor shaft, or even, in some cases, a working part of the motor (figure 3-2). The motor (and hence the platter) speed is compared to a reference provided by an oscillator, which causes it to turn at precisely

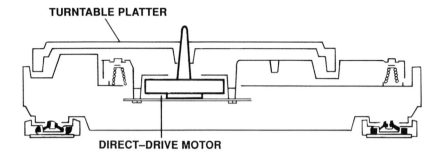

TURNTABLE PLATTER

DIRECT–DRIVE MOTOR

FIGURE 3-2. In a direct-driven system the motor is part of, and concentric with, the platter assembly.

the desired speed. Any required corrections are made directly to the spinning platter.

In order to provide the greatest possible speed accuracy, many manufacturers use a quartz-crystal oscillator in the servo mechanisms of their better turntables. Quartz crystals resonate at a very high frequency, and their error detection potential is in the area of a few parts per million. Quartz-controlled turntables tend to have speed fluctuations — both long- and short-term — which are less than those of the lathes used to cut the records being played on them.

There is a drawback to most quartz-referenced speed-control systems, though: in order to provide variable speed (an option that allows you to change the pitch of the music so that it matches, say, a piano) it's usually necessary to disengage the quartz-lock circuitry. The better turntables employ a system that permits variable speed under the control of the quartz-servo system.

It must be noted that direct-drive systems are not without their own drawbacks. Eliminating the belt also eliminates the isolating influence of the belt upon the platter, allowing any motor-induced rumble to be transmitted directly into the system. This means that a better — i.e., costlier — motor is required for satisfactory performance. By extension, it makes bargain-basement direct-drive models less desirable even though, as mentioned in the discussion of rumble, the published specs might be excellent. Further, a direct-drive system is more difficult to isolate from externally produced shock and vibration than is one in which the platter is belt driven. Again, solutions exist, but they tend to be found in costlier models.

THE TONEARM

As stated in the beginning of this chapter, the tonearm's purpose is essentially to hold the cartridge in position, and to exert the proper amount of force, thus allowing the stylus to properly track the groove. But while the tonearm's job may be described in simple terms, it is one of the most critical members of the audio chain. In essence, it must be two conflicting things at the same time. First, it should have infinite mass, in order that it not resonate. And second, it shold have no mass at all, so that the cartridge can do its job without being influenced by external forces. Clearly, then, some compromises are called for. There are several factors to consider when examining a tonearm's design. They include geometry (the ability of the tonearm to correctly position the stylus), bearing friction, and resonance (which, in combination with the cartridge, is a function of mass and damping).

Tonearm Geometry

Careful attention to the various dimensional and angular relationships within the arm will yield a very low degree of tracking error — and a correspondingly low level of distortion.

Ideally, the tonearm should position the stylus so that it is perfectly tangent — i.e., at a 90-degree angle — to the groove. This would result in a complete absence of tracking error. Of course, with a pivoted arm this is impossible, for as the position of the arm changes, so does the angle which is created at the intersection of the stylus and the groove. But careful attention to the various dimensional and angular relationships within the arm will yield a very low degree of tracking error — and a correspondingly low level of resultant distortion. In addition to tangency, the tonearm designer must make sure that the cartridge stylus rides properly in the groove of the record, when examined both front-to-back and side-to-side.

Bearing Friction

As the stylus tracks the record groove it must move the tonearm inward, toward the center of the disc. Fighting against this motion (and against the arm's ability to track warps up and down) are the bearings at the arm's pivot point. The less friction exerted by these bearings, the better: too much on the horizontal plane will result in uneven stylus wear, as well as channel imbalance. Too much on the vertical plane and warped records will cause the stylus to move up into the cartridge body and/or lose contact with the disc.

Sometimes, in an attempt to reduce friction without paying for high-quality bearings, a manufacturer will use bearings with too much "play" in them. Fortunately, the present state of the art in bearing design is such that any manufacturer that chooses to do so can use bearings that reduce friction to a negligible level while providing the necessary firm support of the tonearm.

Skating

Another force to consider is called skating. Skating occurs whenever a record is played with a conventional pivoted tonearm, and is the arm's tendency to be pulled inward, towards the center of the disc. Skating force, if not held in check, will result in the same ills as high bearing friction. Fortunately, while skating is unavoidable in a pivoting tonearm, it is correctable. A compensating outward force is applied to the tonearm, either via a magnet, or a spring. This force must be equal to that of the inward force that naturally occurs, and when properly applied allows the stylus to track both sides of the groove equally.

Resonance

Much has been made of the shape of the tonearm; straight, S-shaped, or J-shaped. It's worth noting at this point that the shape will have no inherent bearing upon the arm's ability to hold the stylus in its proper position. What will be affected, given equivalent construction materials, is the arm's mass, and hence the resonant frequency of the tonearm/cartridge assembly.

Let's have a look at the nature of this assembly. In essence, it's a bar, pivoted towards one end, and supported by the stylus (which acts as a tiny spring) at the other. Like any object, this system will have a frequency at which it naturally resonates, or vibrates. The resonant frequency is determined by two things: the mass of the

---

Linear Tracking

Because a pivoted tonearm must, by definition, introduce some tracking error, some manufacturers offer an interesting alternative technology. By replacing the pivot with a track, and moving the tonearm across the disc in a straight line, a linear-tracking tonearm is able to hold the cartridge at a 90-degree angle to the groove over the entire surface. At least, that's the theory. Unfortunately, the mechanism used to control the position of such tonearms in all but the very costliest models can introduce sufficient "play" to negate that advantage. Unless you have a great deal of money to spend on a very meticulously engineered linear-tracking record player (which can cost well over $1,000), you will get better return for your dollars with a conventional unit.

entire assembly, and the compliance (or elasticity) of the stylus. Raising the mass and/or the compliance will lower the resonant frequency. Lowering the mass and/or stiffening the spring (by lowering compliance) will raise the resonant frequency.

But why are we so concerned with tonearm resonance? Simple: records are warped, and warps tend to have their own resonant frequencies (or, more to the point, tend to excite specific frequencies in tonearm/cartridge systems). If the tonearm/cartridge resonance occurs at the same frequency as that of the record warp, the results will be chaotic. The stylus will be unable to follow the groove accurately, resulting in severe distortion. In extreme cases, the stylus will jump out of the groove.

Record warps occur at about 4 Hz (for a standard 12-inch LP). Ideally, the tonearm/cartridge resonance should be above that frequency, but below the audible range.

Record warps occur at about 4 Hz (for a standard 12-inch LP). Ideally, the tonearm/cartridge resonance should be above that frequency, but below the audible range. About 12 Hz is ideal, and the best way to achieve that is to make sure that the mass of the arm and the compliance of the cartridge's stylus are appropriately matched. In practice, that's difficult, since there are so many cartridges on the market. It is, however, possible to recognize trends, and since the trend is toward more compliant cartridges (which, as a class, tend to track better), it's reasonable to build turntables with lower mass tonearms. Thus, there has been a tendency among manufacturers to abandon curved arms (which are of necessity more massive) in favor of straight arms.

But a straight arm can have its own problems. Unless a very stiff material is used to make the arm tube, it can have its own structural resonances. Carbon fibre has been found to have an almost ideal stiffness-to-mass ratio, and is often used on better turntables where its high cost can be absorbed.

Dealing with the frequency of the resonance is one thing, but it's also important to make sure that its amplitude (level) is kept in check. The use of damping materials in various locations can compensate for different sorts of resonances, controlling both their frequency and amplitude. Typical locations where damping is used include the coupling between the arm and the counterweight, within the hollow arm tube, and at the pivot.

THE BASE

None of the fine specifications associated with a record player will make any difference if every time you walk within 10 feet of the unit the stylus jumps the groove, or if the howl of acoustic feedback fills

A turntable's ability to withstand shock and feedback is thus extremely important and is, in great measure, a function of its base.

the room every time you crank up the volume. A turntable's ability to withstand shock and feedback is thus extremely important and is, in great measure, a function of its base.

The purpose of the base is to provide support for the turntable and tonearm, and to isolate them from all types of environmental influences (figure 3-3). These might be in the form of vibration (such as might be transmitted through the room's structure by floor-standing speakers) or physical jolts.

The stylus doesn't care where the vibrations it picks up emanate from: they can be induced by the wiggles in the groove, or by external sources transmitted through the record via the base and platter. Isolation of the turntable from external vibration is, therefore, very important. One of the most common sources of such vibration is the speakers. The speakers send their signals through the air and through the hard surfaces of the room. If the turntable picks these signals up, and allows them to get to the cartridge, they will be re-amplified over and over again, in what is called a feedback loop. In a worst-case situation, the howl of the feedback will overpower the music, but more often it will simply cause distortion. This distortion may be manifested as rumble, or simply muddy sound, and it is often blamed on other factors.

While it is almost impossible to completely isolate a turntable from its environment, a well-designed base will go a long way toward eliminating the undesirable effects of shock and feedback. The materials used in the construction of the base should be as resonance-free as

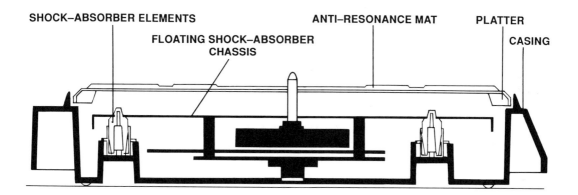

SHOCK–ABSORBER ELEMENTS   ANTI–RESONANCE MAT PLATTER

FLOATING SHOCK–ABSORBER   CASING
CHASSIS

FIGURE 3-3. An important aspect of the turntable's design is its ability to prevent vibration from coloring the sound or rendering a record unplayable. Some models use elaborate multi-phase shock-absorption systems to isolate the platter and tonearm from the base.

possible, and the suspension and feet should be resilient, to absorb vibration before it can get to the tonearm.

When you go shopping, try lightly thumping the shelf your prospective record player is sitting on. If you can hear the result through the speakers or headphones, you may want a more effectively isolated turntable. Obviously, tapping the turntable chassis itself should not result in any audible sounds either. Fortunately, shock resistance and resistance to acoustic feedback tend to go hand in hand, so you need not feel obliged to try carrying out any feedback tests — no easy task in any event.

CONVENIENCE FEATURES AND AUTOMATION

The same high-powered audio buffs who eschew tone controls on their amplifiers (because the amplifier should reveal the pure sound of the recording, and not alter it), and who isolate their listening rooms with weighty poured-concrete walls, tend to opt for totally manual operation of their turntables. This prejudice has its roots in the undeniable crudity of early automatic models. The mechanisms used to move the arm were often unreliable, and could easily do damage to a valuable record. And even when working properly, they depended upon a mechanical trip-lever to trigger end-of-play operation. This put a strain on the arm, preventing it from tracking freely. These problems were solved long ago, but among the *cognoscenti* a complete lack of automation is still *de rigueur*. In fact, in absolute terms better performance may be found in costly manual units whose builders go to great, complicated lengths to keep it all simple. But for most of us a certain amount of automation is almost a necessity.

In absolute terms better performance may be found in costly manual units whose builders go to great, complicated lengths to keep it all simple. But for most of us a certain amount of automation is a necessity.

Why automation? From time to time even a surgeon's hands slip; while we are not talking about so grave an error as connecting someone's kneebone to his wrist, we *are* talking about ruining treasured recordings by scratching them. We are also talking about going out to chop wood while a record is playing, then coming back, blistered and quivering with exhaustion, to find that the disc has been spinning for three hours, the stylus in the exit-groove the whole time.

You should look for *at least* some sort of cuing control — which will let you safely lower the stylus on to the disc — along with a feature that lifts the arm off the record at the end of play. Beyond that, you can save yourself and your records a lot of potential grief with more complete automation. There are plenty of fine, fine units out there that sense the size of the record on the turntable (and, indeed, sense whether there is one there at all — protection against the delicate stylus coming down on a spinning rubber mat), put the arm down in the right place, pick it up again at the end, and turn off the motor.

Beyond that, there are a very few highly programmable models that can play the tracks on a record in any order you choose, repeating any and all according to your whims. There are even a few record changers still on the market (that allow you to pile several records on the spindle), but the old warnings still apply: For one thing, the angle of cartridge to disc changes as the height of the pile of records changes, and the alteration in sound is audible even to a moderately critical listener. Beyond that, with the records in a pile sliding around on top of each other, you will never get them really squeaky clean and thus will never hear really quiet surfaces. Of course, you *can* use the changer to play one record at a time. You can also use a shotgun to catch mice.

PHONO CARTRIDGES

Durable goods are usually defined as consumer articles with a lifespan of more than three years. As a rule, when you plunk down a couple of hundred dollars to buy a consumer durable you get a big hunk of steel for your money; you get something to show your neighbors and a huge carton to put out with the garbage so everyone will know you have enough credit to acquire the latest in computerized refrigerators or washing machines. Even in the high-fidelity field, you generally get some sort of glitzy "proof of purchase": flashing lights, matte black faceplates, wireless remote control units, smoothly operating knobs.

But the hundreds of phono cartridges put on the market by dozens of manufacturers all look more or less alike. You can spend 10 bucks or you can spend a grand (you really can), but all you get to show for it is a hummingbird-sized polygonal form that no one is ever going to see once you have installed it.

Your cartridge and your speakers have more potential for delivering (or not delivering) lots of bang for the buck than any other part of your hi-fi system.

You should, however, be aware that your cartridge and your speakers have more potential for delivering (or not delivering) lots of bang for the buck than any other part of your hi-fi system. Purely electronic devices, such as amplifiers or receivers, are relatively easy to optimize, and terrific performance is fairly common at all price points. Speakers and cartridges are electro-mechanical devices, transducers: they take one form of energy (mechanical, in the case of cartridges) and convert it into another (electrical). There is, therefore, great room for variation among cartridges, both over the price spectrum and within a given price range.

Add to that the fact that we are in a gray, subjective area here. Different people like different kinds of sound and, hence, different cartridges.

What You Must Know

First, figure out how much you want to spend. This should usually be in keeping with the cost of the rest of your system. It is wasteful (and possibly dangerous for the cartridge, which requires delicate handling at this end of the price spectrum) to put an exotic $800 cartridge in a $75 turntable, and just plain dopey to put a cheapie cartridge in a state-of-the-art, cost-no-object installation. A useful, if arbitrary, rule of thumb is that your cartridge should cost (we're talking about actual out-of-pocket expense here, *not* list price — cartridges tend to be very heavily discounted) about one third the cost of your turntable. You should also know just a little bit about the kinds of cartridges out there.

Today, most of them are magnetic. That is, they create electrical output as the result of changes in a magnetic field — in other words, they act as tiny electrical generators. The wavy path of the record grooves (or rather groove: there is only one per side, when you think about it) make the stylus move, the stylus is connected to the cartridge by means of a cantilever, and it is this motion that causes the changes in the magnetic field and creates an electric current.

The logistics of this vary, however, depending on just what that cantilever is connected to, but for our purposes we can divide all magnetic cartridges into two classes: those whose coil is stationary, and those whose coil moves. From the standpoint of the consumer, the main difference between the two types is electrical output. *Fixed-coil* (commonly known as moving-magnet or moving-iron) cartridges produce enough energy to plug directly into a standard phono input. These are by far the most common in the marketplace. *Moving-coil* cartridges, with few exceptions, require additional amplification. Some fancier and/or costlier amplifiers and receivers have this extra amplification stage built in; those that don't will require an external unit.

Knowing a cartridge's output (expressed in thousandths of a volt — mV) and the input sensitivity of your amplifier is thus useful for avoiding the grossest kinds of mismatches, but these are few and far between: most cartridges will work just fine with most amplifiers or receivers, given adequate cartridge output.

The Moving-Coil Cartridge

This brings us to The Question of Moving Coil. Many wealthy audio diehards prefer MC and claim great things for it. They may have something or they may not, but we can make a few generalizations: The MC system is slightly less susceptible to mismatching between amplifier and cartridge. Moreover, while every cartridge (and every *thing* in the known universe) has a frequency at which it resonates, and while resonance makes for distortion, the resonant frequency of moving-coil cartridges tends to be above the musical range. Unfortunately, the extended high-frequency response that results from this can be a disadvantage: the resonant peak can amplify ultrasonic noise in the groove, and any intermodulation distortion in the system's preamplifier will tend to add noise at audible frequencies. Consequently, moving-coil cartridges are generally at their best when used with fairly costly associated equipment.

Stylus Shape

Spherical or conical shaped styli are limited in their ability to respond to the shortest groove modulations. An elliptical stylus is somewhat better in this regard.

A design factor that has significant impact on the tracking ability of a cartridge, and which can account for a price difference between two otherwise similar models, is the shape of the stylus. Generally speaking, spherical or conical shaped styli are limited in their ability to respond to the shortest (high frequency) groove modulations. An elliptical stylus is somewhat better in this regard, and this shape has all but replaced conical models in the low and medium price range. Even better tracking is afforded by styli ground into fairly complex variations on the elliptical theme. They may generally be categorized as "long-contact" elliptical types, and go by various names, including Hyperelliptical, Fine Line, Stereohedron, and Shibata.

Tracking Force

Tracking force (usually specified by the cartridge manufacturer, in grams, as an acceptable range rather than a single number) indicates how much downward force is required to keep the stylus nestled properly in the groove. Since a relatively light tracking force preserves records and the stylus itself, smaller figures are ideally preferable, but it's important not to take this notion to extremes. Best results are likely to be achieved by operating a given cartridge in the middle, rather than at the bottom of its recommended range. Beyond that, you should realize that the difference between a cartridge tracking at one gram, and one tracking at one and a half grams, is — all else being equal — insignificant. Just be sure to choose a cartridge whose rated tracking force matches the capabilities of your tonearm.

The P-Mount Cartridge

That is some of the information you should bear in mind when you go shopping for a cartridge that mounts to your tonearm's headshell using two tiny screws. Such cartridges not only need to be chosen well on their own merits, but properly matched (from the standpoint of tracking force and resonance) to the associated tonearm, all of which requires the cooperation of a skilled — and honest — salesperson. The alternative is to choose a turntable whose tonearm accepts the "P-mount" cartridge format. Such tonearms have no headshell. The chosen P-mount cartridge simply plugs into the end of the tonearm, and that's that. Tonearms accepting P-mount cartridges work properly with *all* P-mount cartridges, so there's no worry about resonance, or tracking force, or any other variable. The trade-off is in performance: the very best cartridges aren't available in the P-mount format, and neither are the very best tonearms. But then again, the best is always very expensive, and if you are shopping in the medium-price range, look into a P-mount system.

4 COMPACT DISC (CD) PLAYERS

Digital audio technology is complicated — so complicated that it makes television, for example, seem as simple as a yo-yo. It is also — in the form of the compact disc — the most significant development in audio since the beginning of hi-fi as a category separate from record players. It is the first major change in music recording and reproduction since 1877, when Thomas Edison discovered that sound could be represented by a squiggly groove on a tin-foil cylinder. Fortunately, there's absolutely no need for anyone who doesn't *already* understand digital audio technology to learn more about how it works than we're about to tell you.

Digital audio is perhaps best understood in relation to the technology it is replacing, called *analog.* Here's the essence of it: Suppose you just composed a very clever melody, and you want to share it immediately with a friend — who happens to live a thousand miles away. You call him on the phone, place the handset next to your piano, and play your tune. Your friend gets the gist of the melody, but there's a lot missing, because the limitations of the telephone system compress the dynamics and alter the frequency response of the original, live event. That's analog. But suppose he's got a piano too, and you call and tell him "first play G-above-middle-C, then play an F..." until you've told him all the notes in your tune. He can then play it on his piano, and if you've been accurate in your description, and he's been accurate in his transcription, he will hear exactly what you intend your melody to sound like. And that's pretty much how digital reproduction works. Because analog reproduction — in the form of pressed vinyl records and conventional tapes — attempts to squeeze a physical representation of the music on to media with restrictive limits, the overall sonic quality cannot, at least on a consistent basis, be as high as that of digital-based systems. The exceptions will occur when the original musical material does not tax the demands of the analog system: for instance, when the music itself has limited dynamic range.

The crux of digital recording is that it doesn't actually store the music; it's an expression of language, of symbols representing the music.

The crux of digital recording is that it doesn't actually store the music; it's an expression of language, of symbols representing the music. What is stored — and later played back — is simply a series of binary numbers, each of which *represents and describes* the music as it existed for $\frac{1}{44,100}$ of a second. Now, because binary numbers are made up solely of zeroes and ones, they can be easily represented electrically by "ons" and "offs" — the presence or absence of a signal — or by the presence of two very different types of signals. It is these numbers — rather than the amount of signal put on the tape — that determines soft or loud, guitar or organ, and so forth. The numbers which represent the music are engraved on disc in the form of a spiral of microscopic pits, each pit usually specified as 0.5 μm wide by 0.1 μm deep by several micrometers long (figure 4-1). The surface is aluminized, so that it can reflect light, and then coated with a protective plastic shield.

Playback is by a laser, which focuses through the protective layer and reflects the encoded data back into an optical sensor. The CD's speed varies from 200 rpm to 500 rpm, depending upon which portion of the disc is being scanned. This enables the laser to scan the

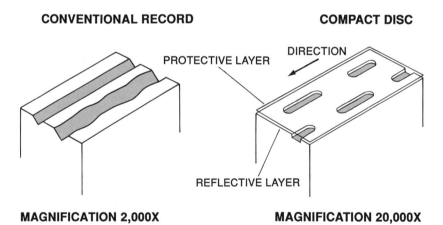

CONVENTIONAL RECORD　　　　　　　**COMPACT DISC**

PROTECTIVE LAYER

DIRECTION

REFLECTIVE LAYER

MAGNIFICATION 2,000X　　　　　**MAGNIFICATION 20,000X**

FIGURE 4-1. The wiggly groove of a vinyl LP record contains a physical representation of the music it contains. By contrast, a compact disc's surface is made up of millions of microscopic pits that describe the music mathematically.

pits at a constant linear velocity, so that the information on the disc can always be processed at the same rate of speed. The digital output is stored briefly in a memory buffer, which holds it momentarily and then releases it in a continuous stream. This buffer eliminates any wow and flutter that might result from rotational inconsistencies. From the buffer, the signal passes into the player's error-correction system, and then to the digital-to-analog convertor. Finally, the signal is filtered to eliminate ultrasonic noise, and then appears at the outputs of the player. The result, as you no doubt have already experienced, can be breathtaking — incredibly clear, detailed, and lifelike.

Compact discs measure a scant 4¾ inches in diameter, and hold up to an hour and a quarter of music on their single playable side. With normal use, the discs don't wear out, fingerprints have little or no effect on them, and scratches on the clear plastic which protects the playing surface usually won't affect their sound. The players themselves range from under $200 to many times that amount. The main *practical* differences between players lies in the features offered, about which we will go into more detail further on. In addition, players will differ in their resistance to external shock and their ability to cope with imperfections in the discs. The nature of the CD format permits various levels of random access and scan functions, along with various display modes, including elapsed and remaining-time indication. Programmability (the ability to select the order of songs for playback) is virtually standard these days, but the *level* of programmability can vary. Some players allow you to program only by track, while others permit you to include sequences defined in a more precise manner — by start and end time, for example.

In addition to "standard" CD players, which accommodate a single disc, there are two types of multiplay changers from which to choose. With one, you place the discs in a magazine, which is then inserted into the player's front panel. Some players of this type will also provide a single-play drawer so you don't have to fuss with the magazine to play just one disc. The main advantage to this type of changer is that their disc magazines can also be used in many automotive CD changers. A potential disadvantage is the relative fragility of the magazines, and the complexity of the mechanism.

The second type of disc changer is called a carousel. It consists of a large platter (which is an integral part of the player and cannot be removed) with five or six recessed areas that hold the discs. A key feature of some examples of this type of changer is that you can gain access to the platter (if, for example, you change your mind about hearing a particular disc) while another disc is playing.

CHOOSING A CD PLAYER

If you've been paying attention to CD player ads you are probably wondering when we're going to get around to discussing techy things like oversampling, the relative advantages of 14-, 16-, and 18- bit systems, and whether or not the 1-bit system represents the wave of the future. Well, we're not, and for a very good reason: they don't matter. Now, we're not saying that all CD players sound the same (although the differences are, in general, so minute as to be nearly imperceptible). It's just that the existence or absence of a given piece of technology in a given piece of equipment in no way reveals anything about the way the equipment will perform in the real world. That being the case, you're better off not giving such matters any weight at all when choosing a player. Instead, concentrate on things that matter.

How do you determine which CD player to buy? What are the differences between players selling for $200 and those for two and three times that amount? Well, you certainly can't use specifications, because they're all superb. You can, however, decide which luxury features are important to you, and which you can live without. You can also make a meaningful assessment of an individual player's ability to withstand shocks: rap it on its top and side to see how much of a jolt it takes to disturb tracking. Determining a player's error-correction capability is a bit more difficult, since it requires a disc with known flaws. Some stores will have special discs designed to test this aspect of a CD player's design.

CD players don't all sound exactly alike, and while it's often difficult to say with any certainty that model A is better than B, you might find that you have a preference.

You can also spend some time listening. As we said, CD players don't all sound exactly alike, and while it's often difficult to say with any certainty that model A is better than model B, you might find that you have a preference.

CD PLAYER FEATURES

Here are some of the more interesting features to consider when choosing a CD player. As you scan them, look for the ones that might relate to the way you'll be using your player. If, for example, you plan to copy all or parts of your CDs to cassette, look for features like peak-level search and tape timing.

A/B Repeat allows you to select random start and end points on a disc and repeat that section for as long as you like. It's usually selected during normal play: you press an "A/B" button at the start of the passage, and again at its end.

Auto Space inserts a few seconds of silence between the tracks being played. This is of interest to those who record tapes for the car, and whose car players have a music scan feature whose operation depends upon sensing these intervals.

Automatic Music Scan is a preview mode which plays a few seconds of each track on the disc. Usually, play may be selected from within scan.

Delete Mode Programming is used to remove a track from the programmed sequence. It's useful for listening to all but one song on an album.

Displays let you know the status of the player. The more elaborate displays can indicate the number of tracks on the disc, the track being played, the tracks selected for future play, the various timing modes (see **Time Display**) and other aspects of the player's operation.

Index Program Search lets you go directly to the intermediate locations, known as index points, that are sometimes used to subdivide the tracks on long discs.

Keyboard Programming makes it easier to select the various tracks for random playback by eliminating the need to step forward and backward through the disc. Often, a deck will offer keyboard programming on the remote controller, but only stepwise programming at the unit itself.

Music Standby is of particular use to recordists as it places the player in the pause mode before each track (or, in some units, user selected tracks) in order to allow the tape deck to be set up or adjusted.

Next/Back sends the laser pickup either to the beginning of the next track or the beginning of the one being played. Pause interrupts play without changing the location of the laser in relation to the disc. Pressing pause again (or, with some players, pressing play) resumes play at the same point.

Peak Level Search scans the entire disc to find the loudest passage. This provides an accurate means of setting the recording levels when you're taping a disc.

Random Access Programming permits you to choose a certain number of selections for playback in any order. Depending upon the player, each selection can be one or more tracks, a timed portion of the disc, a random portion of the disc, an index number, or the entire disc. Programming can be accomplished step-wise, or via a 10- or 11-button keypad. In the latter instance a "10+" button is used to select numbers higher than 10 (to get 15 you would press +10 and 5).

Remote Control allows you to operate the player from your sofa, and you probably already know if you want it. Many remote units have simpler operating controls than the players themselves, including keypad (rather than stepwise) programming. Some even have a volume control.

Repeat is obvious: depending on the player you can program the repeat of either the entire disc, the entire selected program, or any random portion of the disc (see **A/B Repeat**).

Search Modes allow you to fast forward or rewind to a desired point on a disc. Of particular use is audible search, which is found on most players. This lets you hear the music, albeit sped up, during the search mode. Some models have two or even three audible search speeds.

Tape Timing helps the recordist determine which songs on a disc will fit on side A of a cassette, and which must be reserved until after the flip to side B has been made.

Time Display can show the elapsed or remaining time on the disc or selection being played. Some displays are locked into a single mode, while others can be switched to show several in sequence.

Time Programming lets you start play at a specific temporal (as opposed to physical) location on the disc, say two minutes and fifteen seconds into the second track.

5 TUNERS

The tuner's job is probably the most difficult and complex of all the components. It must be able to lock onto one of a possible hundred FM (frequency modulation) broadcast signals, rejecting all others. It must reject myriad other signals, including those from car ignition systems, and atmospheric phenomena such as lightning. (These undesirable signals, by the way, are AM — *amplitude modulation* — sources.) And it must be able to deal with a desired signal whose strength at the antenna might be only a few millionths of a volt, while much stronger signals from closer stations are trying to overpower the weaker one. Once it has done so, the tuner (or tuner section of a receiver) must convert the received signal into useful form so that, further down the line, it can be amplified and finally enter your living room as music.

TUNER SPECIFICATIONS

The tuner is probably the only component whose practical performance capabilities can be judged largely on the basis of specs.

The very difficulty of the tuner's job makes an understanding of some tuner specifications important. In fact, the tuner is probably the only component whose *practical* performance capabilities can be judged largely on the basis of specs. So while convenience features will be considered as well, we're going to concentrate on those specifications which determine the quality of the tuner.

Sensitivity

A tuner's *sensitivity* is simply its ability to receive weak stations. The more sensitive the tuner, the better its ability to lock in on a weak station. But merely receiving a station isn't enough for good listening: if inherent background noise isn't sufficiently suppressed, no one will want to listen. Since the signal-to-noise ratio of a tuner improves as the received signal gets stronger, the sensitivity spec is stated using two numbers: an amount of signal strength (measured in microvolts or dBf) will be related to a signal-to-noise ratio (stated in dB). In other words, for a given amount of signal received by the antenna, you'll get music that's a given number of decibels above the noise.

There are several standards used to state sensitivity, the first being "usable sensitivity." Usable sensitivity is the amount of signal required to yield a 30 dB signal-to-noise (S/N) ratio, in mono. Now, 30 dB is a pretty poor figure. More significant is the spec which calls for the amount of signal required to yield a 50 dB S/N, in stereo. It's generally agreed that 50 dB, while not great, is at least listenable, and that's the sensitivity spec that means something from a practical standpoint. So when you encounter a spec sheet that lists both "usable sensitivity" and "sensitivity for 50 dB of quieting," it's the latter figure to be concerned with.

Selectivity

Sensitivity is of no value unless the tuner also has good selectivity: the ability to lock in on a desired station while rejecting signals from specific nearby frequencies. FM channels are 0.2 megahertz (MHz) apart; 104.3, 104.5, and so on (figure 5-1). Normally, the Federal Communications Commission will not assign frequencies closer than 0.8 MHz to stations in the same listening area. This separation is

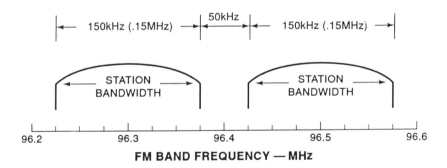

FIGURE 5-1. The FM band has 100 possible station frequencies, established at 0.2 MHz (200 kHz) intervals. Each station occupies 150 kHz of bandwidth, which leaves a 50 kHz "safety zone" between channels.

sufficient to keep interference to a minimum. But listeners in suburban areas are often able to receive signals from two cities, and those signals might be only 0.4 MHz apart. Because it skips every other channel, this is called *alternate channel spacing*. Further, many of the most sensitive new tuners, with the help of outdoor antennas, are able to pull in stations from as far away as 100 miles. In such cases the tuner might be subject to signals that are only 0.2 MHz apart. This is called *adjacent channel spacing*. If the desired signal is the distant one, the nearby alternate or adjacent channel is likely to be much stronger, and could cause severe reception problems.

Selectivity, then, is the ability of a tuner to reject these alternate and adjacent signals, and with them the resulting audible distortion. Generally speaking, the quoted figure called selectivity will refer to *alternate channel selectivity*. It is also referred to as *alternate channel attenuation*. Some specification sheets also reveal adjacent channel selectivity as well; it's worth looking for, because it will indicate a better tuner. In both instances, the spec will be stated in dB, and the higher the number, the better — within limits (70 dB is a pretty good figure). As it happens, when selectivity is taken to the limit other specs sometimes suffer.

High selectivity requires a very narrow bandwidth (the window of signal acceptability). Unfortunately, narrowing a bandwidth will usually yield higher distortion, poorer *capture ratio* (the ability to suppress the weaker of two signals at the same frequency), and lower stereo separation than would otherwise be the case. Thus, many high-end tuners offer variable selectivity (also called variable bandwidth). In addition to the narrow band, which enables the tuner to provide excellent selectivity, these tuners have a second or wide band, with a much lower selectivity spec — often 25 dB or thereabouts (as opposed to a narrow-band figure of 70 dB or better). This wide band is used if interference from alternate or adjacent channels isn't a problem — which is the case not only in certain geographic areas, but at certain areas of the FM dial even when other areas are crowded; the wide bandwidth position achieves the best sound quality. But in the presence of strong interference from neighboring stations, the narrow position can be counted upon to provide the best reception.

Signal-to-Noise Ratio

Since many people live relatively close to their favorite FM stations, and enjoy a strong signal, an important spec to consider is ultimate signal-to-noise ratio. As a tuner receives a stronger signal, it is able to more effectively suppress the background noise. A point is finally reached, though, where the noise is as far below the signal as it will get, and that point defines the tuner's signal-to-noise ratio. The figure (which is expressed in dB) should be as high as possible, and should be stated for mono and stereo. Since the process of stereo broadcasting introduces some noise into the system, the mono figure will always rate better.

Total Harmonic Distortion

As a tuner receives a stronger signal from the station it not only yields a quieter program, but one with lower distortion as well. The *total harmonic distortion* (THD) spec tells the minimum distortion that can be expected, and that spec is reached when a further increase in signal strength doesn't lower the distortion any further. The spec is stated in both mono and stereo, and just as S/N is higher in mono, THD is lower. Generally speaking, the THD spec is given for a 1 kHz test signal. Tuners have higher distortion than amplifiers, and a figure of less than 0.5 percent in stereo is considered to be good.

Capture Ratio

Capture ratio is a very important specification, for it tells how well the tuner can suppress the weaker of two signals appearing at the same frequency. There are two ways that such a condition might occur.

The first involves two separate stations, broadcasting at the same frequency. If a tuner were to be placed 100 miles equidistant from two cities, it's quite possible for it to receive signals from both. When the FCC made its station assignments it didn't take into account the possibility of a tuner good enough to receive signals from 100 miles away. Thus, it's possible — even likely — that cities 200 miles apart will have stations broadcasting at the same frequency. A tuner receiving both stations will have to reject one of them completely, or neither will be listenable (figure 5-2).

The second instance of a tuner receiving two signals at the same frequency is where severe multipath distortion exists. *Multipath distortion* is caused by radio-wave reflection (figure 5-3). The signal from the transmitter should reach the antenna in a straight line, but often this direct signal is followed, a fraction of a second later, by signals reflected off a tall building, mountains, or other objects. This reflected signal is much weaker than the direct signal, but unless it's completely rejected it can cause audible distortion, and in extreme cases a fading of the signal. (Television "ghosts" are also caused by

When the FCC made its station assignments it didn't take into account the possibility of a tuner good enough to receive signals from 100 miles away.

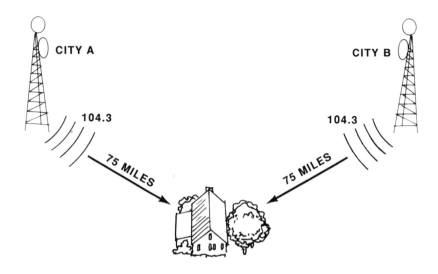

FIGURE 5-2. It's possible for a tuner that is equidistant between two cities to receive signals at the same frequency from different stations. The tuner's capture ratio determines how well it is able to reject the weaker of the two signals.

multipath distortion.) Since the reflected signal is at the same frequency as the direct one, the tuner treats it as another station, broadcasting from a different location.

In both instances, the tuner's capture ratio is a good indication of how well it can cope with the problem. Capture ratio is expressed in dB, and the lower the number the better. This is because the number indicates the difference in strength required for the tuner to select the stronger of the two signals, and reject completely the weaker. A capture ratio of 1.5 dB (which is quite respectable) means that if the weaker signal is 1.5 dB less strong than the desired one, it will be rejected. A good capture ratio, then, is important both in the city — because of multipath — and in suburban and rural areas — because of the high sensitivity of today's tuners.

Separation

Separation refers to a tuner's ability to isolate the two stereo channels from one another. This means, for instance, that if the lead guitar is only on the right channel on the record being broadcast, it won't "bleed" through to the left channel. Most tuner specifications are derived from a test tone with a frequency of 1 kHz fed into only one channel. If we assign an arbitrary level of 0 dB to the original signal going into that one channel, we can then determine the tuner's

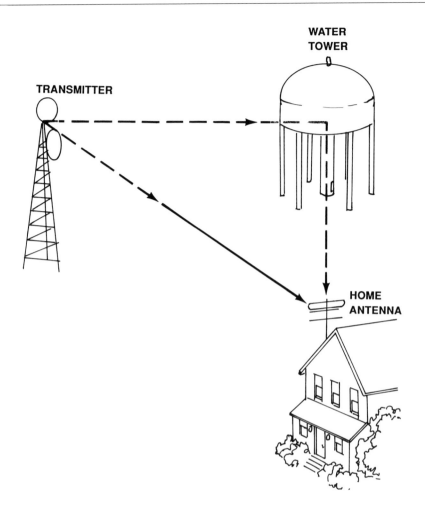

FIGURE 5-3. When a station's signal reaches the tuner both directly and a fraction of a second later, as a result of reflection, the result will be audible as multipath distortion. A good capture ratio can reduce or eliminate the effects of this problem.

separation spec by measuring the level of the signal in the other channel. If it is 30 dB weaker than the original, the tuner is said to have 30 dB of separation at 1 kHz. Some manufacturers repeat the test, and provide specifications for higher and lower audio frequencies as well. A reasonable 1 kHz spec is 30 dB, which is as good as the source material used by most radio stations.

Other Rejection Specs

In addition to these primary specifications, tuners are often measured for AM, IF, and image rejection, all of which are specified in dB. Its AM (amplitude modulation) rejection spec tells how well a tuner suppresses certain kinds of atmospheric interference. It also plays a part, along with capture ratio, in reducing the audible effects of multipath. In areas where there's heavy shortwave traffic, a tuner needs to have good IF (intermediate frequency) rejection, while the reception problems caused by air traffic control at nearby airports call for excellent image rejection. In all cases, the higher the number the better. This is one instance where top-of-the-line tuners are often quite a bit better than low-end models.

TUNING

Tuner design is, of course, important, but so is tuning itself. The slightest deviation from precise tuning results in higher noise and distortion, as well as reduced separation. Up until a few years ago, the user was directly responsible for fine-tuning his receiver or tuner. One turned a knob in one direction or the other, approaching the station frequency gradually. The signal got cleaner until the center of the channel was reached, at which point further tuning in the same direction resulted in a gradual reduction in quality. These days tuning is most often accomplished digitally, using *quartz-referenced frequency synthesis*. This method assures exceptional accuracy, and has all but eliminated the need for tuning aids.

These days tuning is most often accomplished digitally, using quartz-referenced frequency synthesis. This method assures exceptional accuracy.

The circuitry used to provide frequency synthesis thus makes a center-channel tuning meter unnecessary: the only possible tuning point is the center of the channel. Very often, though, a signal-strength meter is provided, in order to aid in antenna aiming.

It's worth noting that while almost all frequency-synthesized tuners feature a digital display of the tuned frequency, it's also possible to provide such a display on a conventionally tuned model. This is done for the sake of convenience, and is certainly a legitimate and worthwhile feature. Just be certain that when looking at a digital tuner you are talking about the *circuitry* rather than just the *display*; an unscrupulous salesperson will deliberately confuse the two.

Tuning Modes

Most frequency-synthesized tuners don't have conventional tuning knobs. Instead, they offer one or more alternate methods of finding a desired station. The simplest method is a pair of buttons, one to send the tuner to the next highest frequency, another to select the next lowest. Of course, more often than not, the next highest or lowest frequency will contain not music, but noise. So the next level up in tuning convenience causes the tuner to scan to the next *broadcast*. An adjunct to this system allows one to vary the threshold (or sensitivity) of this circuit, thus bypassing stations whose reception is marginal. In addition, some tuners also allow the frequency of the desired station to be entered on a 10-digit keypad.

Beyond step, scan, and direct entry tuning — and present on virtually all synthesized tuners — is preset tuning. This enables the user to select a number of favorite stations and store them in the tuner's memory. Once done, a touch of the appropriate button tunes the desired station instantly. There are several ways of setting up the presets. Say, for instance, there are 10 preset buttons. They might be split up into five AM and five FM choices, or each of them might be able to select 10 stations in each band; a shift key might be provided, too, to double the number of possible presets. Random-access presets allow each button to automatically select the band as well as the desired station.

Other features sometimes associated with preset tuning include automatic station scan memorization (which places into preset memory those stations with enough signal strength to be heard clearly), and preset scan, which stops for a few seconds at each preset station.

Some tuners offer more than one setting to be selected for various reception modes. These can include sensitivity (i.e., local/distant), selectivity (i.e., wide/narrow), and stereo/mono. It can be useful to be able to associate the settings that work best for each station with its corresponding preset button.

Preset tuning depends, of course, on the tuner being able to remember the user's programmed stations. Some early tuners would lose their memory as soon as their plugs were removed from the wall. The incorporation of a battery backup system solved that problem, but still lacked consistent reliability. A more advanced solution uses a capacitor to provide backup power to the memory for several weeks after AC power has been interrupted. This capacitor stores energy whenever power is applied, but releases energy in a slow, controlled flow.

Muting

When tuning an analog model, or a digital tuner in step-fashion (rather than via presets), the user must pass through a great deal of

---

How FM Works

....

The letters FM stand for *frequency modulation*, and to understand what that means, and why it's important, it's first necessary to see some of the problems inherent in AM — *amplitude modulation* radio.

With the latter system, the broadcaster sends out a signal on a fixed frequency, which will be somewhere between 540 and 1,600 kHz (kilohertz). The program content causes the level (or amplitude) of the signal to vary (or modulate), and the AM receiver translates these changes in signal level back into music, or news, or whatever. The problem with amplitude modulation is that many of the more common sources of interference have electrical waveforms that appear to the receiver to be desirable signals. A result is, for instance, static during a thunderstorm.

The FM broadcaster, by contrast, is assigned a *range* of frequencies, which extends 75 kHz on each side of his nominal frequency. The nature of the signal being broadcast determines how this "extra" range will be used at any given moment. The amplitude of the signal (its loudness) affects the *amount* of the swing to either side of the center; the frequency (its pitch) determines, quite logically, how often the swing occurs. Therefore, if a broadcaster operating at 104.3 MHz (megahertz) was to send out a pure tone of, say, "middle C" at 261.6 Hz, the 104.3 MHz carrier would shift between frequencies slightly above and below at a rate of 261.6 times a second. The receiver is able to distinguish between the FM nature of the broadcast signal, and the AM nature of interference, and can thus be designed to reject the latter and provide static-free reception.

---

potentially noisy airspace to get from one station to another. The noise that appears between stations can, depending upon volume level, be anything from annoying to dangerous: its high-frequency content can damage speakers if the volume is inadvertently set too high. Thus, most analog tuners (and many digital models with scan tuning) incorporate a muting circuit that cuts the tuner's output during the rough-tuning process, and restores it once the desired station has been located. A second purpose of the muting circuit is to assure that all received stations will be heard with a minimum of background noise. Thus, when the muting is on and a very weak station is tuned, the muting circuit realizes that the noise would overshadow the music, and mutes the output.

Most analog tuners incorporate a muting circuit that cuts the tuner's output during the rough-tuning process, and restores it once the desired station has been located.

High Blend

Most of the noise and distortion inherent in weak stereo signals occurs in the higher frequencies. A drastic solution would be to switch the tuner into mono. This would dramatically reduce the noise and distortion, but at the expense of any stereo effect at all. Depending upon the severity of the problem, another solution is available. By blending the two channels into mono only at the high frequencies — which is where the noise and distortion manifest themselves — it's possible to eliminate (or greatly reduce) that noise and still retain good overall stereo separation. Some tuners take high blend a step further, automatically varying the amount of high blend depending upon the strength of the signal. That way, maximum stereo separation is maintained, while noise and distortion is kept to a minimum. Unfortunately, this can cause another form of distortion, which sounds like a pumping or breathing of the noise.

6 AMPLIFIERS

Amplifiers and preamplifiers can stand alone, or their functions can be combined into single units — integrated amplifiers and receivers (which also contain tuners). In the following discussion, bear in mind that when we say "amplifier" we also mean the amplifier section of an integrated amplifier or receiver, and when we say tuner we're also referring to the tuner section of a receiver (figure 6-1).

An audio amplifier's main function, as its name implies, is to take a small electrical signal and turn it into a large electrical signal. The reason we need an amplifier has to do with the *efficiency* of

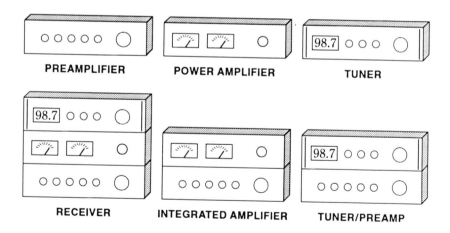

PREAMPLIFIER   POWER AMPLIFIER   TUNER

RECEIVER   INTEGRATED AMPLIFIER   TUNER/PREAMP

FIGURE 6-1. The preamplifier, power amplifier, and tuner are available separately or in various combinations. These include the receiver; the integrated amplifier, which requires the use of a separate tuner for radio reception; and the tuner/preamp, which is used with an external power amplifier.

loudspeakers. Speakers need large amounts of electrical energy to produce sound. The motions of a stylus in a groove don't generate enough power for this purpose; neither do the radio waves received by a tuner; nor do the tiny impulses generated as recorded tape passes a tape head. Simply stated, then, an amplifier's job is to take these very small units of energy and raise their level to a degree sufficient for a loudspeaker to turn them into sound.

An amplifier's job is to take these very small units of energy and raise their level to a degree sufficient for a loudspeaker to turn them into sound.

There are two basic stages of amplification. The first is preamplification. The smallest signals, such as those generated by phono cartridges, are measured in thousandths of a volt. These signals must be preamplified to around one volt. (This preamplification stage is built into tuners and tape decks; their output is at the one-volt level.) Once at the one-volt level, the audio signal is further amplified by the main (power) amplifier to the levels needed for transformation by the loudspeakers from electrical to acoustical energy.

The second function of an amplifier is to provide the controls necessary to a high-fidelity system. It must provide input and output facilities to allow for the connection of various signal sources and outboard devices, and the switching to enable them to function properly. The volume and tone controls, the filters and loudness-compensation switches and circuitry, are all part of the amplifier.

In addition, the circuitry needed to provide proper RIAA (Record Industry Association of America) equalization in the phono stage is part of the preamplifier. RIAA equalization is a standardized non-linear record/playback process which permits records to be cut with less distortion. It's needed because the cutting stylus does not respond to a constant-level signal equally at all musical frequencies. One function of RIAA equalization is to reduce the level of low frequencies to limit the travel of both cutting stylus and playback stylus. (A side benefit is increased playing time on the disc.) At the same time, the high frequencies are boosted to compensate for inherent mechanical losses. In playback, an inverse RIAA equalization is applied by the preamplifier, yielding flat overall response.

The amplification and control sections of an amplifier are available in several formats. Separate preamplifiers and power amplifiers are the most flexible — and the most costly. Generally speaking, the preamplifier handles the low-level amplification (often including an additional stage of pre-preamplification for extra-low-output moving-coil cartridges) and the various switching functions, such as those between signal sources. The power amplifier simply receives the output from the preamplifier/control section and provides amplification, also called gain. But some power amplifiers also feature control functions. Many offer outputs and switching for two or more sets of speakers. Others will accept inputs from two sources, again with switching. Level controls, too, are found on some units. These generally adjust the input sensitivity of the unit — the amount of signal required at the input to achieve a given level at the output — and are used to optimize the volume-control action (and signal-to-noise, or S/N, ratio) of the preamp, depending upon the efficiency of the speakers being used.

Integrated Components

When preamp and power amp are combined in a single chassis, without a tuner, the result is called an *integrated amplifier*. When the same functions are combined with a tuner, the result is called a *receiver*.

There is no inherent reason for separate components to be superior to such integrated units, but engineering realities and the marketplace have seen to it that such is usually the case. Receiver customers generally look for the best combination of features, performance, and value. That is why they opt for a single component, thus saving the cost of extra chassis and power supplies. "Separates" customers, on the other hand, are willing to spend a bit (or a great deal) more in order to get the state-of-the-art circuitry and features not available in integrated units.

The truth of the matter is that while receivers are astonishingly good, it's the separate components that offer the latest technology.

And the truth of the matter is that while receivers are astonishingly good, it's the separate components that offer the latest technology. (In fact, attempts to market "state-of-the-art" receivers, with 200 to 300 watts per channel, were made not too long ago. While the receivers in question were superb, they didn't sell well: customers with the dollars to look for that kind of performance inevitably want separates.)

So we've established that all component systems need both pre- and power amplifiers, and that they are available in several formats. For purposes of discussion, we're going to treat all preamps and all power amps equally, whether they share a line cord and cabinet with one another (or with a tuner), or stand alone.

THE POWER AMPLIFIER

The power amplifier's job is to provide gain: to take a small signal and turn it into a large one — *without changing it in any other way*. This qualifying phrase is very important, for any change other than in level is considered distortion. In other words, anything appearing at the output of the amplifier that didn't appear at its input doesn't belong there, and can be called distortion. A certain amount of distortion is inevitable in any electronic device, but for a given device to be called a high-fidelity component the level and nature of that distortion must be such that it is inaudible. We're going to look at distortion, and the way it's reduced to negligible levels, further on in this section. In the meantime, it's worth looking at some important power-amp specifications (including distortion), and seeing what they mean. The first specification is tied into several others, and logically enough, is power output.

Power

If the amplifier's job is to provide electrical energy, its power spec simply tells how much of a job it can do. Since the amount of power an amplifier is able to provide is dependent upon several factors, it makes sense for the power spec to include those factors as well. In fact, the government (to be precise, the Federal Trade Commission, or FTC) mandates it.

The reasoning behind the government's involvement in the world of consumer audio stems from abuses perpetrated by some dealers and manufacturers in stating the power output of the products they were selling. Because the marketing/sales people did not agree with the engineers on a standard, these merchants were free to quote virtually any power output that could conceivably be achieved by a product, *regardless of how long that power could be maintained*, at what distortion, or over what range of musical frequencies. If one driven channel of a stereo amplifier could be made to reach 100 watts at any frequency, even for the briefest instant, and regardless of the distortion level (which could easily exceed 10 percent) it would be advertised as a 200-watt amplifier (two channels, after all!). Eventually, enough consumers purchased "200-watt" amplifiers, found them incapable of driving loudspeakers with a minimum requirement of 10 or 15 watts, and complained. Ultimately, the FTC stepped in and promulgated the standard which at least provides a modicum of protection for the consumer.

Now, when quoting power output, a manufacturer must state the power (in continuous watts per channel, not just occasional bursts), the amount of distortion present at that power, the *load impedance* (or *resistance*, which corresponds very roughly to the load that a speaker will place on the amplifier) at which the power is measured, and the bandwidth (frequency range) over which that power can be maintained. Further, before it is measured, the amplifier must undergo a period of "preconditioning" where it's run at full power for 20 minutes, and at one-third power for 40 minutes.

The natural question, at this point, is "How much power do I need?" Unfortunately, there is no simple answer — other than "More!" Power is but one of the variables in the equation that, when solved, yields a given volume level in the listening room. Other variables include the efficiency of the loudspeaker being played, and the size of the room. That being the case, the safest approach is to choose your speakers first, and then select an amplifier with sufficient power to drive them to the desired level. If that course of action isn't viable, it's safer to err on the high side — to buy somewhat more power than you really need — since speakers are more likely to be damaged by a low-powered amplifier working too hard than by a high-powered model that's just cruising along. And, if you're absolutely forced to make a more-or-less arbitrary choice, an amplifier in the 50-watt/channel region is a pretty safe bet for all but the most power-hungry speakers (figure 6-2). The rule of thumb is that the vast majority of speakers will work perfectly well with the vast majority of amplifiers.

The rule of thumb is that the vast majority of speakers will work perfectly well with the vast majority of amplifiers.

The reason bandwidth and load must be stated relate to the nature of music, and to the way amplifiers and loudspeakers relate to one another. Generally speaking, amplifiers are capable of more output at the mid frequencies than at either extreme. Thus, an amplifier that can provide 75 watts at 1,000 Hz (midrange) might be limited to 40 watts at 10 Hz (low range) or 25,000 Hz (high range). The frequency range of music extends (with few exceptions) from 20 Hz a full 10 octaves to 20,000 Hz. Further, the lower frequencies require more power output from the amplifier. It's therefore important to know the range, or bandwidth, over which an amplifier can produce its rated power. (At this point in the state of the audio art, virtually all reputable manufacturers specify power from 20 to 20,000 Hz.)

The reason it is important to know the load impedance at which the power was measured has to do with the fact that most amplifiers' power will vary if the impedance is changed. So for the sake of comparison, a common impedance — eight ohms, which corresponded to the majority of loudspeakers when the law was passed — was chosen for the usual power specification disclosure. The resulting power specification of a typical amplifier will look something like this: 40 watts per channel, min. RMS (Root Mean Square, which is technical jargon meaning, roughly, continuous), at 8 ohms with both channels driven, from 20 to 20,000 Hz, with no more than 0.04 percent total harmonic distortion.

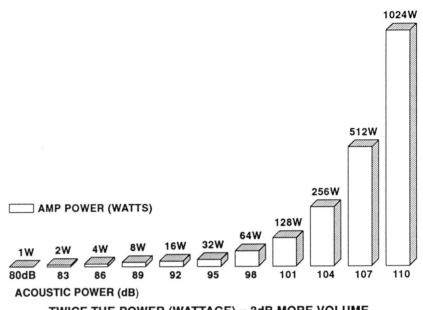

FIGURE 6-2. The small audible difference between, say, a 40-watt amplifier and one having 60 watts is illustrated by this chart. A 3 dB increase in acoustical output in the listening room requires twice as much amplifier power.

Signal-to-Noise Ratio

The signal-to-noise ratio of an amplifier, just as with any other component, tells us how much softer the noise is than the music for a given input signal.

Music is the signal that we want to amplify; noise consists of the non-musical signals that appear as a result of the amplification process. The signal-to-noise ratio of an amplifier, just as with any other component, tells us how much softer the noise is than the music for a given input signal.

In an integrated amp or preamp, it's important to consider the high-level S/N — which deals with the relatively strong signals coming from sources like tape decks and CD players — and the phono section S/N. The latter, since it must have an additional level of amplification to deal with the very small signals transmitted by the phono cartridge, will of necessity have a numerically worse figure. (In a power amp there will be only one, high-level S/N figure, and it might be somewhere in the mid-90 dBs, which means that the noise level will be inaudible.) Because the phono S/N figure will vary

Power versus Current

One of the problems with the FTC system of disclosing power is that, despite the good intentions of that august organization, it doesn't reflect the way an amplifier will perform in real life, and it can mislead the consumer into spending more money than necessary for a given level of performance. Speakers don't behave like the resistors used to measure amplifier power. For one thing, their impedance (or resistance) varies with frequency. This fact has recently been recognized by some amp manufacturers, and amplifiers designed to operate into lower impedances are becoming common. But beyond this impedance shift is the fact that a speaker is *not* solely a resistive device. Rather, it combines resistance and reactance. Let's look at what this means to an amplifier.

Ohm's Law defines a very precise relationship between current, voltage, and resistance. It states that current (measured in amperes) is equal to voltage divided by resistance (measured in ohms). Now, most amplifiers provide a constant *voltage*, regardless of the *resistance* (speaker impedance) they encounter at their outputs. Since, in such an instance, voltage and resistance are "givens," the only available variable is the current. When the resistance drops, then, the current rises, delivering more power to the speaker. At least that's the theory, and it's what many amplifier manufacturers would have you believe happens in practice. Unfortunately it's not as simple as that.

An amplifier's current-producing capability depends upon two factors. First, there are the output transistors, which act as valves, controlling the flow. Think of them as faucets: when fully opened, they allow just so much water to flow through them at a time, and no more. The other factor is the power supply, or — in fluid terms — the water tank. Now, suppose you found that you couldn't fill your bathtub as quickly as you'd like. You could replace your smallish faucet with a big one. But were you to open that big faucet all the way you'd achieve a moment or two of impressive flow, and then a mere trickle. *You've emptied your tank.* It's the same with amplifiers. Output transistors that can handle a large flow of current are of little use if the power supply quickly becomes depleted and can't keep up with the demands of the program material. The bottom line, of course is this: an amplifier's stated "current capability" is often simply a measurement of the maximum flow capacity of its transistors. This can be misleading, and is about as useful, by itself, as knowing the diameter of a length of pipe. It must be related to something *real*. What's real — and what should be considered important — is how much power an amplifier puts out into various low-impedances loads. Good low-impedance characteristics require output transistors with high-current capabilities, that are matched with sufficiently strong power supplies. Therefore, to know how an amplifier will perform in the real world, with real speakers, look for the amount of power an amplifier can put out into low impedances, i.e., four ohms or two ohms.

It's worth noting that there's another way to assure adequate "real-world" power. That's by purchasing an amplifier with much more "FTC" power than is actually required for the application. But while that method will work, it's not a terribly cost-effective way to build a system, since money that's been spent for wasted power can't be allocated towards other, more audibly satisfying ends.

according to the strength of the input signal used to derive the measurement, it's important to make sure that the models you're comparing were measured in the same way. For the most part, manufacturers have settled on a 5 mV (milliVolt) input signal for this purpose. Using such a signal, a S/N figure in the mid-70s dB range is considered excellent for a moving-magnet phono section. If the unit being measured has a moving-coil stage as well, to handle low-output moving-coil cartridges, a reduction of six or so dB (which is an increase in noise) is common.

Total Harmonic Distortion

Simply put, anything present at the output that wasn't present at the input of a component is distortion. Distortion is always measured as a percentage of the total signal, but there are several types of distortion, some of them more significant than others from an audible standpoint. The easiest to understand and measure, and the most often cited (primarily out of habit) is *total harmonic distortion* (THD). This form of distortion is referenced to, and measured at, the amplifier's maximum output. The measuring technique uses a steady-state sine wave input signal — which is a pure tone containing no harmonics — with the device under test connected to a load resistor, an oscilloscope, and a THD meter. The scope picture is examined as the power is increased, and when the sine wave begins to appear distorted the amplifier is said to be *clipping*. And, indeed, the picture looks as though the upper and lower peaks of the sine wave have been clipped off. It is just *below* the clipping point that the THD meter's readout is "frozen" and the spec is determined. It's worth noting that, generally speaking, as a given amplifier's power output is increased, so is its THD. The rate of increase of THD should be as gradual as possible.

Bear in mind, when considering the notion of THD, that from an audible standpoint it is the least offensive form of amplifier distortion. Thus, it's possible to have an amplifier whose THD spec is superb, but which doesn't sound as clean as another amp with a seemingly worse THD figure. That would be because the first amp produced an additional, more audible form of distortion (or because neither level of THD was audible). Let's now look at what that might be.

Intermodulation Distortion

More audible than THD is a type of distortion called *intermodulation distortion* (IM). It occurs when two frequencies — one low, the other high — are combined (as they are in most music) and produce

---

Negative Feedback

••

It's possible to greatly reduce THD by using a technique called negative feedback. Negative feedback (NFB) is a means of self-correction that uses a small fraction of the output signal, and sends it back to the input 180 degrees out of *phase.* (When two moving objects or signals are "in phase" they are moving, say, back and forth together. When they are "out of phase" they are not moving together, and the degree to which they are not together can be expressed in degrees. Since 180 degrees is exactly backwards, it means that when one signal is moving "back" the other is moving "forth," and that they both change direction at the same time — i.e., with no overlap.) This "mirror-image" output is compared with the input, and if there are differences (which there will be) they are cancelled by the application of an inverse or mirror-image voltage. Within limits, the more NFB used, the lower the measurable THD. Because of this, there was a tendency among some manufacturers to use excessive NFB in an attempt to "clean up" a poorly designed amplifier. But too large an amount of NFB, while providing an exceptional THD spec, can also result in a harsh-sounding amplifier. It's now usual to design an amplifier to be as distortion-free as possible from the outset, and then use a small amount of NFB for a final "touch-up."

---

two more frequencies which are the sum and difference of the originals. If, for instance, test tones of 60 Hz and 7,000 Hz were applied to the input of an amplifier, the resulting IM would appear at the output as 6,940 Hz (7,000 minus 60) and 7,060 Hz (7,000 plus 60). In fact, steady-state IM measurements are often made using those frequencies, with the 60 Hz signal four times stronger than the one at 7,000 Hz. Because it results in frequencies that are heard as less "natural" than the overtones of harmonic distortion, IM distortion is more bothersome to the ear.

THE PREAMPLIFIER

The loudness control is designed to enable the amplifier to compensate for the fact that at low listening levels the ear is less sensitive to high and low notes than to those in the middle frequencies.

In addition to handling the phono preamplification and RIAA equalization referred to at the beginning of the chapter, the preamp serves as a control center. What follows is a discussion of the various controls to be found on preamps, integrated amps, and receivers.

Loudness Control

Every amplifier has a volume control, but in addition, most have a switch marked "loudness." This switch is designed to enable the amplifier to compensate for the fact that at low listening levels the ear is less sensitive to high and low notes than to those in the middle frequencies. While each person's response in these areas will differ a little, an average can be described, and indeed has by two scientists called Fletcher and Munson. This average is called the Fletcher-Munson curve (figure 6-3). When the loudness control is switched on, it boosts the high and low notes to a level corresponding to the Fletcher-Munson curves. At high volume levels no high or low boost at all is needed, because the ear's response is "flat." But when the volume is reduced, the bass and treble are boosted, to compensate for the ear's deficiencies. This prevents the music from sounding "thin." The drawback to this method, of course, is that it doesn't take into account the fact that speakers vary in efficiency. This means that for a given position of the volume control, one brand of speaker might be playing softly, while another brand quite loudly. Since the amount of loudness compensation is fixed by the position of the amplifier's volume control, efficient speakers will receive too much boost, while power-hungry models might not receive enough to achieve the desired effect.

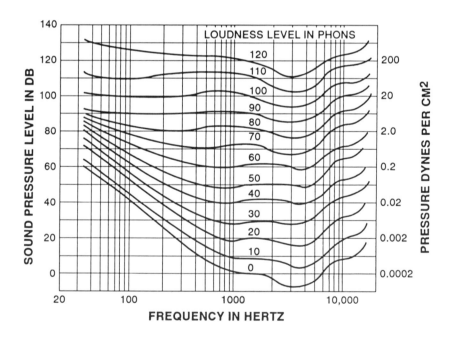

FIGURE 6-3. Applying the Fletcher–Munson curves means adjusting the level of certain frequencies at different loudness levels to compensate for the ear's natural bias. For example, bass frequencies (left side of graph) are boosted at lower loudness levels because the ear doesn't hear those frequencies well at low volumes.

Variable Loudness Control

One solution to this problem calls for a variable loudness control — sort of a secondary volume control. With this setup, the primary volume control is set once, to the highest level likely to be desired. This setting is made with the loudness control turned all the way up. From then on, reductions in *volume* are made by backing off on the loudness control. What this does is lower the *overall* output from the speakers, while at the same time applying the appropriate amount of of relative bass and treble boost for the actual sound level in the room.

Tone Controls

While purists often balk at the use of tone controls, there are times when a combination of room acoustics, speaker characteristics, and program material call for a deviation from flat response. Older records, for instance, often lack the extended high-frequency response present in contemporary pressings. Conversely, older cassettes might have excessive hiss. In each instance, the treble control can be used to compensate. A boost at the high end can also restore the sparkle to a cymbal if an overstuffed living room sofa has absorbed much of it. Or a boost in the bass can help a speaker whose woofer doesn't have what it takes. Oft times, too, the too-bright sound of a badly mastered CD can be tamed with a bit of treble cut, or the excessive boominess on some rock albums reduced by backing down on the bass control.

Some tone controls are more likely to induce distortion than others. The best in this regard are controls which do not use active devices such as transistors to achieve the desired results. Instead, they rely on passive devices (like filters) from which they take their name: passive tone controls.

In essence, tone controls are the most rudimentary kind of equalizer.

In essence, tone controls are the most rudimentary kind of equalizer, but they cannot be used to compensate for problems occurring in a narrow frequency range. They are, instead, broadband devices best suited to making fairly wide range changes in the overall tonal balance.

Tone Defeat

The purists who shun tone controls often find that even when these controls are in the neutral or "flat" position the circuitry has a negative effect on the sound. In order to prevent possible sonic degradation it may be preferable to totally bypass the tone control circuits. The tone defeat switch or circuit serves this purpose, as do tone controls whose neutral position electrically isolates their circuitry.

Balance Control

In a word, this control's job is to balance the output of the two channels. More often than not, it will remain centered, but if conditions in a given listening room cause one speaker to sound appreciably louder than the other, the control will permit compensation.

Mode Switch

Most often, the mode switch simply selects between mono and stereo. If a mono record is being played, switching to mono can reduce some of the noise that is often picked up by a stereo cartridge. (Earlier mono cartridges don't pick up that noise, since their output is the result of stylus motion from side to side, and thus they ignore noise-inducing material on the groove wall that the more flexible stereo styli are able to track.) A more elaborate type of mode control permits the selection of "stereo reverse" (to compensate, for example, when a radio station has reversed the channels during broadcast) and the sending of just-left or just-right channels to both speakers. The latter modes are useful for playing reel-to-reel tapes that have been recorded in quarter-track mono (with separate programs on the left and right channels), for isolating individual instruments on records, and for hooking up monaural video sources.

Tape Monitor

The tape monitor was originally intended to interrupt the signal path to permit the monitoring of the playback signal (during the record process) on a three-head tape deck. While primarily, of course, used for that purpose, the tape-monitor loop also functions as the point at which other signal-processing devices are installed. Equalizers, noise-reduction systems, dynamic-range expanders, et al, can connect via the tape-monitor loop. For this reason (and because many audiophiles own two tape decks) it's common to find two tape-monitor loops (and switches) on many amps and receivers.

Dubbing

One of the reasons to have two tape decks is to make copies, using one for record, the other for playback. To facilitate such dubbing, many control panels feature a special switch which connects the decks together for that purpose, while allowing the user to listen to any other source (or, of course, to listen to either of the two decks). Some systems permit dubbing only in one direction, while others permit either deck to serve as the source.

Separate Input and Tape Selectors

A more flexible set of controls eliminates the tape-monitor and dubbing switches altogether. Instead, the user selects the input (or listening) signal with one control (or set of buttons) and the signal to be recorded with another. Thus, it's possible to tape a concert coming in over the FM, while listening to a CD. To monitor the progress of a recording you simply switch the "listen" control to the same source as the "record" control. An added advantage of this type of system is the presence of an "off" position on the record selector. This prevents any signal from reaching the deck when it's not being used, and reduces crosstalk between sources.

Filters

The most commonly found filter is the subsonic filter, which is designed primarily to keep turntable rumble from reaching the power amplifier, and then the speakers. Generally speaking, the subsonic filter can be left off except when playing records, but because some radio stations have turntables with high rumble, many audiophiles leave the subsonic filter permanently switched on.

The other common filter is the simple high cut, which is useful for reducing hiss on old records and tapes, or from weak FM broadcasts. Since along with the hiss some music is cut, the use of the high filter shouldn't be encouraged.

Phono Cartridge Matching

The output characteristics of cartridges vary from model to model, and the way the phono input section reacts to these variances can effect the ultimate sound quality. The frequency response of moving-magnet cartridges is influenced by the total *capacitance* (which, in this context, is the manner in which a device allows alternating current of various frequencies to pass) of the preamp's phono section and the wiring between the cartridge and the preamp. Too much capacitance will result in a reduction in high-frequency response. Moving-coil cartridges, for their part, like to see specific input impedances. Preamplifiers often have controls that adjust these parameters, along with sensitivity, and can be used to fine-tune the sound of the phono section.

Inserting 20 dB of muting into the system via the mute button permits the volume control to be operated over a wider range, and makes adjustment less critical.

Muting

The muting button generally reduces the output of the system by 20 dB. While that is useful for temporary low volume when the phone rings, it has another important function. If high-efficiency speakers are being used, it might not be possible to turn the volume control more than a few degrees past minimum before the sound gets to be too loud. Inserting 20 dB of muting into the system via the mute button permits the volume control to be operated over a wider range, and makes adjustment less critical. In addition, since the position of the volume control determines the amount of boost applied when the loudness circuit is engaged, 20 dB of muting permits the loudness control to be used in a less severe, more subtle manner.

7 SPEAKERS

A sweeping statement: The finest high-fidelity components in the world will sound mediocre if played through mediocre speakers. Another sweeping statement: Even mediocre high-fidelity components will sound wonderful if they are driving wonderful speakers. For while a hi-fi system is made up of many separate components that work together, the vibration in the air, which we perceive as sound, is created by the vibration of the speaker system. Since what you hear is what matters most, the choice of a pair of speakers is probably the most important one you will make when you put together your audio installation.

HOW SPEAKERS WORK

About the time that Lindbergh flew across the Atlantic, a couple of fellows named Kellogg and Rice invented the loudspeaker as we know it today. Like so many good ideas, the dynamic loudspeaker used a fairly simple concept: Immerse a coil of wire in a magnetic field and electrify it with alternating currents of electricity, thereby causing it to vibrate back and forth with the electrical signal. Attach a sheet of paper, rolled into a shallow cone to increase its stiffness, to the coil, and use this cone to set air in motion. The result: sound at room-filling volume levels unavailable from the primitive earphones of the time, and the prototype driver component of today's loudspeaker systems.

This general concept is still behind most of today's loudspeakers. For reproducing music with good fidelity, several such *drivers*, each optimized to reproduce a different portion of the musical spectrum,

Considering the fundamental simplicity of the dynamic speaker, the level of sonic quality available from the best of such systems is nothing short of amazing.

are used together — *woofers* reproduce bass notes, *midrange drivers* (called *squawkers* in some parts of the world) the middle frequencies, and *tweeters* the high notes. Considering the fundamental simplicity of the dynamic speaker, the level of sonic quality available from the best of such systems is nothing short of amazing. Like the internal combustion engine, or the notion of a republican democracy, the dynamic speaker is an apparently unworkable idea whose success is the result of sheer force of human persistence. In some form or other, dynamic speakers show up in nearly every area of modern life — in automobiles, transistor radios, concert hall public address systems, elevators, and, of course, in headphones.

The earliest objects we would recognize as speakers were little more than telephone receivers with cones attached, and to understand what that linkage achieved, we will have to understand just a little bit about the insides of a dynamic loudspeaker.

An electrical signal, the modulations of which carry the sonic information, comes from the amplifier or receiver output directly to the coil of wire known as the *voice coil*. The voice coil is surrounded by a magnet (the big heavy protuberance at the back of a loudspeaker), and therefore exists within a magnetic field. This magnetic field is of constant strength and, as the signal from the amplifier varies, the electrical relationship between the voice coil and the magnet changes, resulting in a physical movement of the voice coil. The voice coil is attached to the cone (also known as the diaphragm, and the portion of the driver that actually sets the air in motion to produce sound), which is therefore set in motion along with the coil.

If you look at a typical woofer frontally, you will see three concentric circles: the smallest, centermost circle is nothing more than a dust shield, contributing little directly to the sound of the component. The next one out, accounting for the bulk of the speaker's diameter, is the cone or diaphragm itself. And the outer circle — the "surround" — is a very flexible linkage between the cone and the frame of the loudspeaker and, again, is not a functional part of the apparatus except insofar as it must allow full freedom of motion to the cone.

Returning to the early days of speaker making, people used to, as we've said, "listen in" (to radio, for phonograph reproduction was still acoustic) with what amounted to telephone receivers which, if you look inside a telephone, you will see are voice coils with rudimentary diaphragms. It was soon discovered that the sound, such as it was, could be made audible to more than one listener by projecting it through a horn. This system is still frequently used in public address speakers, and in a few home models as well. This type of speaker system is discussed more fully in the section on cabinet design (page 85).

Thus the diaphragm with its vibrations transmitted and amplified by a horn evolved into a horn which *itself* vibrates — the cone — resulting in the type of loudspeaker most commonly found today. (Dynamic speakers may be the most common, but by no means are they the only game in town. Other types — apart from variations on the dynamic theme — include electrostatic, planar, and ribbon speakers, all of which are covered in the section on alternative speaker design later in this chapter.)

Multiple Drivers

Not many individual loudspeakers perform at their best throughout the whole audible range. This is because different frequencies make different physical demands upon a loudspeaker.

Most speaker systems actually consist of two or more drivers — loudspeakers — in a single box. Won't a single loudspeaker do? Sometimes, for certain purposes, it will, and there have always been a number of full-range speakers on the market. But not many individual loudspeakers perform at their best throughout the whole audible range. This is because different frequencies make very different physical demands upon a loudspeaker. The most obvious illustration of this is the fact that you can actually *see* the slow, low-frequency movements of the woofer: the deepest bass frequencies (at high volumes especially) require the speaker cone to travel through quite a distance to move the necessary amount of air. On the other hand, high treble frequencies need a diaphragm which can move much more rapidly. Clearly, it is no picnic to design a single unit which will be able to respond to all those different signals — and to do so instantaneously and evenly, and sometimes simultaneously.

So most loudspeaker enclosures contain more than one speaker, with different drivers designed to perform best in different frequency ranges (figure 7-1). A cone woofer might be paired with a dome tweeter, or a wide-range electrostatic driver might be augmented by a dynamic woofer. Another acoustical, pitch-related phenomenon comes into play here: directionality, the narrowness or broadness of the path a given sound takes when it leaves its source. Low frequencies are omnidirectional; their path is very wide. High frequencies are quite the opposite, and even more so when they are reproduced by diaphragms having a large diameter. All the more reason to assign different drivers to different frequency ranges.

The Crossover: An Electronic Traffic Cop

There are two more important elements in a conventional dynamic speaker system. The first of these is the *crossover network*, which

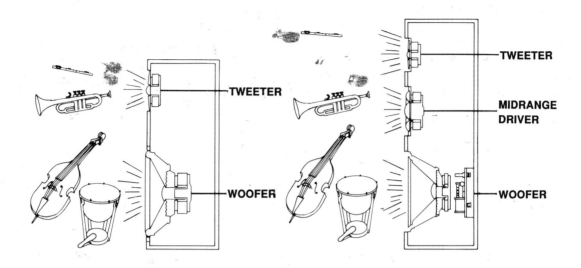

FIGURE 7-1. Most modern speaker systems contain two or more drivers. A two-way system, illustrated at left, will have a woofer and a tweeter. A three-way system will add a midrange driver, which will allow the woofer and tweeter to operate primarily at the extreme frequencies.

channels to each driver the musical frequencies intended for it.

The design of the circuits can be calculated for optimal crossover behavior — the best dissemination of high frequencies to tweeter and low frequencies to woofer — which generally means a relatively gradual transition from one driver to the other, and no excess emphasis of the frequencies around the crossover point. This will result in some overlap: in a two-way system, for instance, both the woofer and tweeter will be reproducing a common portion of the musical spectrum.

Another method of crossing over from one driver to another divides the music into the requisite frequency bands *before* power amplification. This requires the use of two or more power amplifiers, in addition to the often-costly external crossover network, but it allows the user/owner to exert much more precise control over the crossover parameters.

The Baffle

The final element in any conventional speaker system is the baffle. A peek at the cross-section of, say, a cone woofer will set you wondering why, if the front of the vibrating cone sends sound waves forward, the back doesn't propel them backward, too. Indeed, it does, and those backwaves must be controlled or they will wreak havoc with the sound. Control takes the form of mounting the loudspeaker on a board, or baffle, which enables the designer to control the waves by, to name just one method, sealing the sides and back of the baffle in a closed box.

SPEAKER ENCLOSURES

A speaker's performance depends a great deal upon the size and design of its enclosure — this is especially true in the bass region.

When you go shopping for speakers you will no doubt encounter such terms as *bass reflex*, *acoustic suspension*, and *infinite baffle*. It's important to note that these colorful phrases — tossed about so casually — refer not to *speakers*, but to the *cabinets* in which the speakers are mounted. A speaker's performance depends a great deal upon the size and design of its enclosure — this is especially true in the bass region. Enclosures are important: a 12-inch woofer will perform quite differently in the open air or "free space" than in a box. And if the box is sealed it will perform differently than if there is an opening in it.

Most listeners, and even many audiophiles, are surprised to learn that as much sound comes from the back of a speaker cone as from the front. Precisely as much, to be specific. It would be marvelously simple if one could just hang the speaker out in the breeze, unconfined by any sort of enclosure. Unfortunately, the sound from the front of a speaker tends to be cancelled by the sound from the rear, particularly at bass frequencies. Because sound is actually rapid variations in air pressure, a forward motion that increases air pressure will be effectively cancelled out by a backward motion that reduces it.

The obvious solution is to separate the speaker's front wave from its back wave, via a baffle, thus preventing this cancellation. The speaker will then operate without any loss of bass, although the energy from the rear of the cone will be more or less wasted.

The Infinite Baffle

Putting the speaker in a hole in one wall of the room, or a hole in a closet door, accomplishes this purpose neatly, albeit somewhat restricting mobility. It also serves as the textbook example of the infinite baffle enclosure type: a very large enclosure that has no effect on the speaker's output other than to keep the front wave from the back wave. We can also achieve this condition by putting the speaker in a very large box (figure 7-2).

A big box has its drawbacks, though: chiefly that it becomes difficult to find space in the room to seat guests, or indeed to put the remainder of the furniture. OK, then; let's make the box smaller. Good thinking, but now all pretense to simplicity vanishes, because reducing the size of the box will also reduce the bass response of the system. In order to understand the effects a smaller enclosure will have on the response of the speaker we must now examine the concept of resonance.

Resonance

Diverging a bit, we'll begin by noting that an object like a guitar string will tend to vibrate at a certain frequency when plucked, the frequency being determined by the string's *mass* and its *compliance*, or flexibility. Loosen the string, its resonant frequency goes down; increase the string ᵕ mass by making it thicker, its resonant frequency again goes down. Reverse either process, the resonant frequency goes up.

The same is true of loudspeakers. The frequency at which a speaker will naturally resonate (which is also the frequency below which its bass response starts to roll off, or diminish) is determined by the speaker cone's mass and by the looseness of the rubber or plastic-foam edge that surrounds and suspends it. To get good bass

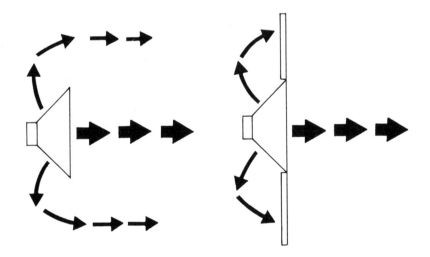

FIGURE 7-2. An unmounted woofer radiates both forward and backward. The waves emanating from the back of the cone tend to cancel those radiating forward. Isolating the front and back waves by placing the woofer on a baffle board eliminates this cancellation effect.

response out of a speaker we can either make the cone heavy or the edge loose (although increasing the cone mass is the less desirable choice because it reduces the speaker's efficiency, drawing more power from the amplifier for a given volume level).

The Acoustic-Suspension Speaker

In our infinite baffle enclosure, the choice is a simple one: we'll simply use a loosely suspended speaker — one with a very floppy surround — in order to get good bass performance. However, if we decide to use a small enclosure, the volume of air inside the enclosure will push outward constantly — just as the air in a balloon is constantly pushing the balloon surface outward — and will effectively stiffen up the speaker. We call this type of speaker — one with a small box that is completely closed — an *air-suspension* or *acoustic-suspension* speaker, because the air in the box acts like a stiff edge, or suspension (figure 7-3). We find, to our chagrin, that in the small box, the final stiffness, and the bass performance, of our speaker will be determined by the size of the box, and not the speaker's own edge.

We have only two choices in our effort to get good bass response from an air-suspension enclosure, therefore: we can increase the cone mass and pay the resultant penalty in efficiency, or else

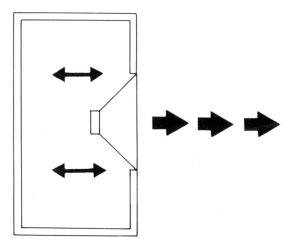

FIGURE 7-3. When a sealed enclosure is relatively small, and the woofer is allowed to move back and forth, with the air in the enclosure acting as a spring, the result is an acoustic-suspension speaker. This provides exceptional bass response for its size, albeit at the expense of some efficiency.

increase the box size and pay the penalty in living space. If, as is usually the case, we have an amplifier of limited power and really *need* a certain degree of efficiency, then the bass response of our speaker inevitably will be controlled directly by the size of the box. "Bigger box, better bass" is the rule with acoustic-suspension speakers, unless you can afford a more powerful amplifier. It must be noted, however, that some manufacturers of acoustic-suspension speakers have taken great pains to increase the efficiency of their speakers. Exotic materials and sophisticated manufacturing techniques allow speakers to offer efficiency that would have been impossible a few years ago.

"Bigger box, better bass" is the rule with acoustic-suspension speakers, unless you can afford a more powerful amplifier.

The Bass-Reflex Enclosure

Suppose we attempt to make some use of the energy from the rear of the cone? After all, it's half of the speaker's total output, and it should come in handy somewhere. Well, we obviously can't use the backwave energy directly, because of the backwave cancellation we discussed earlier. But in a cunning, indirect way, designers do utilize the speaker's rear output, in what is called the *bass-reflex* enclosure type, also called a *vented* or *ported* enclosure (figure 7-4).

In this type of speaker system, the box has a hole or port, sometimes extended inward via a tube, in its front or rear panel. Like the speaker, the volume of air in the box and the port together have a resonant frequency. This resonance is caused by the same phenomenon that generates a musical tone when you blow into the neck of a tall bottle. In the case of the bottle or the speaker enclosure, the resonant frequency is determined by the volume of air in the bottle (or the box), and by the dimensions of the neck (or the port). By careful calculation, the resonance of the box-and-port can be made to coincide with the speaker's own resonance, or even to occur below the speaker's resonance, resulting in deeper bass response. Just as important, the speaker can be made with a somewhat lighter cone than would be necessary with an acoustic-suspension speaker. That, in combination with the fact that the woofer's back wave is contributing to the output, yields improved efficiency, allowing a less powerful amplifier to be used to achieve a given volume level.

Because of the many parameters — speaker mass and compliance, box size, port dimensions — that can be varied by the designer, bass-reflex systems offer greater flexibility in the trade-offs between enclosure size, efficiency, and bass performance. They can offer more bass, or more efficiency, or a smaller box size than a closed-box sys-

Bass-reflex systems can offer more bass, or more efficiency, or a smaller box size than a closed-box system — whichever trade-off or combination of trade-offs the designer chooses.

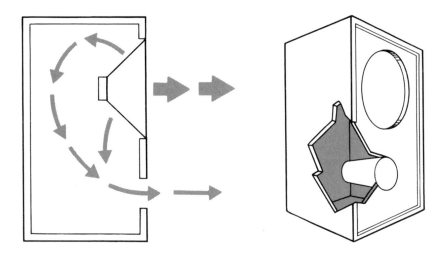

FIGURE 7-4. <u>Left</u>: A vented enclosure directs the back wave of the woofer to the outside of the cabinet to reinforce the front wave. <u>Right</u>: One type of vented enclosure uses a ducted port to tune the output of the rear wave to a specific range of frequencies.

tem — whichever trade-off or combination of trade-offs the designer chooses. Time was when reflex systems were much more difficult to design properly, and less tolerant of physical variations on the components used in them. Until recently, in fact, most reflex systems were designed largely by trial and error, and many tended toward a rather bass-heavy, overly warm character of sound; during the '50s, in fact, they acquired the nickname "boom boxes." In the '60s and early '70s, the results of research on computer analysis of vented systems (and other types of speaker systems as well) became available. This work greatly simplified the process of developing good reflex systems, and vented speakers are now viewed as being on a par with air-suspension or infinite-baffle systems in every regard.

One interesting variation on the bass-reflex approach, by the way, replaces the port with a loosely suspended non-electrically driven cone — a passive cone — which replaces the mass of air in the port, and whose motion supplements that of the driven woofer. Such passive drivers, called *auxiliary bass radiators*. (ABRs), *passive radiators*, or *drone cones*, replace ports where calculations indicate that the optimum port would be too large for the given cabinet (figure 7-5). The majority of the loudspeakers you'll encounter will be either acoustic-suspension or vented designs. This is because those principles are the best understood by designers, and the compromises involved still make it possible to design a speaker system that's acceptable to a wide market.

Alternative Box Designs

Other choices are available to ambitious speaker designers, but they generally require more sophisticated design and greater manufacturing precision. These alternative designs tend, in most cases, to exceed the compromises that most people find acceptable. They may, for example, go full tilt in the direction of efficiency, and demand large cabinet volume, thus creating problems of placement in the listening room. Here are some of the most interesting of these alternative cabinet configurations.

The Acoustic Transmission-Line Speaker uses a long path — sort of a tunnel — behind the woofer that is intended to reduce the level of sound from the rear of the speaker, while simultaneously extending the speaker's response below the driver's resonant frequency. Like a bass-reflex system, the transmission line depends upon the resonance of a column of air to extend bass response beyond what the speaker itself is capable of. However, rather than the bottle-and-neck resonance we discussed earlier, the transmission line causes the long path to resonate, just as the flute or organ pipe does. The virtues claimed for transmission lines relative to vented systems have to do with the transmission line's absorption of unmuted mid-bass, which

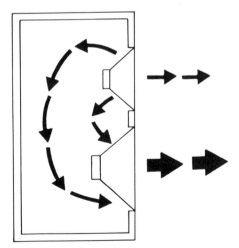

FIGURE 7-5. Some manufacturers use a passive radiator—an undriven woofer cone—in place of an actual vent.

lends it a clean, very dry, un-boomy type of sound. By contrast, some listeners claim to be able to hear rushing noises or hollow-sounding resonances through the port of conventional bass-reflex speakers; this is said to add bass coloration to many bass-reflex systems. The penalties transmission lines exact are in the form of relatively low efficiency and very large cabinet volume.

The Horn-Loaded Speaker employs a horn placed in front of the bass driver (woofer) to greatly improve its efficiency. The horn speaker acts very much like a trumpet horn or megaphone — it matches the resistance of the air directly in front of the driver to the resistance at the end of the horn, and hence achieves a much better coupling between the driver and the room. Horn-loaded systems, though large, are the most efficient speaker types currently available (often able to be driven to room-filling levels by the earphone output of a portable radio). Their most significant drawback, limited deep-bass performance, is derived from the fact that bass performance in a horn is largely controlled by the size of the horn's mouth, and a horn mouth on the order of 15 feet wide is required in order to be able to reproduce the lowest audible frequencies. A number of horn designs attempt to circumvent this problem by using the walls at a corner of the room as an extension of the horn mouth, although this solution is, like many speaker-design techniques, something of a compromise (figure 7-6).

The Electronically Equalized Speaker operates on a very simple principle: boost the level of bass signal going into the amplifier (and eventually into the speaker) to make up for the predictable bass roll-off that small speakers suffer. While logical and straight-forward, this approach has some drawbacks. It places great strains on the amplifier, in that for each 3 dB of bass boost the amplifier power will have to be doubled in order to avoid clipping. Also, since the speaker can only move back and forth a certain fixed distance before it begins to distort, bass boost is useful only when it does not exceed the power handling or the excursion limits of the speaker in question. And since small speakers are the units most likely to require electronic equalization, those limits are frequently not as high as needed to reproduce a wide-range, wide-dynamic piece of music.

ALTERNATE APPROACHES TO SPEAKER DESIGN

Despite the overwhelming popularity of the dynamic speaker, it is not the only means available to transform electrical energy into

Horn-loaded systems, though large, are the most efficient speaker types currently available (often able to be driven to room-filling levels by the earphone output of a portable radio).

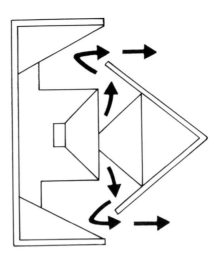

FIGURE 7-6. While difficult to tune for smooth response, the complicated folded-horn enclosure can produce concert levels with very little amplifier power.

sound. It is possible to find alternatives to the dynamic speaker, especially in the field of high fidelity, where maverick ideas are given greater credence than in the workaday world of, say, elevator speakers. Some of these offbeat speaker types, such as the *electrostatic* or *piezoelectric*, are as old as the dynamic speaker itself, while others have been developed within the past dozen or so years. Let's examine both the conventional dynamic loudspeaker and its alternatives, evaluating their operating principles, strong points, and faults, just as a design engineer might when first developing a speaker system.

Of course, understanding the theory behind a speaker doesn't explain the "character of sound" that its supporters claim to hear. The fans of electrostatic speakers claim unusually low coloration and a smooth, open sound absent from many conventional systems. *Planar dynamic speaker* backers make similar claims, with emphasis on the airiness and detail of the high-frequency portion of the music. *Ribbon* devotees often make note of a subjectively "snappier" sound, suggesting that ribbons react more accurately and rapidly to *transients* (sudden changes in volume) than do other types. Piezoelectric drivers are also renowned in some circles for sonic quickness, and are credited with a crystalline, sharply etched sound character. Even with dynamic speakers, there are adherents to particular design configurations.

Whatever the potential benefits of various alternative speaker types, the ultimate realization of those benefits is of course dependent upon the skill of the engineers in integrating the drivers into speaker systems, skillfully reducing the effects of each driver's shortcomings, and blending the driver's performance with the enclosure and crossover to achieve the greatest possible level of realism. Important, too, are the more mundane questions of quality control and reliability, in helping assure that the fragility or variability of a given driver type does not undo whatever benefits its design principle might offer.

Different speaker types involve different sets of compromises, and the wise buyer chooses a system on the basis of how well those compromises conform to his or her own needs.

The upshot of all of this? Simply that a design theory does not necessarily make a superior speaker system. Rather, different speaker types involve different sets of compromises, and the wise buyer chooses a system on the basis of how well those compromises conform to his or her own needs. While a perusal of the theories outlined here may interest you and lead you to audition a speaker you might not have encountered before, allow your own ears to make the final selection.

The Dynamic Loudspeaker

Principle of Operation. As briefly described earlier, a cylindrical voice coil is placed in a narrow cylindrical magnetic gap. Electricity running through the coil effectively turns it into an electromagnet, which then moves back and forth in time with the electrical signal as the coil is alternately attracted and repelled by the fixed magnetic gap. A shallow cone or dome made of paper, plastic, or metal is attached to the rim of the voice coil, and vibrates, creating fluctuations in air pressure that translate into sound (figure 7-7).

Major Advantages. This type of driver is by far the most commonly used in contemporary design, and its behavior is therefore well understood and reasonably predictable.

Power handling can be quite high, since the voice coil (the element within the speaker that will be heated by loud musical passages) is adjacent to the heavy metal parts of the magnetic structure, which act as a heat sink and cool the coil.

The cone size and the back-and-forth distance moved can both be made large, thus giving this speaker type fairly high efficiency and wide dynamic range. Driver sizes are easily varied from very large (30-inch diameter, in a few cases) to very small (¾-inch diameter, in which case the diaphragm is likely to be dome- rather than cone-shaped), permitting a broad range of dispersion characteristics (dispersion is primarily determined by driver size; the smaller the dimension, the broader the dispersion).

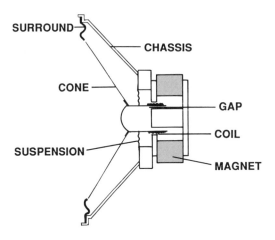

FIGURE 7-7. A dynamic speaker.

Major Disadvantages. A dynamic speaker is driven only at the point where the voice coil is attached, usually near the cone apex or the dome rim. The whole cone or dome surface may therefore fail to follow the motion of the coil precisely. Different segments may bend or resonate independently, a phenomenon generically called cone breakup, and cause peaks or dips in the frequency response and blurring of transient musical signals. To minimize cone breakup and beaming which occurs when a large-diameter driver attempts to reproduce high frequencies, most high-fidelity speaker systems use multiple drivers of varying sizes to reproduce different frequencies. In turn, the crossover network that divides the musical signal into several bands contributes some distortion and some errors in transient response, as does the spacing between the drivers.

The Electrostatic Loudspeaker

Principle of Operation. A thin sheet of plastic film (about the thickness and flexibility of the film used to make household sandwich bags) is stretched over a frame, and placed between two metal screens (plates). The material of the film is chosen because it will take an electrical charge. The central diaphragm is given a fixed high electrical charge, and the metal screens have electrical charges that vary in time with the music. The plastic film is attracted to or repelled by the screens' electrostatic charge, and consequently moves back and forth, setting the surrounding air into motion. Most modern electrostatics use a "push-pull" arrangement, in which one screen pulls the diaphragm towards it while the other simultaneously repels it. This configuration results in low distortion and excellent control over the diaphragm surface (figure 7-8).

Major Advantages. An electrostatic speaker diaphragm is driven uniformly over its entire surface, thus preventing breakup or major resonances of the diaphragm.

The diaphragm is extremely lightweight, and hence capable of reproducing rapid (treble) musical signals. Given the conditions of low mass and uniform driving force, electrostatic speakers can be used as wide-range drivers, bypassing the need for multiple drivers and the consequent potentially troublesome crossover networks. (Many electrostatics, however, are used to cover a limited frequency range, being augmented in the bass range by drivers of other types, usually large cones.)

Major Disadvantages. By virtue of their large radiating area, which is required because of limits in the back-and-forth distance that they must travel, most full-range electrostatics have limited dispersion.

Power handling is limited, because once the short distance the film diaphragm may move has been reached, the technology doesn't provide for a means of dissipating excess amplifier power in the form of heat.

Deep-bass performance is often deficient because the limited excursion of the diaphragm doesn't permit it to move enough air to

Electrostatic speakers can be used as wide-range drivers, bypassing the need for multiple drivers and the consequent potentially troublesome crossover networks.

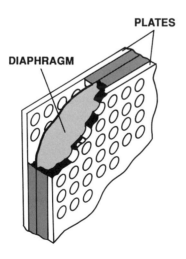

FIGURE 7-8. An electrostatic speaker.

produce very low frequencies. In addition, because most electrostatics are operated with the enclosure back open (an arrangement called a *dipole radiator*), at low frequencies there is cancellation of the bass by the backwave from the rear of the diaphragm, and a consequent bass roll-off. Subwoofers of dynamic design are thus often used in conjunction with electrostatic midrange panels.

Electrostatics present the amplifier with a particularly difficult load, and are therefore incompatible with many medium-priced models. Ruggedly constructed amplifiers, with special self-protection circuits, are often required.

The Planar-Dynamic Loudspeaker

Principle of Operation. This type involves a fusion of the stronger points of dynamic and electrostatic speakers. A thin film diaphragm is again placed between two grids. These grids are simple magnets, rather than electrically charged screens. Nor is the film diaphragm electrically charged. Rather, it has a spidery network of copper or aluminum tracks on its surface. This pattern of lines acts like the voice coil of the dynamic speaker, carrying the musical signal, and therefore taking on the properties of an electromagnet. It is hence alternately repelled and attracted by the fixed magnetic screens, producing sound (figure 7-9).

Major Advantages. As with the electrostatic speaker, nearly uniform force is acting on the diaphragm, reducing breakup to a minimum. Again, the thin, soft diaphragm is not prone to the resonances often encountered in a cone driver.

The low mass of the diaphragm and "voice-coil"-like pattern enables the speaker to reproduce extended treble and also makes possible use of the planar-dynamic format as a full-range speaker — no need for other drivers.

Power handling in most cases is limited only by the melting temperature of the tracks and the diaphragm material, and is usually very high.

The speaker presents a very conventional, easily driven load to the amplifier, thus rendering speakers of this type compatible with even inexpensive, moderately powered amplifiers.

Major Disadvantages. Treble dispersion is often limited, due to the required large area of the diaphragm, when used in the full-range format.

Planar dynamic speakers exhibit the same deficiencies in bass response as their electrostatic cousins, and for the same reasons.

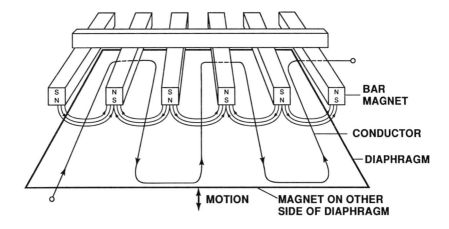

FIGURE 7-9. A planar dynamic speaker.

The Piezoelectric Loudspeaker

Principle of Operation. Certain ceramic and plastic materials will flex or bend when an electrical current is passed through them; the direction of bending is determined by the direction of the current flow. Piezoelectric speakers can be constructed by using one or more chips of such ceramic material attached to the apex of a conventional paper or plastic speaker cone. Alternatively, sheets of plastic film with this property can be formed into cylinders or flat panels, which will bend when a musical signal is passed through them. The back-and-forth bending is what creates the sound.

Major Advantages. The electrical characteristics of piezoelectric materials act as a natural crossover network, with the speaker's impedance rising at low frequencies, thus rolling off response in the bass. No external crossover components need be used.

In the piezoelectric films, uniform drive over the entire diaphragm surface prevents breakup or internal resonance.

Major Disadvantages. Systems that use ceramic chips drive the cone from a conventional position at its apex, and are thus subject to the same sort of cone breakup problems as dynamic speakers.

Full-range piezoelectric systems cannot be constructed, due to the electrical characteristics we've discussed.

The Ribbon Loudspeaker

Principle of Operation. A narrow metal ribbon is suspended vertically in a slot-shaped magnetic field. When a current passes through the ribbon, it is attracted to and repelled from the field alternately; its surface sets air into motion (figure 7-10).

Major Advantages. The diaphragm is composed totally of the electrically conductive metal ribbon, and the entire surface is therefore driven uniformly.

The diaphragm is quite narrow (typically about ½ inch wide), and therefore has excellent dispersion in the horizontal plane. (Remember: the smaller the driver, the better the dispersion.)

Major Disadvantages. The ribbon's range of back-and-forth motion is severely restricted, thus limiting its performance to upper treble applications. (As previously discussed, wider, slower motions produce bass frequencies.) Power handling is thus also usually fairly low.

Generating a magnetic field of any intensity in the long slot requires a large and expensive magnet. Even with such a magnet, efficiency is usually low, unless the driver is horn-loaded to improve its sensitivity.

The ribbon generally requires a matching transformer to render it compatible with the outputs of conventional amplifiers, since the ribbon's impedance is low. The transformer must be carefully (and therefore expensively) constructed to avoid adding coloration to the ribbon's sound.

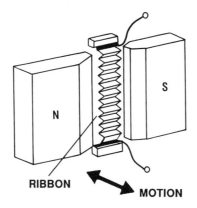

FIGURE 7-10. A ribbon speaker.

The Walsh Speaker

Principle of Operation. The Walsh loudspeaker uses a single inverted cone which acts as a transmission line rather than a piston. The apex of the cone is initially "bent" by the voice coil, and a sound wave originating at the apex moves into the air at approximately 1,100 feet per second. Ideally (and a function of cone material and angle), the ripple travels down the cone at supersonic speed. It takes exactly the same time for the ripple to travel from the apex to the edge as it takes for the sound produced at the apex to travel to directly above the edge at about 1,100 feet per second. The result is a coherent, cylindrical sound field propagated outward over 360 degrees (figure 7-11).

Major Advantages. A properly executed Walsh speaker's coherent sound field eliminates the "time smear" (different frequencies reaching the listener's ear at different times) that is often a result of using multiple drivers.

The use of a single, full-range driver eliminates the need for a crossover network, and its concomitant distortions.

Stereo imaging can be exceptionally good.

Major Disadvantages. In its purest form, the Walsh speaker requires the use of exotic and costly cone materials in order to operate properly. It is also incredibly inefficient. For these reasons, current Walsh speakers (manufactured by the Walsh patent's holder, Ohm Acoustics) utilize an auxiliary supertweeter to obviate the use of exotic cone materials, and a combination of internal bass equaliza-

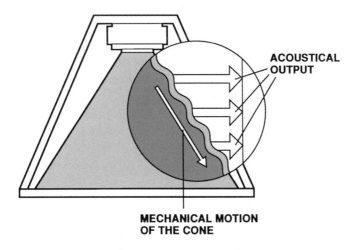

FIGURE 7-11. A Walsh speaker.

tion and sophisticated cabinet design to yield the requisite bass response from modestly powered amplifiers.

SPEAKER POWER

As you now know, one of the basic rules to follow when assembling a hi-fi system is that the speakers are chosen first, followed by an amplifier that's powerful enough to drive them to the requisite volume levels. Now, on the surface that sounds simple enough. Most stores have switching facilities, and you can try various amps and receivers until you've determined that, say, 30 watts per channel are sufficient (making the music sufficiently loud without distorting). Then it's just a matter of choosing the 30-watt unit that has the features you want. Would that it were as easy as that. But while a rose may be a rose may be a rose, a watt is very often not a watt, at least where a speaker is concerned.

You see, amplifiers don't actually produce watts. They produce amperes and volts, which get turned into watts when they pass through a load. Now, that load can either be as simple as a common resistor, or as electrically complex as a loudspeaker. It's relatively easy to design an amplifier that can heat up a simple resistor. It's much more difficult to design one that will work well with the more complicated loads presented by many speakers. The problem is, when measuring power for spec sheets, manufacturers are bound by the FTC rules governing disclosure, and that means stating *continuous power into a resistor*. The upshot is, many manufacturers design their amplifiers so they measure well (i.e., produce the maximum number of watts when measured under FTC conditions) but don't address themselves to the problems the amp will face when a speaker is attached.

The difficulty presented by the complex load of the speaker is compounded by the fact that music is made up of a series of rapid impulses, not by a continuous signal. The type of design that is capable of putting out lots of *continuous power* might not be ideal for reproducing the peaks that are inherent in music.

There are several companies whose amplifiers and receivers seem to put out somewhat less advertised power than you'd expect for the money. These companies are taking a big risk. They're betting, basically, that people will take the time to learn about the realities of power and loudspeakers, and that these people will appreciate the fact that sometimes fewer watts mean better performance. Basic considerations like a sophisticated power supply, high-current capa-

It's relatively easy to design an amplifier that can heat up a simple resistor. It's much more difficult to design one that will work well with the more complicated loads presented by many speakers.

bility, and output capability into low impedances are only a few of the factors that contribute to the ability of, for example, a real 20-watt amplifier to perform better than one whose 100 watts are merely advertising watts.

How do you separate the roses from the thorns? Well, two ways are to read the reviews in the various audio publications, and to study the advertising of those manufacturers who address those issues in their copy. You can also trust your ears. If a 40-watt receiver is driving inefficient speakers to high levels, you can be pretty sure that there's more than baloney inside.

Reproducing Digital Sound

In the past several decades, numerous factors have changed which previously had absolved the loudspeakers of their responsibility to reproduce music faithfully. Now, improved studio design and better microphones have limited background noise at the recording stage. Electrical disturbances are now no longer a significant problem. Noise masking high and low frequencies has been all but eliminated.

In part, this improvement has resulted from the gradual, evolutionary refinement of technology which existed well before the mid-sixties, but the last few years have, in addition, seen revolutionary changes both in recording and reproduction. The revolution which primarily concerns us here is in the area of recording: pulse-code modulation, better known as digital audio. Digital recording has meant that, all of a sudden, speakers — and other equipment — are being called upon to do things which only a short time ago were relegated to the realm of the experimental, and to do them in ordinary living rooms and within ordinary consumer constraints of size and cost.

Digital recording has reduced the noise and distortion inherent in analog recording, and thus increased the dynamic range of recordings. Speakers now have to be able to faithfully reproduce this expanded dynamic range.

What has changed? Essentially, digital recording has reduced the noise and distortion inherent in analog recording, and thus increased the dynamic range of recordings. Speakers now have to be able to faithfully reproduce this expanded dynamic range.

Without going into a detailed explanation of digital recording here, let us just remind you that a digital master tape does not contain information which can be converted to musical sounds by an ordinary tape head; it contains instead a numerical code for each instant (say, $\frac{1}{44,000}$ of a second) of music. When the decoding equipment reads that information, it reads only the code for the music; residual noise on the tape, which we would hear as hiss, is not picked up at all. Therefore, the very quietest of musical sounds — even the silence before the music begins — is not masked by the tape noise which has been present on even the very finest of analog tapes. On the other end of the scale, the loudest music is represented by the same type of numerical code as the softest, so there is no danger that it will overload the tape, which was a constant danger with conventional recording.

Music itself has not changed, so how did pre-digital engineers get around its inconvenient tendency to get very quiet and very noisy? (Or rather, how *do* they get around it: many recordings are still made using analog techniques.) In a nutshell, when the music was very soft, they would boost it to a level at which it covered the noise inherent in the recording process, and when it was very loud they would lower it to a level at which it wouldn't upset the equipment. With digital mastering, they just have to make sure everything is plugged in (not true, obviously: consider that as an artistic, literary use of hyperbole) and they end up with a master tape whose dynamic range is as wide as that of the original performance.

Of course, when the music present on digitally recorded masters is squeezed onto conventional media — LP records and cassette tapes — some of the new system's benefits are eliminated due to the nature and characteristics of those media. We're back to surface noise, tape hiss, and — the key — restricted dynamic range. But when the playback medium is a compact disc, digital audio's potential for wide dynamic range can easily be realized.

Dynamic range: "words so fair as some soft chime had stroked the air"; words on everyone's lips. The effective dynamic range of music is the difference between the ambient noise of the seemingly quiet studio (let's say about 40 dB) — below which the music cannot go, as it would then be masked by room noise — and the loudest *fortissimo* of an orchestra (around 110-115 dB, although that is *exceptionally* loud). That puts effective dynamic range at about 90 to 95 dB. That is a very wide range; put into relative terms, it means that the intensity of the sound at its loudest is approximately 100,000 times that of the ambient noise of the studio! That is a difficult concept to come to grips with; it is like trying to comprehend the age of the earth or the distance to the nearest stars. Best not to think about it. Just realize that not only are the *electronic* circuits at every stage of amplification going to have to deal with that whole dynamic range if they are going to be absolutely faithful to the music, but so are the *mechanical* parts of the transducers, the devices which transform mechanical energy into electrical energy and vice versa: the cartridges and the speakers.

In the digital compact disc, of course, the music is read by a beam of light and then the digital information is translated into an analog audio signal. So the physical limitations that apply to phonograph cartridges and recordings have suddenly evaporated: everything that a digital master tape contains can now be taken home on a CD and fed through your amplifiers into your speakers.

Most modern amplifiers can handle the wide range of today's CDs without undue distortion or combustion, and even those that are less-than-ideal are still pretty good. But for loudspeakers, great difficulties remain.

These difficulties are formidable, especially at the low end of the frequency spectrum, where an unfortunately large amount of high-intensity information occurs, what with drum beats, the odd organ pipe, and so forth. The sheer mass of air which the speaker cone has to shift in order to accurately and loudly reproduce low frequencies is astounding: halve the frequency (thus lowering the pitch) and you quadruple the volume of air the woofer has to move. At the lowest of musical frequencies we are talking not in cubic centimeters, but in gallons!

Then, of course, we come back to dynamic range. In terms of speakers, it comes down to a need for efficiency plus power handling. In other words, with comparatively little amplifier power the speaker must react accurately and audibly; yet it must be able to cope with the huge power — often hundreds of times greater — of sustained loud passages and, even more difficult, *fortissimo* transients, and it must do this without distortion, burning out, or (as has happened once or twice) burning *up*.

With comparatively little amplifier power the speaker must react accurately and audibly; yet it must be able to cope with the huge power — often hundreds of times greater — of sustained loud passages.

Speaker Design Improvements

Until relatively recently, efficient speakers tended to be inaccurate, but at last, the industry has learned to build accurate, efficient speaker systems and, furthermore, speaker systems able to handle the doses of power they must face from the wide dynamic range available from current program sources such as CDs. There are two basic reasons for this new capability, and they occur both separately and in combination. The first is the development of mathematics that enable speaker designers and their computers to optimize vented speaker systems; the second is advances in speaker cone material and design.

The names which come up most often in terms of the mathematics of speaker design are A.N. Thiele and R.H. Small. What those two gents did was work out formulas that allow engineers to juggle five factors and come up with the mix of design features which best suits their needs (needs defined in terms of size, cost, and so on). Those five factors are: (1) the internal volume of the speaker enclosure; (2) the compliance, or flexibility, of the woofer in terms of a volume of air; (3) the resonance of the woofer independent of the enclosure; (4) the resonant frequency of the enclosure; and (5) the strength of the woofer's magnet and voice coil. For instance, once a company has decided on a given enclosure size, it can then work out exactly what to put inside that enclosure to get the most out of it. This used to be done by trial and error or, worse, by hit or miss.

As to the cone materials themselves, in the past they had to be very heavy if they were going to be stiff enough to be accurate and strong. Now, materials are available which are both very stiff and non-resonant *and* very light. This has in turn allowed the acoustic-suspension speaker system, once considered congenitally inefficient, to take its place once again on the shelves and floors of owners of smallish amplifiers.

The numbers of efficient, accurate, wide-range speaker systems and of amplifiers able to deliver the kind of steady-state (continuous) and transient power needed in the digital age are growing. More important to the consumer, they are growing in all price ranges. Inexpensive amplifiers whose ability to drive loudspeakers belie their price and eight-ohm *rated* power are available to those who take the trouble to find them. And $300-a-pair speakers that can do justice to digital source material are also hiding amongst the run-of-the-table-saw.

It's all there to be enjoyed, and as digital reproduction becomes more and more widespread there will be lots more of it. We would like to offer one little piece of helpful advice: remember those first really wide-range digital recordings with cannons and things on them? They sometimes had a little warning on the jackets to the effect that the ultra-loud transient information in the grooves could do damage to your cartridge, and we know a man who used to blow up cartridges as a party trick — a very slick variation on the exploding cigar. Well, those warnings are still applied to CD versions of those records, but they deal with the danger to your speakers.

Your speakers will thrive with the right amount of amplifier power. Too much and they could blow up. Too little, and ditto. In the latter case the warning goes like this: if you hear distortion from your speakers, it's probably your amplifier giving up the ghost. Turn down the volume; a distorted waveform from the amplifier can be deadly to your tweeters. If your problem is too much power, any distortion that you hear probably originates in the speaker itself. Again, turn down the volume, and investigate (with your dealer and the manufacturers involved) the possibility of using fuses to protect the speakers from excess power. Every speaker's requirements in this area are different, so we can't offer any specific recommendations.

DISPERSION

When shopping for speakers, before you set foot in a hi-fi store, before you spend one minute listening, you can disqualify a good portion of the speakers on the market by checking certain specifications. All you need are the specification sheets and a calculator. The information that follows will allow you to draw important conclusions, as long as you apply it to "conventional" speakers with direct-radiating drivers mounted on the front panel of a rectangular box. This, of course, includes the vast majority of speakers.

There are many performance criteria for selecting speakers, but only one of them may be assessed objectively from specifications. This one, uniformity of dispersion, is so overwhelmingly important — and so infrequently satisfied — that you can depend upon it to reduce your shopping list to manageable size.

Uniformity of dispersion is so overwhelmingly important — and so infrequently satisfied — that you can depend upon it to reduce your shopping list to manageable size.

What is dispersion? Think of the difference between a spotlight and a floodlight. A spotlight directs all of its energy straight ahead, leaving the areas to the side in the dark. A floodlight, by contrast, disperses its light over a wide area. Speakers at times behave like either a spotlight or a floodlight.

How important is uniformity of dispersion? If you listen to music in an enclosed space — such as a room — it is very important. In an enclosed space the sound that leaves the speaker at an angle will be reflected back to the listener. If all of the frequencies don't radiate at a wide angle, then not all of them will be equally reinforced by reflection. This will result in, for example, an unstable stereo image: the apparent sound source will tend to shift with the changing frequency of the notes. The music will, in a word, sound "canned." In short, what you should be looking for is uniform, controlled dispersion of sounds of all frequencies.

Calculating Dispersion

Which speakers have uniform dispersion? To calculate dispersion, you need to know three things: (1) the diameter of the driver's radiating area, (2) the crossover frequency, and (3) the speed of sound. The first two are given in speaker specifications (although the driver's actual radiating area is approximately 85 percent of the nominal diameter); the last is a constant — about 13,440 inches per second. Then, all we need to recognize is a simple phenomenon of physics: *sound will radiate straight forward if the radiated wavelengths are shorter than the radiating area, and sound will radiate at an increasingly wide angle if the radiated wavelengths are longer than the radiating area.* Thus we're looking for situations where sound wavelengths are longer than a driver's diameter, indicating a speaker's ability to disperse over a wide area. It sounds complicated, but in practice it's not so difficult.

Let's look at a few examples. The first is a two-way system with a single crossover point and the following specs: an 8-inch woofer, a 2.5-inch tweeter, and a crossover frequency of 3.2 kiloHertz (or, from now on, 3.2 kHz, which equals 3,200 Hertz). To proceed with our formula we have to first determine the wavelength of the crossover frequency and compare it with the size of the woofer. This wavelength is calculated by dividing the speed of sound by the frequency. Dividing 13,440 by 3,200 gives us approximately 4.2 inches. That's the shortest wavelength (i.e., the highest frequency) handled by the woofer, since that's the point where frequencies "cross over" into the higher range handled by the tweeter.

But the 8-inch woofer — even if we count only the cone's 6.5-inch effective radiating area — is much larger than the 4.2-inch wavelength at the crossover frequency of 3,200 Hz, meaning that dispersion will not be at a wide angle. In fact, the wavelength does not equal the woofer diameter until 2,068 Hz (13,440 divided by 6.5). Below 2,068 Hz the wavelengths are longer than the woofer so they disperse well. But the half-octave between 2,068 Hz and 3,200 Hz is poorly dispersed, and this will adversely affect the sound of the speaker in a normal listening room.

With regard to the tweeter, the crossover wavelength of 4.2 inches is larger than the 2-inch diameter of the speaker. This yields good dispersion up to the point where the wavelength is the same size or smaller than the tweeter diameter. That point is at 6,720 Hz (13,440 divided by the 2-inch active diameter of the tweeter), which is high enough so as not to greatly affect the timbre of the music throughout the listening room (but not high enough to give it a truly "open" sound).

A convenient comparative index of dispersion is obtained by dividing the crossover wavelength by the diameter of the lower frequency driver.

But on the basis of the midrange beaming (between 2,068 and 3,200 Hz) one would do better spending time auditioning more promising systems.

Another two-way system shows more promise. It has a 6.5-inch woofer, a 1-inch tweeter, and a 1.8 kHz (1,800 Hz) crossover. Divide 13,440 by 1,800 and we find that the crossover wavelength is about 7.5 inches — considerably greater than the woofer's 5-inch active cone diameter. Therefore, dispersion is good throughout the range of the woofer (since frequencies get even wider as they move further into the bass portion of the spectrum) and up through the higher frequencies to 13,440 Hz, where the 1-inch tweeter becomes directional (i.e., has poor dispersion).

A convenient comparative index is obtained by dividing the crossover wavelength by the diameter of the lower frequency driver. Thus, in the first example the index is .65 (a 4.2-inch wavelength divided by the driver's radiating area of 6.5 inches), and in the second, 1.5 (a 7.5-inch wavelength divided by a diameter of 5 inches). An index of less than 1.0 indicates a definite dispersion problem, and an index of greater than 1.0 indicates reasonably uniform dispersion.

Unfortunately, real life is often more complicated than simple arithmetic, for the transition from wide to narrow dispersion happens gradually over a wide band of frequencies. So far, our analysis has implied that an 8-inch woofer with a 6.5-inch effective cone area will disperse well up to 2,068 Hz and then, at 2,069 Hz — a wavelength of 6.49 inches — will become totally directional. Actually, dispersion loss begins one octave below that point (which is one half the frequency — 1,034 Hz) and severe directionality does not occur until an octave above that point (which is twice the frequency — 4,138 Hz). Given our 8-inch woofer with 6.5-inch effective cone, there would probably be slight beaming beginning at about 1,500 Hz, and obvious beaming above 2,000 Hz. It is also important to note that crossover networks operate gradually, rather than abruptly: if a woofer has a 1 kHz crossover with a slope of 6 dB per octave, it will still be putting out one-quarter the total sound 250 Hz above the crossover point. We must acknowledge the benefit, therefore, of an extra margin of dispersion at crossover points.

That being said, let's use the index mentioned above, and rate dispersion as follows:

1.5+	=	Excellent (little audible effect)
1.0 - 1.5	=	Good (slight audible effect)
0.75 - 1.0	=	Mediocre (obvious audible effect)
Below 0.75	=	Bad (bad)

If you limit your selection to those speakers with indexes of 1.0 or better at each crossover, you'll be getting better sound and you'll make shopping easier.

Dispersion in Three-Way Systems

One obvious solution to the lack of dispersion at the top end of a woofer's response is to cross over to a less directional driver at a lower frequency. In such a three-or-more-way system you must calculate an index for each crossover. Do not assume that multi-way systems disperse well by definition; calculate the indexes. Take, for example, a three-way system using a 12-inch woofer, 6-inch midrange, and horn tweeter, with crossovers at 700 Hz and 4,000 Hz (dividing 13,440 by 700 and by 4,000 yields wavelengths of 19.2 inches and 3.36 inches respectively). Per our formula, dividing 19.2 by the woofer radiating area of 10.5 equals an index of 1.8, which is acceptable. Similarly, dividing 19.2 by the midrange radiating area of 5 inches yields a 3.84 index — also fine. But dividing the upper crossover wavelength of 3.36 by the midrange diameter of 5 yields a problem index of .67 inches. So, when evaluating multi-driver systems, the index to look at is the lowest one.

Factoring in the Tweeter

The highest frequency driver of any system has an upper dispersion limit determined (in the main) by its size. The general rule states that a tweeter will fully disperse wavelengths twice its size. Thus, the fairly common one-inch tweeter diaphragm disperses well enough that only marginal improvements are obtained by going to a smaller unit. On the other hand, a two-inch tweeter (unless it is of a design that reduces the effective radiating area as the frequency rises) is generally not acceptable.

Effective Driver Radiating Area

You've probably inferred that the "nominal" diameter of a driver is generally not the same as its effective radiating area. That's because the nominal diameter includes the "surround" that supports the cone. The best way to determine effective driver size is to examine the drivers and measure them with a ruler. This is an easy, but time consuming process. Since the whole purpose of the exercise is to eliminate the time wasted running around from store to store, use this rule-of-thumb instead. It states that the moving (or effective radiating area) of a driver is approximately 85 percent of its nominal diameter. But in certain situations, complications occur. Here's how to handle them.

Dealing with Odd Shapes. When a driver has different horizontal and vertical dimensions, its horizontal and vertical dispersion will be determined by the respective dimensions. For example, the midrange driver of an unusually configured audiophile system measures 66 inches high by 0.9 inches wide, and operates from 100 Hz to 4,000 Hz. Vertical dispersion is thus limited to about 200 Hz (a wavelength of

67.2 inches), but the far more important horizontal dispersion extends to 15 kHz, far above the driver's operating limit. This driver has, in effect, no vertical dispersion and perfect horizontal dispersion.

More than One Woofer. Where more than one driver handles a given range of frequencies they should be considered as one driver having dimensions encompassing all of them. When two drivers operate in the same frequency range the best results will be obtained if they are mounted vertically. In the case, for example, of a speaker that uses a pair of 7-inch woofers mounted vertically, the maximum dimension that encompasses both woofer diaphragms is 14 inches. But its crossover occurs at 550 Hz — whose wavelength is about 24 inches — and the resulting index is a superb 1.7 vertically. The horizontal index is nearly twice that, because the drivers are mounted vertically.

When two drivers operate in the same frequency range the best results will be obtained if they are mounted vertically.

By contrast, a speaker that uses a pair of side-by-side 6.5-inch woofers operating up to 2 kHz would have a very poor 0.5 horizontal index, in spite of its small cones. Incidentally, drivers that operate in adjacent frequency ranges are, in effect, duplicate drivers at the crossover point. It follows, then, that under most circumstances the best design practice is to mount them in a vertical row as close together as possible.

The Importance of Listening

These maxims, while an effective tool, are not meant to replace your ears. After all, a speaker whose dispersion characteristics are exemplary can still, due to deficiencies in other areas, sound awful. So you'll still have to spend time listening (hopefully using the guidelines that appear elsewhere in these pages) but the ability to eliminate from consideration before setting out on your auditioning rounds those speakers which you would reject anyway, is a valuable and time-saving advantage. After all, it will hasten the day that you unpack, hook up, and begin to live with the speakers of your dreams.

CHOOSING SPEAKERS

Given that there are hundreds, if not thousands, of speakers from which to choose, and assuming that the goal is to buy the best pair that can be afforded, how is it possible to make a choice without turning the process into a full-time career? Can this task, which is often an exercise in frustration, be made a little less daunting? Is there a way to eliminate the time spent in auditioning and rejecting bad speakers? Thankfully, the answer is yes. Certain specifications — such as the dispersion characteristics just discussed — can expedite your shopping by helping you decide which speakers to eliminate out of hand. And there are various other strategies you can apply to seeking out good, accurate speakers, which we'll now attempt to enumerate.

Not too long ago the only way to pick a speaker was by listening and basing a decision on the kind of "sound" you liked best. Did you like a boomy, "present," sizzly sound that made rock and roll really cook? Or did you like a mellower sound that made easy listening even easier? The *real* reason for that kind of approach to shopping was that truly accurate speakers were few and far between — and generally very costly. The situation is rather different now: technology has come a long way, and it is much easier for a conscientious manufacturer to build a speaker whose output more accurately reflects the signal it is being fed.

Building an *accurate* speaker, however, is not as straightforward as building an accurate amplifier: amplifiers and other purely electronic components do not have to do any physical labor, while speakers have to vibrate and to move large volumes of air. The quality spread of speakers in a given price range is thus far wider than that of electronics, and listening — as opposed to comparing specs or features — is still the most important part of the shopper's job. But at least there are now accurate speakers in every price range, given the design constraints imposed by the need to achieve a pricing goal. Once you've got an accurate speaker to start with, you can adjust the sound to your taste by using your amplifier or receiver tone controls, or any of the various signal processing devices, such as an equalizer, you might choose to own.

Speaker Accuracy

How do you tell an accurate speaker from the other kind? It is not all that easy. The very speaker that sounds so impressive in the audio store may be thrusting itself on you with artificially pumped-up bass and frizzed-up treble, and there still are manufacturers who build such inaccuracies into their products for just that purpose: to entrap the buyer, in the knowledge that a *truly* accurate speaker will probably sound mousy next to their doctored one.

To know whether a speaker is accurate or not you have to have something with which to compare the sound it makes. That means that most contemporary pop music is out: their almost universal use of electronic instruments (synthesizers and so forth) and heavy dependence on processors of various kinds make for a sound based not on any acoustic analog, but only on the individual taste of the recording engineer and producer. So even if your teeth ache when you listen to anything but heavy metal, choose your speakers on the basis of listening tests using symphony orchestras, pipe organs, string quartets, or certified unprocessed vocalists or groups. Using such music — which will be primarily classical — you will have something to go by as you listen.

Choose your speakers on the basis of listening tests using symphony orchestras, pipe organs, string quartets, or certified unprocessed vocalists or groups.

You should listen for the kinds of tricks that some speaker makers try to play. If violins sound metallic or strident, the maker may have excessively boosted the treble range; deficient highs will make them sound dull or distant. Cymbals and triangles should sound clear and bright. Cellos and trombones should not stick out: if they do, the mid-bass frequencies may be too prominent, and boosting the mid-bass is one of the old disguises for an absence of true low-bass response.

Dispersion Characteristics

Sweet spots are for tennis rackets, and even there the ideal is for the entire surface to perform well. Too many speakers have sweet spots too: they tend to beam the music (mainly the treble frequencies) out in a straight line, making placement (of both the speakers and the listeners) critical. The ideal, as discussed earlier, is wide dispersion of sounds of all frequencies, so that good stereo perspective will be provided through as large an area of the listening room as possible. (The dispersion characteristics of a conventionally designed speaker can be determined arithmetically. This is discussed in detail on page 99.) Apart, though, from some new, fairly exotic entries, all speakers have limited dispersion, and one of your aims is to buy ones whose dispersion is wide enough to provide a reasonably even sound throughout the listening room.

Speaker Hardware

With a loudspeaker it is sometimes hard to escape the feeling that the more hardware in the package the more you are getting for your money: that a system with three speakers is inherently better than one with two and inherently poorer than one with five; that a big floor-standing model you can hardly move is inherently better than a bookshelf speaker that you can carry home yourself on the bus. These things can, of course, be true, but it is vital to remember that they do not *have* to be true at all. Plenty of small two-way systems outperform big three-way systems in every way, from accuracy to power-handling capacity. Try to forget about hardware when you make your choice (except insofar as it affects installation) and buy on the basis of sound alone.

The Bottom Line: Price

Remember those "design constraints imposed by the need to achieve a pricing goal" we mentioned a few paragraphs back in connection with the availability of accurate speakers at any price point? This, of course, carries with it the implicit warning that a terrific $150 speaker will not be as accurate as a terrific $500 speaker, and this is inevitable, otherwise there wouldn't *be* any $500 speakers (or, more likely, knowing the way the marketplace works, any $150 speakers!). These constraints invariably manifest themselves as trade-offs in the finished product. A serious speaker manufacturer tends to have a sort of house sound: his less expensive speakers often sound very similar to his top-of-the-line models, but not so loud, and with less true deep-bass and high-treble response. In designing these speakers he will have to decide on a set of priorities. One maker may opt to sacrifice some bass response to gain a little extra efficiency (hence, loudness), while another may feel that the additional bass is worth giving up some volume for. In that connection, by the way, it is a surprising fact that, all else being equal, a small speaker is probably going to be less efficient than a big one — that is another design factor that has to be juggled with all the rest.

Whatever you decide to trade off in your price range, however, rest assured that very good speakers for every budget are out there just waiting to be given good homes.

It is a surprising fact that, all else being equal, a small speaker is probably going to be less efficient than a big one.

A Step-by-Step Guide to Speaker Buying

Speaker performance is not readily quantified, so unlike most other components, speakers cannot be chosen on the basis of features and specifications — although, as the section in this chapter dealing with the dispersion specification points out, certain specs can be of some use in *eliminating* bad speakers from contention. To be sure of getting the best speakers for the money you're going to have to do an awful lot of field work, so to make things a little bit easier, here are some steps which, if followed, will make the job easier and ultimately more rewarding.

1. *Invest in a few good compact discs (CDs) to bring to your speaker auditions.* Even if you don't yet own a CD player, you almost certainly will someday. In the meantime, consider these few as an invest-

ment in your system. There are dozens of recordings suitable for testing speakers, but you can get away with three or four and cover just about everything you need to listen for. Carl Orff's *Carmina Burana* contains highly demanding solo-vocal, massed-choir, percussion, and string sections. The Telarc version, under the baton of Robert Shaw, is both the best recording and one of the best performances of the work. From the Denon catalogue choose the Hermann Prey recording of Schubert's song cycle *Die Winterreise*. It's one of the most natural-sounding recordings of voice with piano, and as such is highly revealing of any speaker-induced colorations. Another highly revealing vocal recording is Jennifer Warnes' *Famous Blue Raincoat*. Finally, William Ackerman's *Passages*, on Windham Hill, is one of the best solo guitar discs on the market. The acoustic guitar is fiendishly difficult to record (and reproduce) properly, and this disc, when played back through a good system, can really fool you into thinking that you're hearing live music.

2. *Study your test discs.* The best way to do this is with headphones — good headphones, and the best phones to use for analytical purposes are electrets or electrostatics (more about these later). Dynamic phones *can* be used, but it's risky in that they are, if anything, even *more* variable than the speakers you're trying to choose between. So make a nuisance of yourself in a store that has electrostatic phones on demo (or find a friend with a pair) and study your CDs. You'll quickly find those passages that will offer the greatest challenge to a speaker — and you'll be amazed at how much better the headphones will be than all but the best speakers.

3. *Make a list of speakers to audition.* This won't be a final list, of course, since most dealers will have a model or two that you've left off but should consider. But it helps to have an idea of what's available in your price range, and to reject those that are unsuitable for one reason or other — size, for example. The source of your initial list can be models mentioned favorably in the various audio periodicals, interesting advertisements, friends' recommendations, and past experience.

4. *Audition the complete line of speakers from the manufacturers on your list.* This will be time consuming, and might seem silly since it will probably involve listening to speakers that are well out of your price range. But there is a good reason for this exercise. The better manufacturers use the same criteria for all of their speakers,

and thus they will all share a distinctive sonic signature. So, if you find that the Blastophonic One sounds markedly different from the Blastophonic Four, that could be reason enough to stay away from Blastophonic speakers. The main difference between two speakers from the same company should be in the areas of bass response, power handling, and ultimate output capability. The exception to this rule occurs when a company puts a high priority on spatial characteristics, and the costlier models use more sophisticated techniques to achieve this end.

> *The main difference between two speakers from the same company should be in the areas of bass response, power handling, and ultimate output capability.*

5. *Audition speakers using an amplifier with about as much power as the one you'll be using at home.* Efficiency counts. (It's not unreasonable, though, for the salesman to want to use a more powerful model. Hi-fi store sound rooms are generally a lot more absorptive than living rooms, so it takes more power to achieve a given sound level. Beyond that, some stores have switching systems that sap power from the amplifier being used in order to permit comparison at equal volumes.) If you're planning to use a 30-watt-per-channel receiver at home, and the speakers you're auditioning in the store don't get loud enough with 60 watts, reject them. But if they almost make it with 30 in the store they'll probably be all right at home.

6. *Don't forget the old "one-dB trick."* When comparing different speakers it's crucial that each pair be set to play at *exactly* equal volume levels. Remember this rule: when switching between speakers, the louder pair will always sound better, even if it's not. A few unscrupulous salespeople will set up their demos so that the speakers they intend for you to buy will always be slightly louder than the other pair. If you can't get the salesperson to equalize levels, listen elsewhere; you're wasting your time and not learning anything. And while you're at it, make sure that, for the purposes of this exercise, the amplifier's tone controls are flat, and the filters and loudness control are off.

7. *Don't overload your senses.* The sonic memory is notoriously short. By the time you get to speaker Number 3 you will have no memory of the characteristics of speaker Number 1. First compare Number 1 with Number 2. Compare whichever you like better with Number 3. Then compare the better of that pair with the loser of the first comparison. Ideally, one of the three will stand out as the clear favorite.

8. *Buy the speakers* you *like the best.* This step is the most fun, if only because it means no more schlepping from store to store. It can also be the most difficult, for the speakers you like best might not

be the ones your friends recommend, or the ones that are "top-rated," or the ones that the salespeople want to sell you. Stick to your guns. If you've done your homework and legwork, you've almost certainly chosen a good speaker.

In Search of the $100 Speaker

We've mentioned the fact that below a certain price point a manufacturer must, of necessity, introduce certain compromises into the design of a speaker. This makes things somewhat more difficult for those of us who are attempting to stay within a budget. Even so, speakers with a list price of as low as $100 each (as of this writing) can yield exceptionally satisfying sound. In the late '60s a speaker was introduced that set the $100 speaker market on its ear. That speaker was the Large Advent Utility Model, and compared with everything else that was available for the same money it was a stunner. It was literally the first loudspeaker in its price range capable of providing deep bass and reasonably accurate octave-to-octave balance. At $102 each, it became one of the best-selling speakers of all time — as well it should have. Now think about what else you could buy for $102 in those days: three hundred gallons of gasoline; more steak than you could carry; a good, running Volkswagen. So when you consider speakers at $100 apiece in the '90s, it's well to remember just what $100 is, and to appreciate the technological progress that permits these modest products to sound as good as they do.

It is tempting at this point to list a few good $100 speakers and say "go buy one of these — they're all terrific," but that would be too easy for us, and unfair to you. It will exclude many excellent speakers, for no single reviewer can possibly know them all, and it would fail to provide you with the knowledge necessary in order to make an intelligent choice. So don't be disappointed by the lack of a list of makes and models. A few minutes of reading will give you the wherewithal to ultimately make your own list of contenders, and that list won't be limited to what's on the market at this moment or to what we've been impressed with recently. If you're buying speakers this week, or next year, the information will serve you in good stead.

While it's possible to get a pair of very good speakers without spending more than a couple of hundred bucks, it's important to be aware of those areas in which they are likely to be *not* so terrific. When a manufacturer designs a speaker to sell for that price, he is going to make some compromises, and presumes that you, for your part, can adjust to them. When you spend a great deal of money for speakers you usually get two things that are missing from the bargain models: lots of bass and lots of output. Inexpensive speakers, as a

Speakers with a list price of as low as $100 each (as of this writing) can yield exceptionally satisfying sound.

When you spend a great deal of money for speakers you usually get two things that are missing from the bargain models: lots of bass and lots of output.

rule, don't get very loud and don't go very deep into the bass. (This is not surprising, for even moderately expensive speakers usually have to sacrifice one or the other.) Not only that, you can expect that those $100 speakers with comparatively good bass won't be able to get quite as loud as those with a more restricted bottom end. On the other hand, inexpensive speakers are often able to provide a very convincing stereo image. This is because they frequently are small, and therefore don't have a great big baffle that diffracts the sound before it reaches you.

Another compromise will be in cabinet finish. While there are probably conspicuous exceptions, you can't expect to get genuine wood for $100. Count yourself lucky if the quality of the vinyl is such that it looks like wood from across the room. Better yet, opt for flat black if you've the choice.

While there are loads of other factors affecting the retail price of a speaker, let's consider just the hardware itself for a moment. Basically, a loudspeaker is made up of the box, the raw drivers (i.e., the woofer and tweeter), and the crossover network which assures that each driver only reproduces the tones for which it was designed. If the speaker is designed to *retail* for $100, then the dealer is going to pay the manufacturer somewhat less for it. And if the manufacturer is to make a profit — and he will — it's got to cost him somewhat less to build than he charges the dealer. So you can see that your $100 speaker is built on a very tight budget, which means that no single part of it can be overly expensive. No exotic samarium cobalt tweeter. No hand-rubbed rosewood veneer cabinet. If the speaker is to be any good at all, just about all of the money has to go for performance.

Here are some criteria for choosing $100 speakers:

- *Stick with a two-way system.* The more drivers a manufacturer uses the less he can spend on each one: you're more likely to get a good woofer and a good tweeter if you're not also buying a midrange driver. A three-way $100 speaker is likely to be a three-way solely because the manufacturer hopes to impress the novice who equates "more" with "better." It's not, at least for $100.

- *Learn to judge dispersion by reading specifications.* On page 99 there is a discussion of a method for calculating dispersion using the driver width and the crossover wavelength. In brief, it states that sound will radiate at a wide angle (i.e., be well-dispersed) if the radiated wavelengths are longer than the radiating area.

  Here is an index of performance that will serve you in good stead: divide the crossover wavelength by the woofer's radiating diameter. If the result is over 1.5, dispersion will be excellent. 1.0

to 1.5 is good; 0.75 to 1.0 is mediocre; below 0.75 is bad. The ultimate dispersion of the tweeter, by the way, is somewhat less critical than that of the midrange.

- *Learn to listen.* This should be obvious, but it's all too easy to be sonically seduced by a speaker which, at first hearing, has an "impressive" sound. And be assured that speaker manufacturers know what's impressive to the uninitiated. Thumpy mid-bass, overly forward midrange, and zippy treble can sound very attractive for the time it takes to audition a speaker in the dealer's showroom. But these characteristics will soon become annoying once the speaker is in your living room. Remember: a speaker that sounds initially impressive may have been designed to be sold, not to be an accurate reproducer of music. To listen for accuracy, test it with a disc of unprocessed, acoustic instruments whose sounds you know well. Check carefully for the clear reproduction of those sounds: round, woody acoustic bass; pure, non-piercing violin; crisp, clear drums. No register or set of frequencies should be overly emphasized; the sound should be even throughout the frequency spectrum (unless the music itself emphasizes particular sounds).

While it's not as often the case as it was true a few years ago, many stores will try to sell you "house brand" speakers if you walk in and wave two $100 bills. There's an enormous amount of profit for the store in selling these unknown quantities, and they can seem to be a very attractive value. They often carry a highly inflated "list" price, and you're lulled into thinking that you're getting a very substantial discount. Forget it. You're buying a speaker that has been designed solely as a money-making commodity, and the fact that something resembling music is meant to come out of it in the end has received very little attention. Your ears will quickly weed out these frauds, but to avoid wasting your time with them it is wise to confine your listening to speakers that are nationally distributed and which have a good reputation. The primary thing to remember is that if you first eliminate the speakers that *can't* sound good, and then listen with an educated ear to those that have potential, your $200 will buy a fine pair of speakers.

SPEAKERS AND YOUR ROOM

The auditorium of New York City's Metropolitan Opera House has a gilded plaster ceiling from which hang crystal chandeliers of great size and beauty. The tiers of boxes and seats which rise in five levels above the orchestra are also faced in plaster and have more crystal lighting fixtures attached to them. The walls on each level are paneled in polished rosewood (all, they say, from one massive tree).

The seats are plush velvet and all aisles are heavily carpeted. The very bannisters are snugly wrapped in velvet cozies. Some 3,800 people can be accommodated in the plush velvet seats, and another 250 or so standing, leaning against plush velvet rails: those last figures will give you an idea of the size of the room (a theater *is* a room, you know). Transplanted a few thousand miles westward and flattened out a bit, it could be a pretty respectably sized rodeo palace.

And yet, if you were to stand on the 55-foot-wide stage and munch a bunch of Fritos, someone all the way up in row K of the top balcony would hear you perfectly well. Try *that* in a rodeo palace. Or in your living room (if it is a large one).

Now, if you were to set up a pair of good loudspeakers on the stage of the Metropolitan Opera House and sit pretty much anywhere in the hall you would hear mighty fine music. That is because the Metropolitan is a perfectly wonderful acoustical environment for listening to music. The most important reason for this is no doubt its shape (in a word, boxy), but the balance between hard, reflective surfaces and soft absorptive ones (including those 4,000 human bodies) has worked out to be virtually ideal.

The balance between hard, reflective surfaces and soft absorptive ones has worked out to be virtually ideal.

At home, priorities are different. You have chrome and glass furniture and quarry tile floors (or soft Victorian sofas draped with antimacassars and floors covered with Persian carpets) because you like that style of furnishing, or because it was the style that made itself most readily available; you are not about to throw everything away and buy rosewood paneling and second-hand velvet theater seats — it probably wouldn't result in an acoustic paradise anyway.

When you're setting up the speakers of a stereo system, what you need to do is aim for the best sound you can achieve in the room you've got with only minor alterations.

This concept of "best sound" is, of course, pretty much indefinable, but some of its most important elements are *even sound* (where highs and lows are prominent only to the extent that they are prominent in the musical source material), *realistic stereo image* (preferably throughout as much of the room as possible), and a *lack of any acoustically induced distortion* (which is linked to the first element we mentioned).

It might be best just to go through some of the factors to be considered; then you can pick and choose from among them according to your needs.

The Radiation Pattern

Low frequencies tend to be omnidirectional: they will pretty much radiate all over the place from wherever your speakers are located. The more surfaces with which a low-frequency generating speaker (a woofer or integral speaker system) is in contact, the more those low frequencies will be emphasized. Thus, a speaker in a corner, in contact with two walls and the floor, might tend to be boomy; a speaker dangling in mid-air, suspended from a rope, might sound thin.

High frequencies tend, on the contrary, to travel in a straight line. But small, hard objects like Ming vases, Grecian urns, and empty bottles strewn decoratively about the room in the path of those frequencies will help to disperse the directional highs.

Some rooms have acoustical quirks: two paces directly in front of the second window from the left, for example, might be a spot where frequencies of 259 Hz are unaccountably too loud or too soft.

What we have already mentioned — that hard, smooth surfaces reflect and soft or deeply textured surfaces absorb sound — can also affect acoustic balance in very peculiar and unpredictable ways.

The Elusive Stereo Image

While we must ignore as impractical and excessive the old saw about *true* stereophonic effect being achievable only at "X" feet perpendicularly away from the precise center of a line drawn between two speakers placed "Y" feet apart, we must take note of the fact that it is in an area somewhere between the two speakers that stereo sound is best heard. You will have to decide the axis on which the speakers are placed and the portion of the room that consequently benefits most from the stereo effect. (If the layout of your room is absolutely *impossible*, you should consider a pair of speakers whose design is such that they present a good stereo image over a wider-than-normal listening area. These include the Walsh series from Ohm Acoustics, the dbx Soundfield series, and several models from Bose. As it happens, these speakers are also very good in the other, more conventional performance areas, so you needn't sacrifice overall sound quality in favor of exceptional spatial characteristics.)

If the layout of your room is absolutely impossible, you should consider a pair of speakers whose design is such that they present a good stereo image over a wider-than-normal listening area.

Your Room Creates Distortion

Feedback is the most serious kind of distortion that results from your room. Mid frequencies can ricochet off surfaces and be propelled back to the turntable where they can be picked up as vibration by the phono cartridge. The noise will go through the system over and over again in a vicious circle. In mild cases there may be only an indefinable, but marked, distortion; if things get serious, a howling like that of the microphone at a PTA meeting can actually occur. Low frequencies in such a feedback loop — especially inaudibly low ones — can be even more insidious, muddying sound and wasting power. In either of these cases, speakers, turntable, or furniture will probably have to be moved. As we turn more and more to CDs for our disc-based source material, this will cease to be a significant problem, as CD players are much less prone than their LP analog counterparts to be affected by acoustic feedback.

The live and dead spots we have mentioned — the result of *standing waves* — also effectively constitute a form of acoustic distortion which can often be corrected by moving things around a little.

Reflections from Room Surfaces

Reflections from room surfaces either floor and ceiling or two walls — may cause the reinforcement of some tones and the attenuation of others, depending upon the dimensions of the room and the frequency of the tones. Reflections can be reduced or eliminated by moving the reflective surfaces, or by placing absorptive material in positions calculated to eliminate reflections before they can occur. Sometimes as simple a step as putting a curtain in front of a window, hanging a large oil painting on the wall, or placing a few soft pillows around the room, can effect a dramatic improvement.

Acoustic Absorption

Acoustic absorption is the opposite of reflection, and occurs when a material accepts sonic energy without reflecting it back into the room. This is usually most noticeable in the mid high-frequency range, and makes the music sound dull and muffled. Heavy carpets, drapes, and upholstered furniture tend to absorb sound very well. The ideal room has a mixture of reflective and absorptive surfaces; if you encounter a highly absorptive room there are two possibilities. One is to remove some of the absorptive material; the other is to compensate for the loss of highs by boosting the treble, perhaps with an equalizer. Of course, this assumes that the speakers are not positioned so that their tweeters are firing directly into the back of an armchair; make certain they have a clear "line of sight."

Resonances

A resonance is the frequency at which something — anything — will vibrate if it has the chance. The air within a listening room has a resonant frequency, as do the pictures on the wall and the bronze figurine on the coffee table. The problem with resonances is that they can interfere with good sound: if objects within the room vibrate, they can be distracting. And if the *air* within the room — or, more likely, within alcoves or archways *between* rooms — vibrates, it can cause frequency response problems: certain sounds in the music may be reinforced, for example. Solutions include closing a door (if you're lucky) and placing something large in the cavity (to change the volume of the air).

The problem with resonances is that they can interfere with good sound: if objects within the room vibrate, they can be distracting.

Experiment with Speaker Placement

In many, or even most, rooms, simply putting the speakers in what seems a good, logical location will give you reasonably pleasant results. But if you notice a lack of punch, or pizazz, or sizzle, or sparkle, or whatever you bought your hi-fi system for, you should start juggling the various elements listed above. If the highs are all concentrated on the person in the green wing-chair while you, on the brocade ottoman, hardly hear the tingle of the triangle at all, it may be that you need to look at your guidelines and put some knick-knacks out to bounce the sound around the room a bit.

If, on the other hand, bass notes sound like "I AM OZ, THE GREAT AND POWERFUL"— in other words, boomy — you may want to move the speakers a few inches away from the walls or raise them off the floor.

The possible problems are infinite in their wonderful variety, but then so are the solutions. Don't aim at a Metropolitan Opera House sound, but don't hesitate to move a hassock out of the way of a tweeter if it is blocking all your highs, or to mar the 18th-century symmetry of your drawing room if it means better balance between left and right channels. Experiment, fool around, and before you know it, your speakers will sound as good as they should.

WHERE TO PUT YOUR SPEAKERS: AN ILLUSTRATED GUIDE

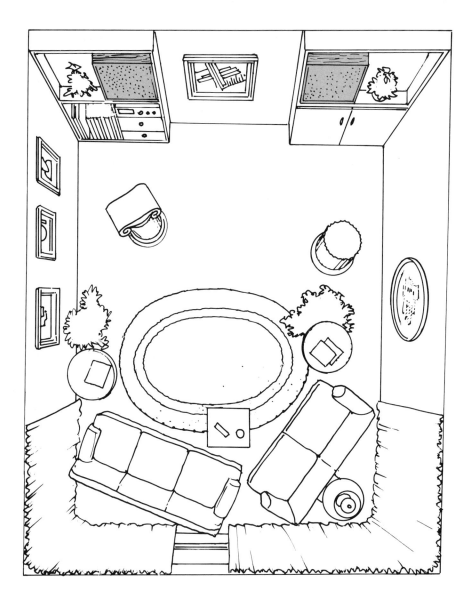

An almost ideal listening room, with the speakers mounted on the short wall, and the distance between them equal to or less than the distance from each to the listening position. The absorptive materials are in the listening area, while the radiating area is fairly live. There are several smallish, hard objects scattered throughout the room to aid in the dispersion of sound.

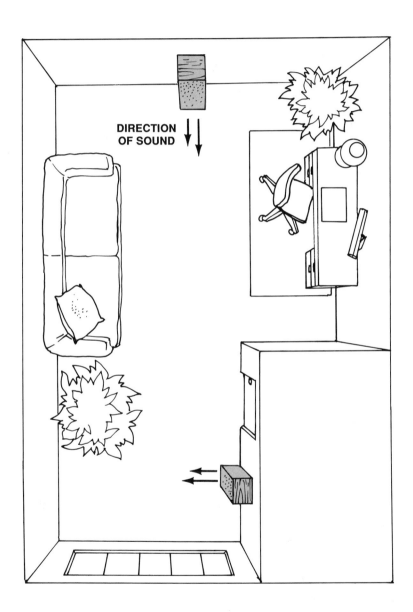

DIRECTION OF SOUND

An L-shaped room is never ideal and, indeed, can be quite problematic. But compromise is possible. This configuration will yield reasonably uniform sound in the primary area, while the desk will receive a somewhat unbalanced perspective. Your receiver's balance control can be used for compensation.

Although the shape of this room is ideal for a single-wall installation, its layout calls for an alternative setup. If one speaker-carrying wall contains shelves, don't worry about mounting one speaker horizontally and the other vertically. Theoretically, you'll sacrifice some of the speakers' imaging potential, but you've already done that by using two walls anyway. On balance, this is a good compromise.

Filling two connecting rooms with sound is ideally done with two sets of speakers. That way, the main room isn't overwhelmed by the volume needed to fill the second room. The smaller speakers in the dining room are ideal for background music; for more serious listening in that room, the main speakers can be played as well, allowing their greater bass output to supplement that of the secondary pair.

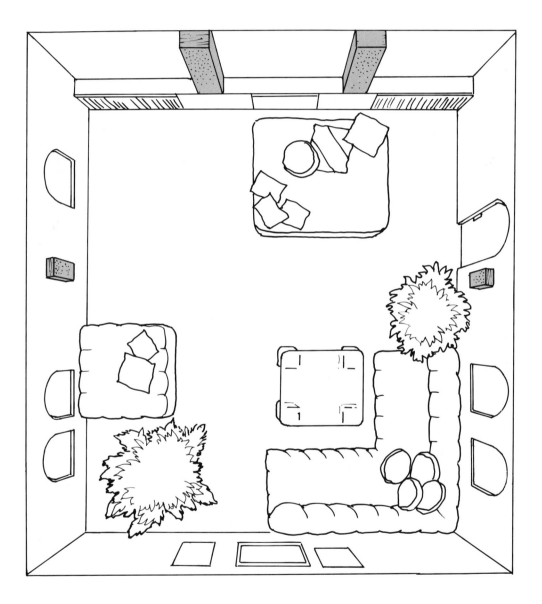

Very large rooms can often benefit from the use of a pair of secondary speakers. This allows a high overall volume level to be maintained without creating an overwhelmingly loud region near the main speakers. In addition, the secondary speakers will serve to reinforce the high frequencies in the far end of the room.

The normal, and ideal, position for a subwoofer in a three-piece system is somewhere between the two ''satellite'' speakers. This eliminates the possibility of the subwoofer's output being heard as a distinct sound source. If central placement isn't possible, the subwoofer in a three-piece system may be placed almost anywhere in the room.

SPEAKER WIRE

If you are like most people who have hi-fi systems, you have connected your speakers to your amplifier or receiver with...well, with wire! A good guess is that 70 percent of you are using so-called speaker wire, color-coded, clear-plastic jacketed two-conductor cable in a very narrow gauge, usually either 20, 22, or 24 gauge (note that as the thickness increases, the gauge number decreases). Another 22½ percent of listeners have heard about thicker wire having less electrical resistance, and have switched to 16- or 18-gauge lamp wire, or, as it's often called, "zip cord."

System Connectors

The connections between the various electrical components in a system, such as those between turntable or CD player and amplifier, do deserve some attention. The combination of low signal level and the nature of the connection itself can make it worthwhile to seek out cables whose quality is higher than those the manufacturer tossed in the box.

The so-called RCA phono connector that is used on virtually all system components was created about four decades ago for ease of use and economy of manufacture. It is, to put it mildly, one of the less secure plug-jack designs, and the least bit of corrosion can result in noticeable aural problems.

Here, the cable manufacturers have managed to come up with products that address all the potential problems at once: not only does the structure of the cable itself meet the electrical needs of high-quality, low-level signal transmission, but the gold-plated plugs completely eliminate the corrosion problem. For the latter quality alone, these cables are worth considering, especially if your installation is such that fooling around with your cables is an awkward task; they are all the more useful if for some reason you need especially long (longer than about 36-inch) cables. There is no need to spend $100 on three feet of cable; good cable with gold-plated connectors is available at any electronics store.

The remaining 7½ percent have probably gone out and bought one or another of the fancy audiophile cables now on the market. These cables are available in a wide range of types, and each of the various kinds is said to solve a different problem or set of problems inherent in the connection of loudspeakers to amplifiers.

The simplest of these problems, already hinted at in our reference to zip cord, is electrical resistance. The greater the impedance of a given type of cord, the greater the power drain. What actually happens is that some of the amp's output is wasted on literally heating the wire instead of driving the speaker cone. So thick, less resistant wire is in principle a good aim for any hi-fi system.

Anything that you read or hear that purports to attach significance to other aspects of speaker wire design has never been proven in any reliable testing. For most people, lamp cord will do nicely; for really long runs, or for top-of-the-hill systems where any degradation is too much degradation, going a gauge or two heavier, without spending more than hardware store prices, will be more than adequate.

For most people, lamp cord will do nicely; for really long runs, or for top-of-the-hill systems, going a gauge or two heavier will be adequate.

HEADPHONES

Like speakers, headphones have the final say about what your music is going to sound like. This is hardly surprising since, in essence, a pair of headphones *is* a pair of speakers, even if they are mounted on your ears instead of on your bookshelves. Thus, they must be auditioned as carefully as loudspeakers and will inevitably be chosen on subjective, musical grounds rather than purely on the basis of a specification sheet.

There is another kink, however, with headphones: since they are sitting on your head, they must be comfortable. If they are not, no matter how good they sound they will wind up gathering dust.

Headphones either isolate the listener from his aural environment or do not. The former surround the ears, usually sealing them off with a flexible gasket of some cushy material, and make it well near impossible to hear the phone. The non-isolating kind sit *on* the ear, allowing you to be *of* the world as well as *in* it.

That is the first choice you have to make: to hear outside sounds — like the telephone — or not to hear them. Unless a peculiarity of your listening space dictates one or the other type (people who live next to airports, for instance, might well prefer the isolating kind — they may even choose to wear them when they are not listening to music), this is a matter of taste, although you should bear in mind that by and large non-isolating phones are more comfortable over the long haul than the generally heavier isolating models.

Once upon not too long a time ago, all serious headphones were of the isolating type, since good bass response was thought to depend upon the creation of a sealed chamber over the ear, which seemed to require a bone-crushing clamp around the head. Technology, however, is always on the march, and developments in the way that diaphragms (the headphone equivalent of a speaker's cone) and magnets are made permitted the creation of light-weight open-air headphones. At their best, these phones have a more speaker-like, airy sound and enable you to "sense" the acoustics of the room you are sitting in, not merely that of the recording you are listening to.

So generally speaking, non-isolating, open-air headphones provide a more spacious sound, as well as more comfort, but at the expense of some — but not all that much — bass response. Hybrid models, which surround the ear but still permit some outside sounds to reach the listener, are often the best compromise between comfort, overall sound quality, and bass response.

Everything we've said so far applies primarily to conventional phones, known as *dynamic headphones*: those that work like miniature conventional loudspeakers. Most buyers opt for these, for several reasons, not the least among them cost and compatibility: they are available at a wide variety of price points and, almost without exception, simply plug into the jacks provided on most amplifiers, receivers, and other hi-fi components.

There is another entire sub-class of headphones: if you consider yourself truly bitten by the audio bug, or if you plan to use headphones for critical listening, even as a primary sound source, maybe you should consider *electrostatic* or *electret headphones*, which are quite unlike anything we have discussed: they use a totally different technology to create sound, and they require a special junction box which connects directly to the speaker outputs of the amplifier. In the case of electrostatic models, the junction box generally is also connected to an AC outlet, while electret models derive the necessary charge from the audio signal itself. Both types are costly, but the best of them provide uncanny sonic realism.

Uncanny sonic realism is very nice, but it has one big drawback: any flaw in the rest of your system will be mercilessly revealed. Tape hiss, record surface noise, hum...these and the other glitches that are filtered out by lesser headphones (or by the ambient noise in the listening room when listening to speakers) are presented in all their glory by electrostatic headphones. So be sure that the rest of your system is up to snuff before you write out a check for $150 or more for a pair of such phones.

Another thing about electrostatics: they can be power-hungry. As noted, just about any pair of dynamic headphones will work fine plugged into the front of just about any old amplifier. The purchaser need hardly bother with the efficiency specification of the conventional phones he is looking to buy (unless he has a real 98-pound weakling of an amplifier). This is not quite so true with electrostatic

Glitches that are filtered out by lesser headphones (or by the ambient noise in the listening room when listening to speakers) are presented in all their glory by electrostatic headphones.

models. If your amp is not up to powering them, you will have to crank it up to full volume to reach normal listening levels, and that will probably result in distortion, which will turn out not to be the fault of the headphones at all. Mind you, if you are looking at a grand's worth of headphone (and electrostatics can cost that much and more), your amplifier is probably up to the job. The danger level is around 50 watts or less per channel: at that point or lower, be sure you can take them home and try them before you make a commitment.

The ultimate rule about shopping for headphones is the one that applies to the choice of speakers — only more so, since comfort is a factor as well as personal taste in sound. Trust your ears, don't buy headphones that hurt, and audition the models you're considering using the same criteria you would when judging speakers. If you do, and if you stick with a brand that will probably be around in the unlikely event that you ever need service, you won't go wrong. A careful choice will mean fine sound and comfort, which in turn will provide a guarantee of good listening.

8 SIGNAL PROCESSORS

Certain audiophiles refer to the ideal amplifier as "a straight wire with gain." This phrase implies that what goes in (from the program source) will be just the same as what comes out (through the speakers or headphones)...except louder.

There are not many amps or receivers out there that live up to that ideal. All introduce some minuscule percentage of distortion, and virtually all permit the user to modify that incoming signal in some way, either through simple bass and treble tone controls or through more complicated multi-band equalizers. This ability to adjust the sound makes many audio purists uncomfortable, and they tend to favor components which have some sort of tone-control defeat circuits built in.

The less radical among the cream of hi-fi hobbyists — and certainly the rest of us — acknowledge that, while audio equipment is *meant* to reproduce music as faithfully as possible, the limitations of equipment, software (i.e., records, tapes, CDs, and radio broadcasts), and environment make the achievement of that goal extremely problematic. Most of us hear music which has been compressed in its dynamic range, laden with extraneous noise, distorted — in short, which is not all that much like the original live performance when you come right down to it. Noise, most often in the form of hiss, can find its way into the signal during non-digital taping, FM transmission, and tape playback. And even if the medium is theoretically capable of reproducing the full range of peaks and valleys of live music (as CDs, for instance, are), the manufacturer will probably have been unable to resist the temptation to compress it just a wee bit.

With LPs, this is understandable, and necessary, for the mechanical constraints imposed by the format — primarily in the stylus/ groove interface — prevent it from handling the full dynamic range of music. Likewise, FM broadcasters must effect a certain amount of compression to avoid overload and to raise the volume of soft passages to a level that will be heard over the airwaves. With CDs, the reasons are less apparent.

In the realm of frequency response, no hi-fi system is perfect. There is always that plus or minus so many decibels next to the otherwise impressive frequency-response figure. Your amplifier and CD player may have nearly flat response, but there isn't a cartridge or a speaker made that doesn't have a peak or a valley *somewhere* in its response curve. Added to that are the acoustical quirks of the room in which you have the system installed. That room becomes a part of the system, and its own resonances and other influences become a part of the system's frequency response. And if it isn't that, it's the recording engineer, who may have made a whole disc sound too bright or boomy for your taste. In any case, it is amazing that hi-fi sounds as good as it does.

It is amazing that hi-fi sounds as good as it does. However good that is, the listener can make it even better, using one or more kinds of signal processors.

However good that is, the listener can make it even better, using one or more kinds of signal processors.

These devices change a "pure" signal in some chosen fashion to deliberately alter the output that you hear from your speakers. Signal processors can be used in two ways. One is to compensate for the problems we have outlined, the goal being to restore the signal to its theoretical original state. The other is to tailor the music to personal taste — an equally valid goal in view of the lack of a live equivalent to much of today's pop music, which is generated largely by electronic instruments.

The "tone" control on a pocket radio is a rudimentary signal processor. Indeed, the most common, and probably the most useful, category of processors — equalizers — is made up of glorified tone controls. Equalizers, by acting to boost or cut specific segments of the sound spectrum, enable you to compensate for these factors, besides catering to your own taste in sound and minimizing such problems as clicks and hiss.

EQUALIZERS

Amplifier designers, despite the astonishing complexity of the products they create, have it easier than the poor souls who develop speakers. The operation of an amplifier is far less susceptible to interference from external factors than that of a speaker, so the designer can be pretty sure that if he does a good job, the product will work well. The speaker crafter, by contrast, can have no idea where his brainchild will ultimately wind up. And, since the room plays such an important role in determining the overall sound, the speaker's design may have to be compromised in order that it work reasonably well over a wide range of acoustical conditions. True, many speakers come with instructions like "Place each speaker 1 meter from the side wall, 1.2 meters from the rear wall, and 3 meters from each other," but let's face it: not many people are able (much less willing) to make acoustical considerations the primary focus in establishing their decorating priorities. So, given the imperfect nature of speakers, and the relatively unpredictable way in which they interact with the listening room, many music lovers choose to modify their sound with an equalizer.

What Does an Equalizer Do?

An equalizer is, in essence, a sophisticated tone-control system whose capabilities and flexibility far exceed that of conventional bass and treble controls. The basic operating principle of any equalizer is simple. The broad range of audible frequencies — 20 Hz to 20,000 Hz — is divided into segments (called *bands*), and each segment is given its own volume control. When you twist your bass or treble control, what you are actually doing is raising or lowering the volume of a portion of the musical spectrum — the bass portion or the treble portion. By dividing the spectrum into narrower bands, an equalizer allows you to make finer adjustments to the relative levels of various parts of the music. This allows you, for example, to emphasize a singer's voice without also raising the level of certain accompanying instruments.

By dividing the spectrum into narrower bands, an equalizer allows you to make finer adjustments to the relative levels of various parts of the music.

Making the Connection

The typical equalizer is easily connected to virtually any audio component system, regardless of whether that system uses a receiver, an integrated amplifier, or a separate preamplifier/control chassis as its central component. Since an equalizer is intended to intercept the audio signal, work its magic, and then return it to the normal path, it is easily plugged into the audio system via those ever-present tape-out/tape-in jacks commonly referred to as the tape-monitor circuit or loop. In most cases, the jacks on the amplifier or receiver now taken up by the added equalizer are replaced by similar in/out jacks on the equalizer itself, so that a previously connected tape deck need not be abandoned in favor of the equalizer.

The Two Types of Equalizers

Before we consider the desirability of equalizers in an audio system, let's briefly consider the two basic types available: graphic and parametric.

A *graphic equalizer* is one which is equipped with as few as five and as many as twenty or more separate controls (usually of the slider type, as opposed to a knob), each of which can adjust the response of a relatively narrow band of frequencies. In this way, the graphic equalizer provides a more diverse range of adjustments than would be possible with a simple bass and treble tone control, or even a bass, treble, and midrange tone control now commonly found on some amplifiers and receivers. A five-band graphic equalizer might have controls which operate around center frequencies of 100 Hz, 250 Hz, 1,000 Hz, 2.5 kHz, and 10 kHz, for example. A ten-band graphic equalizer (the most common variety available for home systems) might have controls centered precisely one octave apart (an octave is a doubling of frequency) at, say, 31 Hz, 62 Hz, 125 Hz, 250 Hz, 500 Hz, 1 kHz, 2 kHz, 4 kHz, 8 kHz, and 16 kHz. Usually the amount of boost or cut available at these center frequencies is about 10 or 12 dB.

While most graphic equalizers are intended to operate over the entire frequency range, some are designed to be more specific in their application. There are models available, for instance, which divide the bass into five distinct bands. By doing so, they are able to compensate for room-induced response aberrations such as standing waves (vibrations of the air in the room which will cancel certain frequencies and reinforce others).

A *parametric equalizer* is based upon the theory that in most instances there are only three or at most four regions of frequency in any sound system that require correction or compensation. The regions, however, may occur anywhere in the audible spectrum. Thus, a parametric equalizer may have only three or four adjustment bands, but each of these may be moved over a wide range of frequencies. In most cases, the bandwidth of frequencies may be varied along with the amplitude (amount) of boost or cut introduced by the control. As an example, one set of controls (one band) of a parametric equalizer may be centered at any frequency from, say, 500 Hz to 3 kHz, and the width of spectrum handled by that control may be varied from a fraction of an octave to a full octave. Once you have selected the center frequency and the bandwidth, you adjust the amount of boost or cut.

Do You Need an Equalizer?

While experts may argue the merits of parametric versus graphic equalizers, there is a more fundamental question that needs to be addressed: Does an equalizer in whatever form belong in a home audio system at all? The probable answer is: Yes, if it is used correctly.

Does an equalizer in whatever form belong in a home audio system at all? The probable answer is: Yes, if it is used correctly.

Those in favor of using equalizers with home audio systems argue that most hi-fi speaker systems do not have anything resembling flat or uniform frequency response over their entire useful range. Indeed, those few manufacturers who do publish response curves for speakers show curves that are replete with peaks and valleys, many of them several dB in amplitude. And of course, such response curves are usually taken in acoustically "dead" or inert rooms, whereas actual listening rooms add substantially to the aberrations in frequency response exhibited by any speaker system. And so it is argued that a properly used equalizer can counteract those response-curve errors, yielding a net response in the listening room which is very close to "flat" or ideal.

Simple bass and treble tone controls could not hope to accomplish the same results since each such control covers too broad a swath of frequencies. If you try to compensate for the minor dips and peaks in response using such tone controls, you can neutralize the peaks and dips but in so doing you will falsify other, nearby regions in the audio-response curves of the system as a whole. It follows that the greater the number of bands in a graphic equalizer, the more accurately it can compensate for room and system-response variations. In the case of parametric equalizers, the narrower each of their bands can be set, the more accurately they can compensate for errors in system response (and the more difficult they are to use).

This justification presumes, of course, that the owner of an equalizer will end up using it correctly. Unfortunately, that is seldom the case. If the only test instrument you have with which to adjust your newly purchased equalizer is your own pair of ears, the odds are great that you are going to end up with a system which may be *less* accurate and have poorer overall response than if you had not bothered with an equalizer in the first place. That is because human hearing is, in itself, anything but flat in response and varies greatly depending upon the volume level of the music (see the Fletcher-Munson curve on page 70).

Unfortunately, many owners of equalizers, faced with the inability to use them properly, end up using them as sound-effects amplifiers. They turn up the bass slider controls, crank up the extreme treble, and sit back thinking that they have now compensated for the deficiencies inherent in their speaker's woofer and tweeter sections. The sudden emphasis of bass and treble, though sometimes startlingly impressive, is anything but an accurate reproduction of musical sounds. On an aesthetic level this presents no real difficulty, since the listener's taste in sound is his or her own business. But electronically, there is a problem. Such arbitrary boosting of certain frequency bands (especially at the bass extremes) makes extremely heavy demands upon the amplifier used with the system in question. Remember, a boost of 10 dB for any frequency band on an equalizer (an amount obtainable on just about all equalizers) calls for a 10-to-1 power increase from a connected amplifier every time musical frequencies which fall within that band occur in the program source to which you are listening. That means that if you have been coasting along at 20-watt peaks when the equalizer's controls were set to their flat or center positions, the amplifier will suddenly be called upon to deliver *200 watts per channel* when frequencies within the boosted band occur in the music source. If the amplifier can't deliver that much power, it simply clips and distorts the signals every time such power demands are made upon it. It is for

Many professionals prefer to adjust response by attenuating certain bands to achieve flat response — cutting bass frequencies, for example, rather than boosting the treble.

this reason that many professionals who use equalizers prefer to adjust response by *attenuating* (i.e., reducing the level of) certain bands to achieve flat response — cutting bass frequencies, for example, rather than boosting the treble.

Another argument against equalizers has to do with their inconvenience. Let's say you have meticulously adjusted the controls so that the music sounds flat when you're in a particular listening position. A change in your position may require a readjustment of the equalizer settings to get the same overall sound. Understandably, some hi-fi owners feel that the aural benefits of EQ just aren't worth the bother. Such listeners simply choose their other components (especially loudspeakers) with extreme care and are content to take the frequency response as it comes in their particular listening environments.

Perhaps the best way to decide on whether owning an equalizer is worthwhile is to have your dealer demonstrate what the device can do, even in the less than ideal surroundings of a retail audio shop. If you are impressed with the sonic results and feel that music reproduction suddenly seems more natural and accurate, then there is a good chance that the equalizer will do as much for your system at home — providing you adjust it properly.

Setting Up Your Equalizer

Some manufacturers, aware of the problems that can be encountered by a neophyte trying to adjust a newly installed equalizer, assist the consumer by providing a test record as an aid in adjusting the device. This test record often contains individual noise bands, each of which corresponds to the frequencies governed by each of the slider controls on the equalizer. The idea is to adjust each slider as each noise band is heard so that all the noise bands sound equally loud. As many purchasers of equalizers have quickly discovered, this is almost as difficult a task as trying to adjust the equalizer's controls while listening to ordinary music. Again, our ears easily deceive us into thinking we can judge equal loudness levels at different frequencies when in fact we are incapable of doing so.

A few manufacturers go a step further and even supply a sound-level meter in addition to the test record. With this combination, it is possible to do a fairly good job of equalizing a system, though the procedure is somewhat tedious, since every time you adjust one band of the equalizer for a reference-level reading on the sound-level meter, you generally have to go back and re-adjust the levels on adjacent band controls.

The most sophisticated method of adjustment of an equalizer involves the use of a device called a *real-time spectrum analyzer*. This type of instrument, usually equipped with a calibrated microphone and a source of wide-band noise frequencies, displays a complete response curve (using light-emitting diodes, or LEDs) which varies as the equalizer's controls are adjusted. Being able to observe the entire response curve of one's system at a glance is a great aid in equalizing a sound system, and reduces the time required for this procedure to just a few minutes. Several equalizers are now available which incorporate built-in real-time analyzers as well as the needed source of noise and the calibrated microphone. Thanks to integrated circuitry, these all-in-one combinations, though not cheap, are within reach of those dedicated audio enthusiasts who feel that correct equalization is essential to their enjoyment of music played on their audio systems.

The ultimate in equalizer convenience is afforded by those few models whose on-board computers automate the entire equalization process. You simply place a microphone in your listening position and press a button. The equalizer sends a test signal through your speakers and compares what it "hears" through the microphone to the original. The electronic equivalent of the normal sliders move as if by magic, and the resulting equalization curve can be stored into the unit's memory. Several memory positions are provided, so you can save different EQ curves. This means that you can make adjustments for different types of music, or save a flat setting for both full and empty rooms.

Of course, it's important to remember that the uniform response you work so hard to achieve will remain flat only if you remain at the exact listening position where the calibrated microphone was placed when the initial adjustments were made. If you move even a few feet away, to another chair in the same room, the equalizer will have to be readjusted. Such are the vagaries of room acoustics.

Other common types of signal processors are as follows: *dynamic-range enhancers*, which restore some of the breadth of louds and softs to music which has been compressed in the recording process; *noise-reduction systems*, most often used in conjunction with tape decks (and generally built into them), do just what they say, cutting down on hiss without cutting down on the music (as a simple equalizer inevitably does); and *ambience simulators*. The latter come in many flavors. Some are simple reverberation or echo devices, while others much more sophisticated.

AMBIENCE SIMULATION

Go to a concert and close your eyes. You will be able to judge, without any visual clues and with a fair degree of accuracy, how large a room you are in, how far you are from the performers, where the performers are situated relative to each other, and even (with some practice) whether the room is full or half-empty. The same holds true for, say, your dining room.

Every room, be it Carnegie Hall or your dining room, has a sonic signature — a set of characteristics that define its acoustics. When you listen to live music in a reasonably large space, the sound doesn't all reach your ears at the same time. (It doesn't even reach both of your ears at the same time.) Some arrives directly, but most of what you hear is reflected off the various surfaces of the room, reaching you fractions of a second later. The nature of this reflected sound — the amount of delay before it reaches you, the directions from which it arrives, how it's blended with the direct sound, and how long it lasts after the source ceases — provides the ambience information that makes live music sound "live."

At home, however, when listening to your hi-fi, the ambience of the concert hall (or whatever) is replaced by the ambience of your living room. Now, it's true that many records have a certain amount of ambience "built in," but for the most part what you are hearing is

No matter how good your conventional sound system is, it cannot, by itself, re-create the ambience of a large room within the confines of your small one.

your room. The music lacks the sense of immediacy and depth that is part and parcel of the live music experience. No matter how good your conventional sound system is, it cannot, by itself, re-create the ambience of a large room within the confines of your small one.

The situation is compounded when you add video to the equation. Everyone agrees that TV is enhanced by the addition of a good sound system, and towards that end many products are available to integrate audio and video components. But flanking your TV screen with a couple of good speakers only cures some of the sonic ills that have plagued TV watching for so many years. In order for an audio/video system to be truly effective, the visual information presented by the screen needs to be audibly confirmed by the sound system. If you are watching someone yelling into the Grand Canyon, for example, the audio coming through your speakers ideally should sound cavernous and reverberating.

Quadraphonic's Broken Promise

In the mid-seventies, quadraphonic sound had the technical capability of providing the requisite ambience. Quadraphonic sound used four channels of amplification and four speakers, giving it the theoretical ability to replicate with great precision the ratio and nature of direct sound versus reflected sound heard in a concert hall. Why, then, did it fail on the marketplace?

First of all, it required specially encoded software to do a proper job, which meant that new records had to be purchased. Now, there's nothing inherently wrong with this notion: witness the popularity of CDs today. But in the case of quadraphonic there were several competing systems, and they were not compatible with one another. CBS records couldn't be decoded by a device meant for RCA's, and so on. Further, rather than trying to provide a more lifelike musical experience, the record companies often relied upon gimmicks rather than sound musical judgment when they produced four-channel records. While placing the listener in the middle of the band, and then having the instruments spin around his head, might be an interesting technical achievement, it has little to do with the authentic spatial reproduction of a live performance. In all, quadraphonic sound was a consumer's nightmare, and consumers finally said "no thanks."

Time Delay with Extra Speakers

Around the time of quadraphonic sound's demise, several products appeared that offered a much more viable means of re-creating the acoustics of a large space within the confines of a small one. They, too, required the use of a second stereo amplifier and speakers, but did not rely upon specially encoded software. Instead, they used time-delay circuitry to duplicate the reverberant field (and other sonic characteristics) of various acoustical spaces. The secondary speakers provided the ambience information, and weren't intended to be specifically heard: the idea was that you turned them up until you could just hear them as distinct sources, and then lowered their volume slightly until they disappeared. Some models "interlocked" the control over various acoustical parameters, reasoning that in real life as one changed, so would the others. Others provided separate controls, and permitted a greater range of adjustment, making them both more flexible and more difficult to use (and more prone, perhaps, to bizarre sonic results). In the main, these systems worked very well, but were costly. The better models ran from $600 to over $1,000 — a lot of money even by today's standards. And then you had to buy speakers and an amplifier — more money. Further, they were complicated to install and operate, and could — with improper use — result in some pretty awful results. It's no wonder, then, that you'll have to search long and hard to find one of the remaining stand-alone time-delay ambience simulation systems.

Image Enhancers

A much simpler (and less costly) alternative to ambience simulation via time delay goes by the generic term *image enhancement*. It's possible to fiddle with the signal going to your standard stereo speakers in such a way as to significantly alter the sound stage they present. Never mind how they work: there are several methods and for our purposes they all boil down to "they do it with mirrors." Image enhancers are simple to install and operate: they're generally inserted into the tape monitor or processor loop (or between amp and preamp) and have very few controls. They're also inexpensive, starting at around $100, and peaking at not much more than twice that. Variables which affect their sonic results include (beyond, of course, the sophistication of the device being used) the nature of the recording being played, the type and position of the speakers in the room, and the position of the listener. Some of the units claim to analyze and extract hidden ambience in the recording; others synthesize it.

For the most part, you'll want to stick with more-or-less conventional speakers, radiating directly into the listening room. Further, you'll need to point them at your primary listening area, which itself might be somewhat restricted for best results. But those results can be pretty astonishing. For the most part, conventional stereo systems present a sound stage that's limited in size and scope to the space between the speakers, and the front-to-back imaging is chancy at best. The better enhancers, on the other hand, can present an almost uncanny sense of width and depth. And, acting on those cues (and especially in a darkened room) your brain does its own bit of psychoacoustic synthesis and adds apparent size to the listening room.

The better enhancers can present an almost uncanny sense of width and depth.

Ambience Replication

The most exciting sort of ambience processors are those that use digital computer circuitry to store and — using at least four and sometimes as many as seven speakers — re-create in your living room the acoustic characteristics of actual night clubs, concert halls, and arenas. These systems can be frightfully expensive in themselves, and the total cost must include not only the processor itself but the requisite speakers and amplifiers.

Video Processors for Audio

Audio/video systems present their own particular problems, and offer their own unique rewards. The problems, as we already mentioned, have to do with the differences between what we see and what we hear. It's all well and good that we can now easily get wide, flat frequency response and loads of dynamic range, but for the true video aficionado that's not enough. Real movie buffs the kind who actually go to the movies in theaters — know that many soundtracks contain lots of non-dialogue audio, usually ambience information intended to be played back through rear- and side-mounted speakers (the sound of a car driving by, for example). It's called Dolby Stereo (from the same folks who brought you Dolby Noise Reduction) and aside from providing depth, these ancillary speakers give out off-screen cues. This means that when James Bond is about to be conked on the head, we know that said conker is tip-toeing from behind that parked car whose bumper we can just see in the corner of the screen. It also means that when you see a space cruiser appear on the screen as if from above and behind you, you'll have heard it coming, and probably couldn't keep from ducking your head.

But can we, in our modest living rooms, get similar results? Definitely. Most stereo video tapes are encoded with the same multichannel information that you hear in the theater. What you need is a way to get that information off the tape and into your room. To do that you need a decoder and at least one pair of additional speakers at the rear of the room. These decoders are available from a number of sources, some specifically licensed by Dolby Labs to use circuitry specific to their system, others using their own circuitry to achieve similar results. As a bonus, they can also be used as ambience-simulation systems when you're listening to conventional stereo sources.

Receivers with Ambience Enhancement

The miracle of microchip technology has enabled receiver manufacturers to incorporate some fairly competent ambience enhancement systems in their better receivers. Some are simply front-speaker image enhancement systems, while others make use of the "B" speaker taps to drive rear speakers for credible surround-sound processing. The most elaborate models include separate rear-channel amplifiers, along with a wide range of processing options, often including Dolby Surround for video signals.

Once you've spent some time listening to a system with good spatial characteristics, you'll be reluctant to go back to simple stereo.

Don't forget, in the excitement of contemplating the notion of owning a system that allows you to transcend the boundaries of the living room, that none of these processors mean a thing unless they are operating within the context of a decent hi-fi system. First make sure that you've handled the basics, and then you can be sure that the embellishments will do their job. One thing's for sure: once you've spent some time listening to a system with good spatial characteristics, you'll be reluctant to go back to simple stereo.

9 THE PURCHASING STRATEGY

Knowing the inner workings of all the hi-fi components will certainly enhance one's ability to choose and purchase an entire system. But we're all operating under certain financial constraints, and before embarking on the purchasing odyssey you'll need to know how to allocate percentages of a total budget to different components.

At the same time, your overall budget — along with other factors — will dictate where you decide to purchase your system: a hi-fi specialty store, a large hi-fi chain store, a discount house, or a mail-order service.

Let's first take a look at what can be done with the budget you have chosen.

BUDGETING YOUR SYSTEM

When putting together your budget, don't forget to account for any possible future purchases, like video equipment or additional audio sources. Failure to plan for future growth could make your present system obsolete.

Over the years many formulas have been devised to aid the hapless consumer in allocating a percentage of the total budget to each of the various components. Each formula is intended to make sure that you don't wind up with an unbalanced system, and each has some validity. We're going to offer some guidelines to consider in several price ranges, but bear in mind that no inflexible rules exist. Only *you* know, for instance, whether the speakers you're buying today are going to be replaced in six months, and that you therefore need a receiver that can handle the future acquisition. When putting together your budget, don't forget to account for any possible future purchases, like video equipment or additional audio sources. Failure to plan for future growth could make your present system obsolete. In the examples that follow, we're going to presuppose a 20 percent discount from list price. You might get more, and you might get less, depending upon your choice of dealer and equipment. And bear in mind that when dollar figures are cited, you must take into account any inflation that may have accrued since the time of this writing.

System 1: $500

Given a 20 percent discount, we're looking at $625 worth of equipment at list. You can buy an awfully good receiver for $200, from just about any of the major manufacturers. They won't be powerhouses, but they'll get the job done, and should certainly be able to drive most of the $250-a-pair speakers you'll be considering. Such speakers are available from a wide range of manufacturers, both full-line and specialist. If at all possible, audition your speakers with the receiver you're considering: in this price range you won't be dealing with tremendous power reserves, so it pays to make sure you have enough. In order to maximize sound quality, a $500 system can't have a wide range of signal sources. In addition to the FM and AM tuner provided by the receiver, you should limit yourself to a single additional component. With $450 already spent, you have $175 remaining for a record player, cassette deck, or CD player. If you choose a conventional record player, don't stint on the cartridge: plan on allocating $50 and make sure that you get a nationally advertised model rather than a "house brand" that might or might not be of equivalent quality. If you opt for compact discs, your choice will be limited to models lacking some of the latest convenience features, but don't discount the notion of buying last year's model on closeout if it offers a feature or two that isn't within the budget on a newly introduced unit. Another idea is to put off the purchase of a second source and get even better speakers. Now subtract 20 percent and if you've chosen each component carefully you've got a first-rate $500 system.

System 2: $750

Your choices in this range are a bit more varied. You can, for example, simply add an additional source to the $500 system. Another possibility is to move up to a $300 receiver, $400 speakers, and $200 worth of record player or CD player, which still keeps the system well balanced. Many receivers in this price range offer some video and surround-sound functions (although in the latter instance you have to factor a second pair of speakers into the equation). You might, however, decide that you want your long-term speakers now, and are willing to wait a while and upgrade the electronics sometime in the future. In that case, any of the better $200-to-$250 receivers, coupled with a $175 cassette deck, record player, or CD player, will permit you to buy a pair of very fine speakers. If you take this route, once again be sure of your chosen speakers' power requirements. There are some speakers in this price range that will work very nicely with 20 watts per channel, while others may require several times that amount.

System 3: $1,000

With $1,000 to spend you don't have to make nearly as many compromises. Once again, you must decide whether to opt for one or two very fine pieces and other more modest components, or a completely balanced system, but in either case you should wind up with very good equipment. Even if you opt for several source components (and it *is* possible to buy a receiver, speakers, record player, tape deck, and compact disc player for $1,000) we recommend that you live without one of them for a while and upgrade the rest of the system first. Regardless of approach, though, it's still crucial to choose speakers first, then amplification, and finally sources. A reasonable mix might have speakers listing for up to $500 a pair (more, if they're very efficient), a receiver at $300, and a cassette deck and record or CD player at $225 each. The total is $1,250, or $1,000 after the discount. If sound quality counts for more than the convenience of a tape deck you can put $225 into better speakers and electronics.

System 4: $1,500

If you are ready to spend $1,500 on a system you probably have some clear ideas about what you want, which is a good thing, considering the myriad options that are unavailable in the lower price ranges. You can choose either a receiver or separates (tuner, amp, and preamp), and can certainly include a turntable, a CD player, and a cassette deck. (Again, however, it might be wise to go for quality rather than quantity, and limit your sources to one or two, rather than all three.) In this range you can also expect to get video and ambience enhancement facilities, either in the receiver or as a separate component with switching and signal processing functions. Something to bear in mind is the tremendous efficiency range of loudspeakers selling in the upper price ranges. Even with speakers listing for $1,000 a pair, you have to determine your power requirements and budget your electronics accordingly.

In this range you can also expect to get video and ambience enhancement facilities, either in the receiver or as a separate component with switching and signal processing functions.

The One-Brand Shortcut

Many manufacturers, some of them well known and greatly respected, offer an alternate route for those consumers who do not want to deal with all the choices involved in putting together a component system. These are the one-brand systems we see advertised so heavily, especially by department stores and the larger audio chains. Such systems are made up of separate components, and range from simple setups selling for $300 to $400 to complex arrays which can include everything from separate power amps and preamps to CD players and equalizers. These one-brand systems, which often feature a single remote-control unit that handles the entire system, are often substantially less expensive than multi-brand systems of comparable configuration.

Are these systems worthwhile, or are they just jazzed-up consoles without the cabinetry? Assuming we are talking about serious hi-fi companies, these one-brand systems can offer very good value indeed. They are stocked by the stores as a package, thus reducing the need for huge and varied inventory; the electronic components are often as good as others from the same manufacturer; and the manufacturer can optimize the performance of each component relative to the others.

The Problem with One-Brands.   There are two potential problems inherent in one-brand systems. The first is that very often what appears to be a stack of individual components is actually a single unit. In some instances, a single large front panel is styled to give the appearance of separates; in other cases the separate components are electrically linked in such a way as to share a single power supply. Both schemes can result in electrical performance that is inferior to that of true separates. In addition, and perhaps as important in the long run, they prevent any possibility of upgrading a given section by replacing it with a better one. So the first thing to do when considering a one-brand system is to look at the *back* of the components and make sure you're getting separate components.

Speakers in One-Brand Systems.   The second drawback to the one-brand system lies in the final, all-important component, the loudspeakers. The best loudspeakers are still made by loudspeaker companies, not by electronics giants. Speakers supplied with one-brand systems are designed to be both inexpensive and visually impressive, while sonic considerations are often secondary. This approach is what permits one-brand systems to be such an apparent bargain.

The best loudspeakers are still made by loudspeaker companies, not by electronics giants.

Hence this warning: Unless the speakers in question happen to sound good (which *can* be the case), keep away from the one-brand systems unless (a) you can buy them without the speakers and (b) they still represent good value even in speakerless form. In that event, you will be virtually assured of a system that is well-matched electronically and aesthetically. It could also be that the price, even with the mediocre speakers, is so good that you just cannot resist. So go ahead and buy the system anyway. You might find the speakers to be adequate for a while, and then, if the price really was all that low, you can give them to the Salvation Army or a young niece, replacing them with speakers you will truly want to listen to for years to come.

WHERE TO BUY YOUR SYSTEM

Deciding where to buy your hi-fi system can be almost as important as selecting the components themselves. Indeed, the choice of a store will influence not only the nature of your "shopping experience" but — at least potentially — the long-term pleasure you can expect from the system itself. The kinds of stores that sell hi-fi equipment nowadays are many and varied. There are specialty hi-fi stores of varying degrees of exoticism; there are chain stores, department stores, and discount stores, both walk-in and mail-order.

Choosing the kind of store will depend largely on how much you want to spend, where you live, and how much dealer support you need. The larger the percentage of full retail price you pay, the more expertise and the more after-sale support you can expect to be buying (although there certainly are exceptions).

Hi-Fi Specialty Stores

This is where you will find the most enthusiastic and expert salespeople, people who love hi-fi and should be able to explain every item they sell in great detail (but don't let them drown you in techno-babble that you don't understand — and don't feel embarrassed if you don't understand it). They will help you put together a well-matched system, allowing you to audition components at length in well-equipped listening rooms. Often, they will have their own service shops and will supplement manufacturers' warranties with their own arrangements. Some of them will even let you take things home to see if you really like them, crediting the price of returned items toward the purchase of other equipment.

That, and more, is what you get when you shop at an audio specialty store, and there is no way on earth that a small business can provide this kind of service without charging full retail price, or nearly.

Large Chains

There *is* a way to get something of the service and expertise of an audio boutique without paying full price: there are chain stores that deal exclusively in hi-fi and related equipment. It's possible that they will be staffed with the same kind of salespeople who work in audio boutiques: enthusiastic, knowledgeable, and taking genuine pleasure in helping you to choose the best system you can afford. Since these are chains, often large ones, they benefit from the purchasing power that a small retailer never can, which is reflected in their prices. Dealing with a firm that buys in large quantities has an additional advantage for the consumer: closeout sales. Often, the chain's warehouses will be overstocked with a certain item, which will then be offered at an unbeatable price.

If you are looking for something particularly out-of-the-way (some sort of terribly expensive hand-made "cult" item, say — or just something terribly expensive), you are not likely to find it at an audio-chain store, and will probably have to go back to the specialty shop to get what you want. On the whole (and there are exceptions), chain stores cannot offer quite the kind of personalized service that you'll find in the boutiques, but they often have their own service departments and offer their own extended warranties. If you are looking for a good balance between price and service, one of these stores will probably be about the best place for you to shop.

Department Stores

You'd be surprised: although we still do not really associate department stores with anything more circuit-laden than a pop-up toaster, the fact is that many department stores devote thousands of square feet to such non-traditional merchandise as computers and electronics. Some of them even hire (or train) salespeople who can answer hard questions.

If you don't feel comfortable dealing with specialists (and you can believe that not all of them are out to make you feel comfortable), you will certainly feel at ease in the store where you buy sheets and pillow cases. As long as you are careful about "house" labels or off-brands, you will find certain advantages in department store shopping, the same ones, in fact, that apply to any purchase: you can charge the equipment to your department store charge, and if it doesn't suit you for any reason you can simply return it. Just beware of salespeople who tell you that you can save money by buying only one speaker — they're probably the ones who were selling shelf-lining paper the day before and have no business in the hi-fi department.

Discount and Catalog Houses

Be careful: the people who work in most discount houses and just about all catalog houses know little about what they're selling, whether it is a variable-speed drill or a variable-capacitance amplifier. It's not their fault; they're not hired to do anything more than fill in sales slips. Nor can you expect to be able to examine carefully, much less audition, your potential purchases. You make your selection, either from a display or from a catalog, pay for it, and take it home. The kind of merchandise you'll find here is middle-of-the-road equipment, nothing too fancy. You won't get much in the way of dealer support and if anything goes wrong you will have to deal with the manufacturer yourself, under his warranty. But the price will be right. If you know what you want and aren't afraid of taking care of everything yourself, you might want to try these places.

There are also discount houses that deal only in electronics; in general, the same warnings apply, but these stores may well have their own service centers, warranties, and listening rooms, however rudimentary. According to the advertising for these hi-fi discounters, prices will be very low. You may have to do without the manufacturer's warranty, however. This can certainly be a good place to buy, but know what other stores are charging for what you want before you cross the threshold.

Mail Order Houses

Walk-in hi-fi stores of the various kinds we have outlined are numerous, but for some people it will be far more convenient to shop by mail order. Mail order houses offer few services, have low overheads (after all, all they are doing is taking a box off a shelf and sending it out by carrier), and, hence, sell at good discount prices, sometimes very close to the actual dealer cost. Among the services they *don't* offer is a house warranty, so check into the terms of the manufacturer's obligation, and indeed that of the United States distributor of the product (if the product was imported directly by the retailer, you may find that your only recourse is in Seoul or Osaka). As with the discount houses, though, if you know what you want and if price is a primary consideration, mail order may serve you very nicely.

10 SETTING UP THE SYSTEM

Here are a few procedures you must follow — and some you must *not* do — when you get a new stereo system home. Most of this will be absolutely, transparently obvious, but it's easy to forget the most obvious things in the heat of the moment (many audiophiles are notorious for leaving the tape monitor on and wondering why the speakers are dead when they try to listen to the weather report.) The proper connection of your equipment is just about as important as its careful selection. If you make serious mistakes you can look forward to silence at best, major damage at worst. Minor errors can result in downgraded sound and gradual, but no less serious, deterioration in your equipment.

First of all, the byword in the setup process is patience. Five minutes can seem like as many hours when you're eager to get listening, but by taking your time and sort of counting to 10 before doing anything as serious as turning a power switch on, you will be a lot happier in the medium and long term.

A small point related to the issue of patience: if possible, let the store deliver the equipment. Even if components are getting smaller and lighter by the minute, there is still the matter of liability for damage. The stuff is so well-packed that there is almost no chance of this, but things do happen. Better the store or its shipper should bear the responsibility for getting everything to your house safe and sound: if you drop a CD player while fumbling for your keys it's your hard luck, but if a trucker damages it you will be reimbursed (hopefully).

Once the equipment has arrived safely, unpack everything carefully, throwing nothing away. Do not even throw away the boxes and packing materials unless you have absolutely no room for them.

For transporting appliances of any kind, whether for moving or repair purposes, nothing beats the original cartons.

Now read the instruction booklets for everything from the cartridge to the speakers — however straightforward a component may seem, there can easily be some quirk which can cause mild palpitations in the hardiest audiophile if not known about in advance.

With luck, and given that the manual writers have had more than their usual three-hour crash course in English, your hour or so of light reading will probably tell you everything you need to know about installation and interface between components. (But don't put down this book yet; there may be a couple of informal hints that didn't find their way into the instruction manuals.)

There are various opinions about the sequence of events, but we feel that convenience should prevail over theory, at least until anything is plugged in. We'll go through one possible installation sequence here, but, whether or not you choose to follow it, you should, first of all, work out where everything is going to be. Ideally, the individual components should not be stacked — individual shelves are the best arrangement for both ease of access and best heat dispersal. If you must stack components, don't put the units that generate the most heat, such as receivers or amplifiers, at the bottom. Try to arrange items so that there will be the neatest possible tangle of wires behind the scenes. The idea of neat stereo wires may sound utopian (and the notion of a neat tangle contradictory), but if you work the arrangement out on paper you certainly can minimize the chances of strangulated cable.

Ideally, the individual components should not be stacked — individual shelves are the best arrangement for both ease of access and best heat dispersal.

This plan will help you decide the order of connection: If tuner A, CD player B, and turntable C are to be plugged into preamp D, it makes simple sense to connect them all before hooking up preamp D to power amp E.

SPEAKER SETUP

Most people still buy receivers as opposed to separate tuners, preamplifiers, and power amplifiers, so if you want instant music you can always wire your speakers up to the receiver and listen to the radio for a while before proceeding.

The best idea for speaker wire is relatively low-resistance wire. For normal lengths, ordinary lamp cord is fine (throw away the narrow-gauge "speaker wire" many audio stores insist on throwing at you as you are leaving the premises). Some speaker manufacturers recommend the following gauges for various lengths (when in doubt, always use the heavier — lower-numbered — gauge rather than the lighter). For runs of 25 feet or less, use 18 gauge (which is standard "lamp cord"); for 25 feet and more, 16 gauge.

Try to keep cord length as short as possible. If your speaker leads have to get past a doorway, try to go along the floor, because going up, across, and down a door jamb can add very nearly 20 feet to the run of wire.

Be sure that the speakers are connected right and left speakers to right and left outputs, respectively, and in phase — that is, the "+" connector of each speaker is linked to the equivalent lug on the back of the amplifier or receiver. Any cord you may use will be coded in some way to facilitate this matching: either it will be color coded, or there will be a ridge running along one side of the cable or, sometimes, a thread running along one of the cable's connectors. (If you use U-brads or staples to fix the cable to walls or baseboards, try not to pierce the insulation.)

Don't strip too much of the wire; one-half inch or a bit more will be fine for screw connectors and about one-quarter to three-eights for push connectors. Once they are stripped, twist the strands of the wire into a coherent bundle; loose wire, caused by untwisted ends or by too long an exposed area, can result in short circuits, blowing fuses or equipment. Wrap the screw lugs clockwise so that you don't dislodge the wire when you tighten the connectors. And if you connect your speakers to outputs labeled Speaker A, don't expect much music if you have the amplifier's selector switched to Speaker B.

If you have more than one set of speakers to connect, know which are which, and if you have more sets than your amplifier has outputs, do not go out to an electrical supply store and buy a cheap switching device. Invest in a proper speaker switch box, and when you are running several pairs of speakers at one time, pore through the amplifier or receiver manual to make sure that the combination of impedances will not pose a problem for the amp. A truly good switch box will make certain, as a part of its design, that the impedances are not too low.

CD PLAYER SETUP

If you've included a compact disc player in your new system you will probably want to get that hooked up right away. The electrical connection is simple: just connect the Left and Right Out jacks on the player with the Left and Right CD (or, in some units Aux) input jacks on the preamp or receiver. Some CD players provide two sets of output jacks: fixed and variable. Use the latter if you want to match the CD player's output to that of your other source components, eliminating nasty surprises when you switch from one to another. A few of the new players also provide digital outputs, designed primarily to facilitate the use of outboard digital-to-analog converters. It's a virtual certainty that at this stage of the game you have no use for these outputs, so just ignore them.

The mechanical setup is not quite so straightforward; the requirements of every unit seem to be different, so alas, all we can tell you is to read the manual and believe it implicitly. Many CD players have some sort of transit screws that will have to be loosened, tightened, or removed (and *don't* lose them if they are the removable kind), and some need to be placed more precisely level than others. Sensitivity to shock is something that varies from model to model, but you can take it for granted that the sturdier a foundation you provide, the less likely you are to run into problems in that area.

Sensitivity to shock is something that varies from model to model, but you can take it for granted that the sturdier a foundation you provide, the less likely you are to run into problems.

TURNTABLE SETUP

Very likely the turntable will already be mounted on its base, along with its tone arm. Just as with CD players, screws may have to be loosened or tightened so that the table will float freely on its suspension — refer to the instruction booklet (which you will, of course, already have read) and be sure that you have removed (and saved) any bits and pieces which are there for shipping and not for operation. If you do not have one of those easy-to-use P-mount plug-in cartridges, try to have the store personnel install and adjust the cartridge; if this is impossible don't try to do it while the tonearm's headshell is attached. Loosen the collar or set-screw that holds the headshell on and remove it to a desk or table with good lighting. Mount the cartridge according to the manufacturer's instructions; believe him when he stresses the importance of alignment, because if your cartridge is in cockeyed it will sound cockeyed.

Get your turntable leveled; use a bubble level and get that bubble right into the center of the field. A sturdy foundation is also important, in order to minimize the effects of acoustic and surface-borne feedback. (You don't want to have to walk on tip-toes when you're playing a record.) Especially with an automatic turntable do not plug the unit in until you've got the tracking force and anti-skating adjusted (again, according to the manufacturer's instructions). If the stylus should slam down onto a moving platter, *sans* record, it could be ripped off its cantilever, or the whole cantilever could be ripped out of the cartridge.

The leads, obviously enough, go to the Phono In jacks on your receiver or preamp. As with speakers, note whether you are going into Phono 1 or Phono 2, and if you have separate inputs or a switch to choose between moving-coil and moving-magnet cartridges, be sure you know which you have and act accordingly. Further, if your amp has adjustable capacitance be sure to set it for the right figure as indicated in the cartridge manufacturer's booklet. When the system is all set up you will want also to set the phono sensitivity level (if your preamp or receiver has one) so that the phono volume level is about the same as the FM level.

TUNER SETUP

Speaking of FM: if you have a receiver, you're pretty much set, except for the antenna. The flat wire dipole antenna that probably came with the unit should be connected to the 300-ohm antenna input; any other antenna you may wish to use instead should be attached to whichever input is specified by its manufacturer. As to the position of the antenna, if you are using the wire dipole you should move it around until you find a position that yields the best reception. At the least, try to get its arms spread out — or you can give it a try under the carpet. Other antennas will come with instructions of their own (and will always yield better results than the flat dipole).

With a separate tuner, once again look for the Tuner In jacks, plug left to left and right to right, and plug the electrical cord into a switched outlet on the back of the amp. In all cases, whether you use these convenience outlets is just that — a matter of convenience; if wall outlets are easier for you, by all means use them. However, do not use *switched* convenience outlets for mechanical components — tape decks, CD players, and turntables; these are best turned on and off by the user when they are not in the middle of a play cycle.

TAPE DECK SETUP

Tape deck setup is relatively simple: connect tape deck Out (or Play) to Tape In (or Monitor) on the amp, and Tape Out (or Record) on the amp to tape deck In. But beware of some exceptions: a few manufacturers inexplicably reverse this nomenclature, so read the instructions.

That covers it, unless you have other components like signal processors or extra units that don't fit into any of the jacks on the back of the amplifier. Some of them are meant to be plugged into tape-monitor inputs and outputs; others between preamplifier and power amplifier. If you still have excess components you don't know what to do with, leave them unconnected for the present and get down to listening with what you have. Later on you can investigate the various available program route selectors intended to serve as electronic traffic cops in such complex systems as yours. Take a map of your system with you so that you and the store can figure out just what you need.

Some final pieces of advice: If your turntable has a dust cover that lifts up on hinges, be sure there is enough shelf clearance for it to open and stay open. Provide some source of light near the turntable and tape deck, and also have a little flashlight and a mirror handy for fiddling around behind the components. Clean back there with a vacuum or feather duster from time to time. Leave room for record cleaning devices and whatever other little gadgets you like to have nearby.

If you have done everything right, the reward will come as soon as you turn the system on and listen to that first CD or cassette.

11 TROUBLESHOOTING

Most people who are at ease with their stereo systems will tell you that 90 percent of audible problems in a home system could be cleared up by the user if only he knew how to locate them. You would be amazed at how many horrendous situations can be traced back to such simple things as loose wires. They key is finding which wire is loose — a key known as troubleshooting.

Troubleshooting means applying your knowledge of the path a signal follows in your hi-fi and tracking the precise point on that path at which the signal is going astray. A simple example: You know the signal goes from amplifier (or receiver) outputs to speaker inputs. If there is no sound in the left speaker, either the speaker is at fault, or the wire leading to it, or the left-hand portion of any of the electronic equipment which generates and amplifies the signal (or the cables interconnecting that equipment). By trial and error you ascertain that the speaker is OK and the amplifier is working; checking the speaker wire reveals that it is faulty. You replace the cable and all is well. Knowing the possibilities and checking each of them in turn — that is troubleshooting.

We are going to lead you through several of these possibilities, beginning with general problems affecting the whole system and working down to more specific difficulties. Once you get a feel for the theory of it, you should be able to work out your own procedures for checking on various problems you might encounter, but we think that this guide will take you through most of what you need to know.

No sound at all, from any program source

- Is the amp or receiver turned on?

- If so, is everything properly plugged in?

- Is the tape monitor knob turned to Source or Tape? If it is on Tape, all program sources apart from the tape deck will be silent.

- If you have a speaker selector (Speakers A, Speakers B) is the selector switched to the terminals to which your speakers are connected?

- Are your speakers connected properly, or at all?

- Are the wall outlets okay? Check them by plugging in something like a lamp or hair dryer. Does it work? If there is no juice, check the house fuses. If they are all right, try another outlet or call an electrician.

- Check the fuses in your amp or receiver and, if necessary, replace them. If a fuse has blown, but blows again as soon as you have replaced it, bring in an expert.

No sound at all, from one program source only

- Is the program source plugged in and turned on?

- If it is plugged into a convenience outlet on the back of the amp or receiver, try plugging it into a wall outlet instead.

- In the case of a unit with multiple jacks on the back, such as a tape deck, make sure that the source's *output* is connected to the amp's *input* — and that it is the input to which the program selector is switched.

- Twist the knobs back and forth a few times, jiggle the connecting cables, and disconnect and reconnect the unit from the amplifier. This may sound a little like the give-the-unit-a-whack school of repair, but sometimes a dirty control or connection can be at fault and the friction can clean up that dirt.

- Check and if necessary replace the unit's fuse.

- If none of that works, have the mute component checked out by an expert.

Bad, interrupted, or no sound, all sources, both channels

- This is not a good sign; unless it happens that both loudspeaker connections are loose at the same time, you've probably got amplifier problems. If you have an integrated amp or a receiver, check the connection with the wall outlet for the heck of it. If that is all right you will have to seek guidance from a repair outlet (although you can always try hitting or throwing out the unit or waiting for it to cure itself).

- There is also the chance that someone has turned the volume up all the way, damaging both speakers. If the speakers both sound muffled, the tweeters could be blown. If the bass sounds distorted, the voice coils could be rubbing. Plugging the speakers into a friend's amp will quickly reveal whether the problem is with them or with your own amplifier.

- If you have separate pre- and power amplifiers, you have to determine which one has the problem. Turn the power-amp gain as low as possible (if your unit has a gain control), and connect a high-level source with a volume control, also set low (tape deck, for instance) directly. If the problem disappears, the fault lies with the preamp; if it persists, the power amp is the culprit. Either way, the hi-fi doctor will probably have to be consulted.

Bad, interrupted, or no sound, all sources, one channel only

- First step: Make a visual inspection of the connecting wires between the amp and the speakers. Tighten any loose connections and redo any frayed connections.

- If that doesn't do the job, try reversing the left and right speaker connections, hooking the left speaker to the right channel output and vice versa. If the same speaker continues to act up, there is probably an internal problem in that speaker. If any of the individual drivers are fused, check those fuses. If the speaker is self-amplified, check the speaker amp's electrical connections for looseness. If you have no luck that way, exploratory surgery will have to be performed inside the speaker box; don't do it yourself, since you will probably be in violation of the guarantee. A speaker may not seem to be as susceptible to home handyman damage as a receiver, but you can still mess things up if you are poking around and put a screwdriver through an unexpected crossover network.

- If, after you reverse the channels, the problem migrates from one speaker to the other, the problem lies in the amplifier and if you have an integrated amp or receiver, it's professional time. If you have separates, try reversing the connections between them; if the problem remains in the same channel, the faults is within the power amp. If the problem reverses, the fault may lie either with the preamp or with the cable connecting the preamp to the power amp. Try tightening a possibly loose or dirty connection, or using a new cable, before you cart your preamp to the veterinarian.

Bad or no sound, one channel only; you only have one program source

If you have multiple program sources, the fact that all of them are on the blink at once is an indication that the fault lies not with any of them, but rather with some element they have in common: either the amplifier or a speaker. But with a single source system, the difficulty could be anywhere along the line.

What you need to do is follow the procedures outlined for systems with multiple program sources; but you must follow them all the way back to the turntable, tuner, tape deck, or whatever. Check all the fuses and connections, jiggle the connections a little to cut through any possible dirt, reverse them to see at what point the problem no longer migrates with the reversal.

SPECIFIC COMPONENTS

All those procedures will, we hope, lead you to the source of your hi-fi problem; sometimes, however, the source will be obvious. If, for instance, the phonograph stylus is jumping out of the groove, you will not have to go through any long diagnostic rigmarole to work out that it is the turntable that needs attention. However you determine the site of the damage, here are some ways to find out its nature and even some ways of rectifying it.

Tape Decks

- If there is no sound, double-check the tape monitor control on your amp or receiver. If it is on the Source, move it to Play or

Tape or whatever your amp calls it. Likewise, check that the monitor switch on the deck (if it has one) is pressed. If there is still no sound, go back to the procedures outlined earlier and check connections, both within the system and to the house current, for looseness, breaks, and correctness of path.

- If the sound is poor or severely downgraded from what you know your machine can do, the first thing to do is to clean the tape heads and the rubber rollers. If the heads are dirty and clogged, sound quality will suffer; if the rubber parts are dirty, the speed of the tape past the heads can become uneven, with audible results. (By the way: it's a good idea to perform these cleaning chores on a regular basis — *before* a problem occurs.)

- If poor sound persists, try other tapes. There could be a mechanical defect in the tape housing (if a cassette deck is what we are discussing; on an open-reel machine a severely warped reel or a badly stretched tape are similar problems).

- If the tapes you have been playing are home-recorded, try a tape which was made on another machine, or a commercially prerecorded tape. This will tell you whether it is the record or the playback section of your machine which is the root of the evil: if the problem disappears when you use a tape you yourself did not record, then the playback section is guiltless and you must look to the machine's recording section.

- If all the tapes in question were recorded from a single source, say, FM radio, make a test tape from another source. If that one comes out all right, check the connections from the defective source. If the problem is the same on all sources, check once again that the amp or receiver Tape Out cables are securely connected to the tape deck's inputs; try new cables if necessary.

- If problems persist, try making a recording with microphones (if the deck has inputs for them). This will tell you whether the problem lies with the line input or with the recording circuitry itself. If both mic and line inputs result in poor tapes, you will have to resort to the audio wizard's expertise. In fact, you will have to do so in either case, but you will be armed with specific information that will make his job easier and you more credible.

- Now, if the problem exists on one channel only, the same procedures must be gone through, except supplemented this time with the Old Switcheroo Test: reversing cables at all possible stages of connection will tell you where the problem lies.

- If, on a cassette deck, you cannot get the unit to go into record mode, check to see that the safety tabs on the back edge of the cassette have not been removed. If they have, and if you are sure that you want to record over the material on the cassette in question, a piece of cellophane tape placed over the hole will do the job.

- If all electronic and transport controls look right, but the tape isn't moving, check to make sure that the Pause control is not engaged. Likewise, if it is moving, but not recording, check the Record Mute control.

Record Players

Whether the sound is poor or absent, whether this is so on one or both channels, the first thing to check is the connections of the cartridge to the headshell, the headshell to the arm, and the turntable to the amplifier. Just make sure everything is good and tight and that there is no visible dirt that might be fudging the electrical contact. Also, clean your phono stylus and check it for wear. Use a soft brush with a bit of alcohol, or one of the very clever stylus cleaning devices available at most audio salons.

- If the sound is downgraded on one channel only, reverse the cables leading to the preamp, amp, or receiver. If the poor sound stays put, then the phono preamp section is at fault and Dr. Fixit will have to be consulted. If it moves to the other side, continue your investigation: Switch the actual cables; one of them might be defective. Try reversing the connection of the cartridge to the headshell (if it is not a P-mount model, and permits such monkeying around); if the problem remains in the same channel, there is a fault within the turntable's wiring that a professional will be happy to check for you. If the problem migrates to the other side, it is your cartridge that needs attention — probably replacement.

- If the sound is downgraded on both channels, try jiggling everything, including the source selector switch. Make sure that, if you have multiple phono inputs, the turntable is connected to the right one. Try to borrow another turntable and connect it to your system. If the problem disappears, its origin was your record player. Make sure your cartridge's rated output is compatible with your amp or preamp's sensitivity (this will apply primarily to older electronics, but extreme cases still do exist). Otherwise, it's repairman time. If the problem persists with another turntable, the phono section of the preamp is probably at fault. Also repairman time.

- If the problem is simply that the stylus is jumping out of the groove, the first thing is to clean it. Inspect the record on which the problem is occurring for dirt or pitting and for severe warping — any of those can bounce a tonearm like a pothole can bounce an old jalopy. Try a new record.

- Check stylus pressure, anti-skating force, levelness of turntable. Some cartridges simply weigh too little for some tonearms and will have to be replaced. If the recommended tracking force is, say, .75 to 1.25 grams, don't track the cartridge at .75 grams (unless you have some whiz-bang tonearm and a very well-isolated turntable). Take the middle road, and use a force of about a gram or even a little above.

- Check the vertical alignment of the cartridge. If it is out of whack, warped areas in the outer rim of the disc can physically hit the cartridge body.

- If the jumping occurs toward the inner grooves, double-check the anti-skating compensation control. Even try a new setting, for on some turntables calibration is not 100 percent accurate. Or the automatic return mechanism may be binding a bit; move the arm manually. Can you feel any resistance?

- See that nothing is impeding free movement of the arm, like a strangulating wire.

- If the problem is a very audible humming noise, the turntable could be improperly grounded. Be sure that the ground wire is connected to an appropriate place on the rear of the amp or receiver — most amps nowadays have a screw post to which turntable ground wires can be connected.

Tuners

Most of what we say under this heading will be applicable both to separate tuners and to the tuner sections of receivers. Where we discuss switching wires, however, this is clearly applicable only to cases where the tuner and amplifier are distinct units. There are those of you, unfortunately, who just live in bad reception areas. For you, better tuners or better antennas may be the only solution.

- Is the sound bad on one, some, or all stations? If it is only one, the station is probably experiencing technical difficulties, or it may be a remote station which you shouldn't be listening to at all. If a number of stations scattered across the dial do not sound up to snuff, it could be that those originating from a specific transmitter or locality are either too far away or are having problems themselves. In New York City, for instance, some stations transmit from the Empire State Building, while most have moved their facilities to the World Trade Center. There are areas of New York's upper West Side which have trouble picking up signals from the latter location, and there's not much they can do about it. If everything on your tuner sounds poor, then the unit itself, or its antenna, is probably at fault.

- As usual, the first step, once you have decided that the malfunction is yours and not the broadcasters', is to jiggle all the controls and wires to see if a speck of dust in the works is at fault. Give special attention to the antenna connection.

- If your tuner allows various reception parameters — bandwidth, sensitivity, and so on — to be adjusted either manually or automatically, try overriding the automatic setting. Does the sound improve when you switch from stereo to mono? The circuits that sense too-weak stereo signals may be set to too low a threshold. Conversely, if you are setting things manually, see if returning control to the tuner's own decision-making circuitry yields an improvement.

- If the sound is poor only on one channel, try reversing, then replacing cables. If this test comes up positive, then the tuner's circuits for the offending channel are out of kilter.

- If sound is poor on both channels and on all stations, examine all antenna connections (including, if applicable, those at the outdoor antenna itself). If no luck, try reorienting your antenna. Has there been a wind storm recently? This can move or loosen things. If you have just bought your tuner, you may have chosen the wrong one for your reception area. A better antenna or tuner could be your only choice.

Compact Disc Players

All of our comments vis-à-vis switching cables to determine whether the problem lies within the suspect component unit or elsewhere apply to CD players. If cable switching and replacement causes you to determine that, for example, only one channel of the player is working, it's a job for Dr. Digital.

- If the drawer won't open, make sure you have loosened or removed the transport screw that the manufacturer has included for protecting the mechanism during shipping.

- If there is no sound at all when you press Play, check to see whether the unit's time display indicates that the disc is, indeed, being read by the laser. If it is, make sure that the player's own volume control isn't the culprit. Check the player's mute switch, too.

- If the display indicates that the disc isn't being recognized by the laser, open the drawer and make sure the disc isn't upside down. (It can happen to anyone.) If the disc is positioned properly, try giving it a quarter of a turn so that the laser's initial contact point is different. You'd be amazed at how often this works.

- If discs that previously played fine suddenly begin to skip or stutter, the problem could be dirt — either on the disc or on the player's lens. In the latter instance, try a camel's hair artist paintbrush or one of the commercial lens cleaners. Discs may be cleaned manually, but we'd recommend the purchase of one of the commercial products that automatically provide the radial motion that is necessary to do a proper job.

Caring for Your Records

When caring for LP records it is important to realize that, despite your best efforts, they will eventually develop tics and pops. The temptation, then, is to say "Why bother?" and forget the whole thing. This would be a bad idea, for while no amount of maintenance will completely prevent surface flaws from appearing, a modicum of care will go a long way toward minimizing them. Further, playing a dirty record greatly speeds up the rate at which both it and your stylus wear out. Proper care — in the form of sensible storage — can also prevent warps, the worst of which can render an LP unplayable.

Fortunately, record care is a fairly simple matter. When you're not playing them, they should be stored vertically (rather than stacked), with sufficient pressure on either side to keep them from leaning one way or the other. It's also important to remove the plastic shrink wrap from the jacket, for it can shrink and cause the record to warp. And always use the inner sleeve, which is much smoother and less prone than the cardboard jacket to releasing debris onto the LP. Indeed, particularly treasured records will benefit from the use of "accessory" sleeves made of special rice paper or polyethylene.

There are many approaches to cleaning records, ranging from simple velvet-like pads to automatic wet/dry vacuum systems that cost several hundred dollars. If you happen to own a radio station, or have an LP collection that the Smithsonian is eyeing covetously, the latter approach might be justified. Otherwise, one of the brand-name cleaning devices should be more than adequate. Granted, the simpler methods don't "deep clean" the groove, but they will remove the bulk of the loose dirt. You should use such a cleaner each time you play a record — preferably both before and after.

If you're dealing with particularly hard-to-remove debris, say, the remains of a peanut butter sandwich, a more drastic approach is called for. The simplest and most effective strategy is to pay for the use of an industrial-strength cleaning device. Many audiophile stores keep one on hand for this purpose, charging so much per disc. Good results may also be obtained with a weak solution of Ivory Liquid and a soft, lint-free cloth. Just be sure to rinse long enough to remove all of the soap.

Proper record maintenance also means keeping your stylus clean. Many cartridge manufacturers sell small bottles of suitable fluid, along with the appropriate brush.

Caring for Your Cassettes

The best way to take care of your cassettes is to take care of your cassette deck. Following the manufacturer's instructions, clean and demagnetize the heads and capstan(s) on a regular basis. Beyond that, common sense dictates that cassettes not be stored where they're likely to get dusty or dirty. You should also keep them away from heat and excess humidity. And, of course, make sure you don't keep them near any strong magnetic fields: on top of your speakers is the wrong place for your tape library. It's also a good idea to store your tapes without fast winding them. If you only listen to one side of a tape, don't rewind it until just before you're ready to play it again.

Caring for Your Compact Discs

The results of too casual an approach to CD care won't be noticeable in the short term, so it's tempting to ignore the issue entirely. You've probably noticed that even dirty, scratched CDs often play properly. What you might not be aware of, until it's too late, is that the player's error-correction circuitry is busily trying to compensate for the incomplete information caused by those surface imperfections. Eventually, the result could be audible distortion, and then the outright inability of the player to track the disc. Therefore, it's important to keep the playing surface of the disc clean, and both sides free from scratches. (Scratches on the label side can be more damaging than those on the better-protected playing side, since they are more likely to destroy the portion of the "sandwich" on which the music is recorded.)

Fortunately, it's a fairly simple matter to avoid touching the surface of the disc, and to keep it in its jewel box between plays. CDs should be cleaned radially, from the center outward, rather than 'round and 'round as you would an LP. There are several inexpensive hand-cranked devices that do the job very nicely, and for not more than the cost of two or three discs.

GLOSSARY

A/B Test If you listened to speaker A yesterday and are listening to speaker B today in the hope of making a choice between them, odds are you won't be able to remember the sound of speaker A well enough to make an educated decision — unless one of the two is grossly inferior. Getting both set up in the same room with a way of switching quickly back and forth between them is the only true A/B comparison, and an A/B comparison is the only real way to tell which of a given pair of items you prefer. Never buy critical components without such tests to help you narrow down your shopping list. But beware: the more efficient (hence, the louder) of the two speakers will always seem more appealing, so make sure the volume levels are equivalent.

Acoustic-Suspension Speaker Like an **infinite-baffle speaker** system, an acoustic-suspension enclosure separates the front from the back of the drivers that make up the system. It differs in that the actual suspension of the speakers is looser, allowing a longer movement of the woofer. In the past these speakers have tended to be quite power hungry (that was the price you had to pay for compact size and good bass performance), but the march of technology has made many of them considerably more efficient.

Air-Suspension Speaker Another name for an **acoustic-suspension speaker**.

Ambience Simulation When we refer to acoustic ambience, we're talking about the influence the environment has on the way we hear sound in a given space. For example, the ambience of a heavily draped small room will be "dead" when compared to that of a huge concert hall with hardwood floors and plaster walls and ceilings. Ambience simulation is a broad term which encompasses any of various methods of re-creating the acoustics of one space in the physical environment of another. Through electronic control of such elements as **reverberation**, echo time, and **phase** relationships, the impression of a cavernous space, for example, can be presented in a small living room. Some systems depend on the use of extra or specially designed speakers to achieve the desired effect.

Antenna Any device — from a simple length of wire to a very fancy multi-element system on a rotating roof mast — that captures energy at radio frequencies (i.e., as broadcast) and converts it to electrical energy for use by a receiver (whether radio or television). For the best reception in any area, an antenna tailored to the specific needs of that area is required.

Anti-skating Anti-skating force is applied to a pivoted tonearm to counteract its natural tendency to be pulled towards the center of the disc. (See **Skating**)

Auto or **Automatic Reverse** This feature is found on a growing number of tape decks; it simply means two-way operation. At the end of the tape, the transport reverses and the other side of the tape is played. In the past, difficulties in achieving precision tape-head alignment (see **Azimuth**) made it difficult to come up with an economical way of providing this feature in the record mode, but those obstacles have been largely overcome. While many two-way decks still can't offer performance quite as good as their unidirectional counterparts, they are much improved.

Automatic Turntable Generally speaking, this term refers to any turntable between a purely manual one (which has no automatic functions) and a changer (which adds the ability to play a stack of records to any other features it might offer). That is to say, it does some of the work for you but only does it one record at a time. Early automatic turntables were often scorned by purists because their sensors placed a drag on tonearm, interfering with proper **tracking**. That's often not the case now, with optical sensors replacing mechanical systems. Some automatics (often called semi-automatic) merely lift the arm at the end of play and return it to the rest. At the other end of the scale, some models can play the cuts on an album in any order and as many times as you choose. Since we all have butterfingers at times, some degree of automation is usually desirable to prevent damaging the nearly extinct LP.

Azimuth To the user of a tape recorder this term refers to the angle at which the tape head's pole-piece slot (the gap that exists where the positive and negative poles of the magnet face each other) meets the tape. This angle should be 90 degrees and highly consistent between record and playback. Improper azimuth results in a loss of high-frequency response, and a comprehensive program of maintenance should include a periodic check of tape-head azimuth.

Baffle The board on which a speaker system's **driver** or drivers are mounted, and which keeps the energy radiated by the back of the driver from interfering with that radiated by the front. Depending upon the type of speaker system, the baffle can drastically affect the sound and performs different acoustical functions in each speaker enclosure type.

Balance A musical and a hi-fi term, it can refer to the relationship (in volume) between various sections of the orchestra or various performers, or to that between the two channels of a high-fidelity system, or to the relationship between the several frequency bands of the audio spectrum. Respectively, these different types of balance can be controlled by: the conductor (or recording engineer); your balance control; and an equalizer or set of tone controls. The placement of loudspeakers in a room can have an enormous effect on the latter two kinds of balance, and a surprisingly noticeable one on the first.

Bass-Reflex Speaker A member of the class of **vented speaker systems**, the bass-reflex system takes advantage of the fact that any driver radiates sound backwards as well as forward. It releases through a port the sounds that would otherwise be directed away from the listener, thereby reinforcing the sound waves that come from the front of the driver. This results in improved bass response and greater efficiency, when compared to a sealed speaker system (i.e., one with no port) of otherwise equivalent specifications.

Bias In a tape recorder, a high-frequency signal applied to the tape along with the music being recorded. The purpose of this signal is to allow the tape to respond more accurately to the musical signal. Different types of tape require different amounts of bias, and most tape decks provide switching to accommodate a wide range of tapes.

Cabinet The enclosure that contains the drivers and other components of a loudspeaker system. It may appear to be a simple concept, but it is critical to a speaker's performance. Size, proportions, materials, construction — all these factors, plus many others — must be optimized in each speaker's design. Reading through this glossary you will find several references to different kinds of cabinets or enclosures.

Capstan On a tape recorder, the capstan is a polished shaft which turns at a precisely calibrated speed and is responsible for moving the tape past the heads at an equally precise speed. Generally, the tape is held against the capstan by a rubber pinch roller and both it and the capstan itself must be kept clean if speed accuracy is not to suffer. (See **Dual Capstan**)

Capture Ratio When two radio signals are at the same frequency (be that the result of two distinct stations or **multipath distortion**) it is the capture ratio that expresses a tuner's ability to choose the stronger of them. The more sensitively it can distinguish between the two, the better. Thus, the smaller the number of decibels expressed in the tuner specs, the more impressive the capture ratio.

Clipping One of the ways distortion is seen visually on an oscilloscope is by a flattening of the top and bottom of the waveforms. This indicates that the amplifier has literally run out of clean power and has begun to generate serious **distortion**. The power level at which this begins to happen is called the clipping level, and the solution is to turn down the volume before the speakers are damaged.

Coloration In the absolute, coloration is **distortion**, plain and simple. But in real life, the line between coloration and distortion is a fuzzy one at best, and coloration is the term used to describe audible distortion of the sort that isn't really nasty: the (sometimes subtle) alterations a component makes to the complex timbres of music. Generally speaking, purely electronic components are the least likely offenders in this area. On the other hand, transducers — phono cartridges and speakers — do inevitably color the sounds they emit, and it is a question of pure taste what sort of color you like added, as long as you remain within an acceptable range. There were plenty of early speakers on which you couldn't tell a violin from a trumpet, but that is an extreme example which, we hope, you'll never encounter. The ideal, of course, is that a component should add no coloration of its own, other than that which, by the judicious use of tone controls and the like, you request.

Compact Disc The official name for those 4¾-inch discs whose rainbow-colored surfaces carry up to 74 minutes of digitally encoded music. Also known as digital audio discs (DAD), they have quickly become the *de facto* standard for home playback of **digital** audio. No special equipment besides a CD player is required to enjoy them, but many people find themselves upgrading to the finest amps and speakers they can afford in order to do proper justice to the discs.

Compander A combination of the words **compressor** and **expander**, a compander is a signal processor that, upon recording, compresses the music's dynamic range and, upon playback, expands it, resulting in an improvement in dynamic range and in lower noise.

Compliance This word is used mostly in connection with phonograph styli and loudspeakers. In both cases it is the amount of "give" in a substance. A high-compliance **stylus**, for example, will yield readily and quite a bit to the tiny forces exerted upon it by the record groove. A sweeping statement about the desirability of a highly compliant stylus cannot be made, because the mass of the associated tonearm must be taken into account as well and a proper match is more important than any single characteristic of either. Regarding loudspeakers, because of the complexity of the design process it is of little use to the consumer to know anything more than the fact that compliance is one of the balls that the engineers juggle when they work out how to achieve the sound they are out to get.

Compressor A component which acts to reduce the dynamic range of a musical signal. Such compression allows the signal to be recorded with lower distortion than would otherwise be possible. Best used in conjunction with an **expander**, either separately or as part of a **compander**. Because compact discs have such great potential for wide dynamic range, some players offer a (defeatable) compression circuit. It is useful both for making cassette tapes and for listening when wide dynamics aren't desirable (especially for automotive playback, where the ambient noise of the car tends to mask the soft passages of highly dynamic music).

Crossover The device within (or outside) a loudspeaker that divides the signal from the amplifier into two or more frequency ranges, sending each range to the appropriate driver. Some audiophiles use an external "active" crossover, which divides the spectrum after the preamp stage, and sends each band to its own individual power amplifier. Such a system is often used with separate **subwoofers**. The electrical characteristics of capacitors make them simple crossovers in themselves, and they are often used as such.

Crosstalk This is a sort of musical seepage. One sort of crosstalk involves the tracks on a tape head and causes material on one track to be heard faintly on another. The other major category is crosstalk between channels, where material from the left channel leaks onto the right channel and vice versa.

Decibel (dB) This is the touchstone unit of a rather complicated system of measuring audio power. It is not an absolute measurement but rather an expression of a relationship between two levels. For reference's sake, note that the smallest difference in sound that is easily audible is roughly 1 dB, that 3 dB reflects a doubling in power, and that 10 dB represents a doubling in perceived loudness.

Digital Digital has several usages when confined to the world of hi-fi. The oldest relates to tuners, where it describes a very precise method of locking in on a station and of digitally displaying the tuned station's frequency on the front panel. More recently, the term digital has been used to refer to a new means of recording music, using computer technology to describe the music as a series of numbers which can be recorded on tape and translated once again back into sound. Using this method, traditional tape-related problems such as noise, wow and flutter, and lack of headroom don't exist. Record companies have been recording digitally for several years, but we've only recently been able to enjoy true digital playback at home, via the **compact disc**. The term "digital ready" is often applied to components, especially speakers. This term implies the component so described is capable of handling the superior dynamics inherent in digital sources. Except in those cases where a power handling test has been published (such as in the better magazines), there is no way, other than by listening, for the consumer to reach a conclusion about the truth of such claims.

Digital-to-Analog Converter Unless the digital signal from a CD player is converted into analog form at some point you'll never recognize the digital expression as music. The digital-to-analog (D/A) converter handles that task, and differences in their design and construction can account for sonic differences between players.

DIN Performance and mechanical and physical standards in Europe — not only in high-fidelity equipment, by the way, but in such things as automobiles, too — are handed down under the initials DIN, which stands for *Deutsche Industrie Norm.*

Dipole In the most common usage, this refers to the simplest of the FM antennas in general use (the T-shaped wire which comes with most tuners and receivers). In a broader sense, dipole refers to any device with opposite effects of polarization at opposite ends. Thus, a speaker which radiates its energy equally to its front and rear is dipolar (as opposed to omnidirectional — radiating energy equally in *all* directions). The most common dipole speakers are planar and electrostatic panels, which make use of the back wave, and whose placement in the listening room is thus very critical to prevent phase cancellation of bass frequencies. (It's worth noting that conventional cone drivers are also dipolar, but they most often aren't used that way, their backwave being either damped by a sealed cabinet or altered by one which is vented.)

Dispersion The angle through which a speaker radiates its sound. Low frequencies are naturally omnidirectional — that is, they have a wide angle of dispersion — but this is not the case for higher frequencies, which tend to be highly directional.

Displays let you know the status of a given component. The more elaborate displays can indicate (on a CD player) the number of tracks on the disc, the track being played, the tracks selected for future play, the various timing modes (see **Time Display**) and other aspects of the player's operation. On elaborate receivers the display can reveal such items as the source program, equalizer settings, and ambience simulation mode.

Distortion If in passing through your audio system the original signal has been appreciably altered and no longer accurately represents the quality of that original signal, it has been affected by distortion. Distortion, a relative term, can be caused by electrical or mechanical shortcomings, and is almost inevitable. While distortion cannot perhaps be completely avoided, it can certainly be minimized. For quite a while now many of the quoted specifications associated with audio equipment have reflected distortions that are well below the threshold of audibility. Essentially, the lower the distortion, the higher the fidelity. Unfortunately, the mechanical parts of a system are more prone to distortion of various kinds, and speakers inevitably introduce some (which is often called **coloration**).

Dolby Noise Reduction This now-common method of noise reduction was responsible for taking the cassette format out of the voice-only realm and making it a sonically viable hi-fi product.

Driver Each separate loudspeaker of a speaker system is known as a driver. Types of drivers include **tweeters**, midrange drivers, and **woofers**.

Dropout When, owing to crumpled or dirty tape, damage to the magnetic media, or any other cause, there is a lapse in contact between a tape head and the moving tape, dropout occurs. If the lapse is serious, obviously there will be momentary but complete silence, but if only a portion of the tape moves just a slight distance from the head, there will be a brief degradation in high-frequency response.

Dropout, CD When, owing to a flawed or very dirty or scratched CD, there is a lapse in the laser reading of the recorded CD surface that is greater than the ability of the error-correction circuitry to overcome, a dropout occurs.

Dual Capstan Most tape decks use a single capstan, placed after the head block, which pulls the tape along its path. A second capstan, placed *before* the head block, isolates the portion of tape at the block from the rest of the transport, creating what's known as a closed loop, and providing (at least in theory) more stable tape motion and better performance. Dual-capstan transports are frequently found in **auto-reverse** decks, where they help provide uniform performance in both directions.

Dub To copy material from one source to another. Dubbing can be from disc to tape, or tape to tape. In recognition of the popularity of dubbing, many receivers and amps have switching which makes the process simple. It's also possible to buy a single dubbing tape deck with two transports, one to play back, the other to record. Often, this occurs at twice the normal speed, cutting dubbing time in half.

Dynamic Headroom In amplifiers, the amount of power (beyond its federally mandated "continuous" or RMS rating) available for momentary musical peaks. Bear in mind that most musical events are simply a bunch of peaks strung together, and you'll see the importance of dynamic headroom. It's not as though an amp can deliver *one* peak and then has to rest for twenty minutes. Recovery time is usually very brief. Dynamic headroom is measured in **decibels** (dB), so a figure of 3 dB means that twice rated power is available: a 40-watt amplifier can momentarily deliver 80 watts if it has 3 dB dynamic headroom.

Dynamic Range The gamut of volume from the softest to the loudest sounds. In the past, technology significantly limited the dynamic range available from a home hi-fi system. More recently, though, with the greater capabilities of modern home equipment and media, dynamic range is being restored to a breadth more nearly that of live music. This is particularly true of so-called audiophile recordings, and certainly of compact discs, but the situation is improving throughout the general consumer field as well. Wider dynamic range means that your speakers must now respond accurately to a far broader spectrum of power without undue distortion and certainly without causing damage.

Efficiency What it sounds like. Its most usual application is in reference to loudspeakers, where it expresses (although not precisely) how much power the speakers require to drive them to listening level. A very efficient speaker might need only a few watts to fill a large room with sound; an inefficient speaker might require a hundred watts or more to reach similar levels.

Equalization is the raising or lowering of a portion of the frequency range in order to achieve a desired result (which is usually flat response in the listening room). Equalization occurs at many points in the chain of musical reproduction, often without any intervention on the part of the user. LP records, for example, are recorded with certain parts of the range boosted and others cut according to an equalization curve which is standard throughout the industry. Your amplifier must compensate for this with, as it were, a mirror image of that curve built into its phono section. Similarly, tape decks are built to compensate for the various response curves of different tape formulations.

Another class of equalization is in the hands of the listener. The simplest equalizers are the basic bass and treble tone controls, but separate equalizers — with many frequency bands and great flexibility — are available for the knottier problems of home equalization. Some speaker systems have simple equalizers of a kind built in, such as knobs or switches which enable the listener to set the system response for, say, bookshelf or floor placement.

Error Correction When related to digital audio the term refers to the computer circuitry within a CD player that analyzes dropouts and fills the resultant gaps with music.

Expander Referring to dynamic range, an expander broadens it, either by restoring dynamic range removed by a compressor or artificially improving an originally dismal situation. Compression/expansion (see **Compander**) can be a great aid in cutting down noise, and expansion on its own, when done by means of sophisticated equipment, can add sonic dimension to mediocre recordings.

Flutter Rapid fluctuations in the speed of a turntable or tape transport, usually measured and stated together with **wow**. The audible result of flutter is a warbling or vibrato effect.

Folded-Horn Speaker A marked contrast to the **acoustic-suspension** design of speaker systems, the folded-horn system, which forces the sound of the driver to take a circuitous path within the cabinet before being released into the room, is the most efficient type of speaker available to the consumer. It is also probably the most difficult to make sound accurate, and advances in other technologies have made it even less common than it was before.

Frequency Modulation (FM) In an FM broadcast signal, the musical or other information determines the frequency of the "carrier signal" — as opposed to AM, in which it is the amplitude which varies. FM broadcasting is the system of choice for music, for while it doesn't reach as far as AM signals, it provides greater clarity and lower noise.

Frequency Response The range of frequencies (cycles per second) to which a given piece of equipment will react is its frequency response but, by itself, the specification provides only the roughest guideline of how wide the range of a component is. Unless this is defined by a plus-or-minus-so-many-decibels qualification it can be very misleading. To give an extreme example, a cassette deck might claim a frequency response of 20 Hz to 20 kHz, but an examination of its response curve shows response at 20 kHz to be 15 dB below the midrange. Clearly, its high frequency response is awful, and the 20 Hz – 20 kHz spec meaningless. So look not only for wide frequency response, but smooth or flat response as well.

Front Loading is found on all but a few CD players and a very few turntables. A motorized drawer opens up to accept the disc, and closes for play. Some, but by no means all, players key the "close" button into the drawer itself, so giving it a gentle nudge causes it to close. A design advantage of front-loading players is that they can be stacked with other components.

Gap The distance between the pole pieces of a tape recorder head: a critical distance. It is partly because of this that a two-head tape deck (which uses a single gap for both record and playback) rarely achieves the performance level of a three-head machine (whose separate record and playback heads allow each to have a gap optimized for the purpose). A compromise in gap width must be made when record and playback are handled by a single-head gap.

Graphic Equalizer An equalizer whose only adjustable parameter is amplitude (level), and whose controls are a series of sliders which provide a visual (graphic) display of the equalization curve being used.

Ground refers to a point of zero voltage, generally in a power circuit. Some form of grounding is necessary for completion of a circuit (think of birds perched on high tension wires, safe from harm because they are not grounded) and this may be provided by a third wire in the cable or a separate ground wire. In low-voltage systems particularly it may be integral with the power cables, in which a separate wire won't be present. Picturesquely referred to by British manufacturers as "earth." In pro systems, a long copper rod is actually driven into the earth.

Harmonic Distortion Harmonics, as noted below, are what determine the timbral quality of any sound. When a speaker (or any other hi-fi component) adds harmonics not present in the original, or changes them around in some way, this is the dreaded harmonic distortion, usually expressed as a percentage of the total output.

Harmonics When we talk of "middle C" as being at a frequency of 261.6 Hz, we are simplifying matters: in any musical (as opposed to pure electronic) tone, the sound consists of a fundamental tone (in this case 261.6 Hz) and a number of frequencies which this tone generates, which are a series of multiples of the fundamental. These are the harmonics and it is their distribution which determines the timbral quality of a sound: why a flute sounds different from a clarinet, for example.

Headroom describes a component's leeway, or margin for error. In a tape deck, for instance, it refers to the ability to "push" the meters into the red during recording, without incurring audible distortion. In the case of an amplifier, it is its ability to provide momentary power beyond its nominal rating.

Hertz This term has gradually (and officially) replaced the older (and more straightforward) "cycles per second" (cps). It comes from the name of the German physicist H.R. Hertz, who died in 1894. Abbreviated as Hz. Note that one kiloHertz (1 kHz) is one thousand cycles per second.

Hiss Specifically, the annoying high-frequency background noise on tape recordings, which may be caused by equipment shortcomings (at either the recording or the playback stage) or by residual tape magnetism. In a broader sense, it refers to any similar noise in other components, such as amplifiers. Audio neophytes, when encountering good equipment for the first time, often comment on the amount of hiss the speakers have. What they are hearing, of course, is tape hiss, or record surface noise, being "properly" reproduced for the first time.

Hum As a rule, hum originates from the leakage of 60 Hz alternating current, originating in the house wiring, into the sound system. This most often happens at the phono cartridge stage and may be caused by a number of problems. The easiest hum to check on and correct is that generated by improper grounding.

Idler Wheel This communicates motion from a powered revolving shaft such as that of a motor to a third wheel, such as a turntable. Since the idler wheel acts as an intermediate gear, its size determines the speed of rotation of the third wheel, and speed changes may be effected by altering the size of the idler wheel. Idler-wheel drive is no longer common on turntables, but is still often used to communicate motion to a tape-recorder capstan shaft.

Impedance The degree of resistance that an electrical current will encounter in a given circuit or device. While even highly conductive materials have some degree of electrical impedance, this is too small to be taken into consideration even when long-distance wiring is being considered in an audio system. Of more general interest are the impedance ratings of various components such as speakers, for here amplifier output may be directly affected. Note that rated impedance is something of a chimera: in actual use, a speaker's impedance can fluctuate widely, and the use of additional speaker systems has a dramatic effect on overall load, which can cause amplifier problems. If using more than two pairs of speakers at once, do invest in a switch box with some sort of protection circuitry in it (unless your amplifier is one of the very few equipped to handle more than a couple of pairs).

Infinite-Baffle Speaker There are two basic ways of dealing with the fact that sound comes out of the back of a driver as well as the front. The infinite baffle works on the principle of suppressing this backward output completely by mounting the speaker on a baffle board and using a very large enclosure in which the rear-firing sound waves can be "lost." This makes for an unwieldy system, but a very efficient one with bass response potentially better than one using the same drivers in, say, an **acoustic-suspension** enclosure.

Intermodulation Distortion (IM Distortion) Like **harmonic distortion,** IM distortion involves the introduction of a new and unwanted signal. But the concern here is not the harmonics themselves, but newly created frequencies that are the sum and difference of existing ones. If, for instance, test tones of 100 Hz and 1,000 Hz were applied to the input of an amplifier, the resulting IM would appear at the output as 900 Hz and 1,100 Hz. When IM distortion is bad, terrible blurring or smearing of the sound can be the result.

ips Inches per second is how tape speed is measured. The rule has always been: The faster the tape speed, the better the quality of the sound (everything else being equal) — and it still is. But with the advent of cassette technology we have all had to rethink the subject. Cassettes traveling at 1⅞ ips are nowadays achieving results rivaling open reel (which can move at 7½ or 15 ips). This is because of various noise-reduction and headroom-extension systems that assure that everything else is not going to be equal. So know what ips is when you see it, but be flexible in your assumptions about the bottom line.

Jack The female part of a plug/receptacle pair. The place where you plug in headphones, for example, is a jack. Different types of jacks and plugs are used in different parts of the world, so if you have bought hi-fi equipment abroad you may need adapters to mate it with units made for the U.S. market.

kHz This is the abbreviation for kiloHertz, or 1,000 Hz.

Level Basically, the strength of a **signal** — any signal. Not a term with precise technical meaning, this can also refer to listening level or to the level of an electrical signal.

Logic A name for electronic circuits that make sure events happen in the proper order. For instance, when you press Play while a tape is rewinding, logic circuitry might automatically insert an intermediate Stop command to make sure the tape doesn't break or spill.

Loudness In its broadest sense, this means what it sounds like it means. As applied to the "loudness" control on an amplifier, it is short for **loudness compensation.**

Loudness Compensation When we listen at very low volume levels our ears do not hear certain parts of the musical spectrum as well as they normally do, particularly in the bass area. Loudness compensation boosts these areas when switched on, making our perception of the music closer to what we would hear at louder levels. As the volume is raised, the amount of boost is reduced, until — at the highest volume — none is present at all. Since the position of the volume control, rather than the actual sound level, determines the amount of boost, the effectiveness of the circuit will depend upon speaker efficiency and the boost curve chosen by the manufacturer. A more effective means of providing accurate loudness contour uses a continuous control that allows speaker efficiency to be a factor.

Metal Tape Up until the late '70s all recording tape coatings were made of metal oxide formulations, but new developments have permitted the use of pure metal particles. Evidence shows that high-frequency response and maximum output level are much improved with metal tape. On the down side, the tape costs more than the best oxide formulations, which are currently very good.

Microprocessor A computer-on-a-chip, just like the one in your Apple or IBM PC. The ones found in audio equipment perform myriad functions. On tape decks they operate the random and search transport modes and any automatic tape-to-deck matching, like bias optimization. Some turntables use them to control tonearm motion and turntable rotation. Tuners use them for memory operation, as do receivers, which sometimes have settings for several EQ curves and other variables. On CD players they perform most functions.

Modulation In general terms, the word refers to the act of controlling or varying something. As used in expressions like **frequency modulation**, it describes the way one electrical or radio signal modifies or controls another signal for such purposes as enabling it to carry information. The way in which a record groove carries information also goes by this name.

Monaural Single-channel audio. Some high-end stereo equipment is simply monaural equipment times two: this can result in extraordinarily high stereo separation and minimal crosstalk.

Monitor When your guests are mingling and listening to Strauss waltzes in the living room and you are slaving in the kitchen crushing ice and squeezing lemons, but have a little speaker over the Cuisinart so you can tell when to go and change the CD, you are monitoring the music. The term has also taken on a qualitative meaning as applied to speakers: the implication seems to be that a speaker good enough to be used by a record company to "monitor" their recordings must be very good. Regrettably, that's not necessarily so. Monitors are chosen for a variety of reasons, sound quality being only one and often not even near the top of the list. In tape-recorder vocabulary, a monitor head is a playback head positioned just past the record head so that the newly recorded tape can be instantly listened to — or monitored. (The monitor head is not in addition to, but *is* the playback head when it is separate from the record head.)

Multipath Distortion Ghosts on your TV are caused by multipath, which is what happens when the same signal reaches your tuner at two different times. Usually, it's caused by a reflection, such as off a mountain or tall building. The reflected signal arrives a moment later than the original, and the result, in audio systems, is distortion. The best cure is a highly directional **antenna.**

Multiplex The primary application of the word is to FM stereo broadcasting, where the two channels are combined on a single carrier signal in such a way as to permit them to be separated again at the receiver.

Noise Any undesirable external signal (as opposed to internally generated distortion) which has found its way into the material you are listening to. It can have its origins anywhere in the chain of recording or playback — from poor mastering, to bad microphones, to dust on the record, a poor connection, or dirty contacts within switches and knobs.

Octave Musically, an octave is the distance between like notes, for example between middle C and the next C above it on a piano keyboard. It is worth remembering when looking at speaker specifications (which is no substitute for listening) that the musical relationship known as an octave involves a two-to-one ratio in frequency. Thus, in the bass, the seemingly short step from 40 Hz to 80 Hz is an octave, as is the apparently huge treble leap from 10,000 Hz to 20,000 Hz. It's also worth noting that the lowest note on a bass guitar — its open E string — is about 42 Hz.

Oxide When a metal combines with oxygen, as in rust, an oxide compound is formed and such compounds are used in audio to provide the magnetic coating for most recording tape.

Parametric Equalizer An equalizer that enables you to control not only the amount of boost or cut but also the steepness of the curve (i.e., the width of the frequency band being acted upon) and even the center frequency at which it acts. Such equalizers are most useful for correcting known deficiencies in a system or room acoustics, but they are good for bringing unruly speakers into line, too. With such an equalizer you can, for example, tame a nasty peak in your speaker's response without affecting nearby frequencies.

Pause interrupts Play in a CD player (or, in the case of a tape deck, Play or Record) without changing the location of the laser in relation to the disc or the tape in relation to the head. Pressing Pause again (or, with some players, pressing Play) resumes play at the same point.

Peak The level of an instantaneous burst of power or signal. As a rule, equipment is capable of handling or producing peaks far greater than its rated capacity or output. (See **Headroom**)

Phase The position in time of a sound (or other) wave when compared to a second wave. If you think of a sound wave as a series of humps and valleys and superimpose two of these series so that they match up, you will be imagining a pair of waves *in phase*. If you shift the position of one of these series forward or back, the waves are now *out of phase*. Varying degrees of importance are attached to phase coherency in the audio world, but empirical evidence shows that equipment designed for accurate phase response sounds better — for one reason or another — than equipment where phase response has been left to chance. When hooking up your loudspeakers you can ensure that they at least are in phase with one another. This is achieved by making certain that the positive (+) input of each speaker is connected to the positive (+) output of its respective amplifier channel, and that the negative (-) terminal is connected to the negative (-) output. (One audible result of not doing this is a loss of bass.) Another form of phase coherency involves all the musical information from a speaker system arriving at your ears at the same time. Some speaker designers even place various drivers in such a way as to ensure that the distance from the sound-producing portion of the woofer to your ears is the same as that for the tweeter. This "stepped" effect can also be achieved electronically, with short timing delays built in for the drivers which are physically closer to the listener, so that the drivers which are further away have their sound perceived simultaneously.

Phase-Locked Loop (PLL) An FM multiplex decoding system based on feedback control of an oscillator. It is a very accurate tuning system, and tends to retain its reliability with age with no need for realignment. Phase-locked loop circuitry is also used to control the speed of motors in some turntables and cassette decks.

Phone Plug The relatively bulky plugs of ¼-inch diameter that generally come at the end of headphone leads intended for home use. The name comes from the fact that they were used on telephone switchboards.

Phono Plug The small plug which is used throughout the U.S. for interconnection of high-fidelity components. Also called RCA plug, and not to be confused with **phone plug**.

Playback Head In a tape deck, playback functions can be combined with record functions in one head, but for various reasons it is desirable to use separate record and playback heads. Two of the reasons are that the characteristics of each head may be optimized for its function, and that the playback-only head can act as a monitor head. This allows the recording to be checked as it is being made.

Power In practical terms, an amplifier's power is the amount of energy it is able to deliver to a loudspeaker. This is expressed (somewhat inaccurately and misleadingly) in watts. For the specification to mean anything at all, it must be linked with a couple of other numbers as well, first of all, the frequency range through which that power is available. Then this must be further qualified by a statement of the distortion levels that will be reached at that power. And then, the impedance of the load into which the power was being fed when measured must be taken into consideration. A sample published power specification might read as follows: 35 watts per channel into 8 ohms at 0.5 percent total harmonic distortion from 20 to 20,000 Hz. The problem with a power specification based solely upon watts is that it can't truly express the real-world ability of an amplifier to make a pair of loudspeakers play in a listening room. Speakers and music, unlike test signals and load resistors, are dynamic, and place a different sort of demand on the amplifier. The voltage and current capabilities of an amplifier at various loads are important, and can make one 20-watt amplifier sound great and another awful, playing the same music through the same speakers.

Preamplifier An amplifier which takes the tiny signal from a phono cartridge or other sound source and increases it sufficiently to be able to pass it on to a power amplifier for further amplification and transmission to the speakers. Some preamplifiers — favored by a group of audiophiles — do that job and that job alone, while other types incorporate elaborate control facilities, including things such as fairly complex equalization systems. Preamplifiers are available separately, or combined in a single chassis with a power amplifier (called an integrated amplifier) or as part of a receiver. Phono cartridges with especially minuscule output, such as moving-coil types, may require *pre*-preamplifiers for use in a normal system, although many models (including integrated amps and receivers) include circuitry to handle them directly.

Repeat is what it sounds like: depending on the unit you can program the repeat of either the entire tape or disc, the entire selected program, or any random portion of the tape or disc.

Resonance When you pluck a guitar string, the note you hear is determined by the string's resonant frequency. That is the frequency at which it will vibrate if left to its own devices. Everything has one, including the Brooklyn Bridge. The problem with resonances is that they can interfere with good sound: when a part of your system is exposed to a note at its resonant frequency, it will vibrate in sympathy, with annoying-to-disastrous results. That is why, for example, turntable isolation and tonearm/cartridge matching are so important: resonances can't be eliminated, but they can be reduced. Speakers, on the other hand, *use* certain resonances to enhance their performance. The bass response of a speaker is dependent, *inter alia*, on the relationship between the resonant frequency of the woofer and the design of the cabinet.

Reverberation The gradual dying away of sounds in any enclosed space caused by the sound bouncing around from surface to surface in that space.

Rumble Low-frequency vibrations caused by the motor or other mechanical parts of a turntable can be transmitted into your audio system through the record surface and the cartridge. This is rumble: it might or might not be in the range of audible frequencies, but even if it is not, it will be present in the signal and will send confusing messages to your amplifier and speakers, degrading the sound. It can also modulate higher frequencies.

Saturation When a solution can accept no more of what is being dissolved, it is said to be saturated. The same principle exists for recording tape in that it can only hold so much magnetic information. When the tape coating has had all it can take, it too is saturated, the result being audible **distortion**.

Search Modes allow you to fast forward or rewind to a desired point on a tape or disc. Of particular use is audible search, which is found on most players. This feature lets you hear the music, though sped up, during the search mode. Some models have two or even three audible search speeds.

Selectivity A different concept from **capture ratio**, selectivity refers to a tuner's ability to tune in to a station that has other very strong signals coming in on adjacent (200 kHz away) or alternate (400 kHz away) frequencies. It's measured in dB, and generally speaking, the higher the better. However, if there *aren't* problematic nearby signals, lower selectivity can yield lower distortion and better overall sound. To provide the best performance in all circumstances, some tuners and receivers offer variable selectivity, either manually controlled by the user, or automatically adjusted by the unit's own circuitry.

Sensitivity The minimum amount of signal needed at a component's input in order to achieve a given level at its output is that component's sensitivity. It is this specification that determines, among other things, whether a preamplifier will need a pre-preamp for a moving-coil cartridge. In a tuner, it refers to signal strength required and must be stated in conjunction with a signal-to-noise figure to be meaningful.

Separation The absence of **crosstalk,** or, to put it in a positive light, the segregation of two stereo channels. Separation can be enhanced or downgraded through good or poor speaker placement.

Signal Musical or other information carried in electrical form. It becomes sound again through the speaker's translation of electrical energy to acoustical energy.

Signal-to-Noise (S/N) Ratio The expression in dB of the relationship between the musical or other signal strength in a component and its accompanying noise. When various noise-reduction systems are doing their jobs, it is the S/N ratio they are improving.

Skating However smooth the surface of a record groove, and however smooth the finish of a diamond stylus, a huge amount of friction is generated when a record is played. This friction generates a force which pulls a pivoted tonearm toward the center of the record. Compensatory force is applied in the form of **anti-skating**. Linear-tracking tonearms, which are not pivoted, don't require anti-skating. Nor do CD players.

Speaker Enclosure The various kinds of speaker enclosure most popular today are defined separately, but the basic criterion for defining an enclosure is whether or not it acoustically isolates the front of the woofer — and other drivers — from the rear. For example: an acoustic-suspension system does provide this isolation while a bass-reflex system does not, but makes use of the speaker's rear waves after assuring that it will be in phase with the front-firing waves.

Squawker This word once stood proudly with **woofer** and **tweeter**, referring to the driver intended to reproduce the midrange. Someone had the sense to say "enough is enough" and the term has fallen out of use in this country.

Standing Wave This is a phenomenon that can have a fairly dramatic effect on the bass response of an audio system. Sometimes, the relationship between the wavelength of a frequency and the dimensions of the listening room can result in the sound wave actually being reflected back on itself, which creates a form of audible resonance known as standing-wave distortion. This, along with the related but more subtle type of standing wave that *eliminates* certain frequencies, can be combatted by moving things around in the room (including the speakers), or by the use of sound-absorbing materials.

Stylus Commonly referred to as a needle (which is basically what it was half a century or more ago), the stylus is the end of the phono cartridge that makes contact with the record. It consists of a tip (usually diamond) bonded to a shaft (called the cantilever). The record groove imparts motion to the stylus, which in turn causes the cartridge to act as a tiny generator whose output contains an electrical analog of the music on the record.

Subwoofer This much-abused term literally describes a speaker whose output is in the range below that of a conventional **woofer**, or roughly from 20 to 50 Hz. More commonly, it is used to describe the physically separate bass section of a speaker system whose midrange and high frequencies are reproduced by shoebox-sized "satellite" speakers. Such subwoofer/satellite systems are particularly useful when the listening room cannot readily accommodate a pair of large conventional speakers.

THD When **harmonic distortion** is expressed as a specification in the form of a percentage, this abbreviation, standing for total harmonic distortion, is often employed.

Time Display can show the elapsed or remaining time on the tape, disc, or selection being played. Some displays are limited to a single mode, while others can be switched to show several in sequence.

Tone Controls These can take many forms, from the simple tone knob, which is in fact nothing but a treble-cut control in most cases, to very complicated systems of equalization with 10 or more precisely defined frequency bands. In between, there are the usual bass and treble controls and sometimes added midrange control. All these controls may be used to change the character of a system's sound either for simple reasons of personal taste or to compensate for the acoustic eccentricities or shortcomings of a given room or loudspeaker system. Many speakers, in fact, have their own, usually rudimentary, tone controls, used mainly to "customize" the speaker for a variety of installations.

Tracing As distinct from **tracking**, tracing is the capability of a stylus to react accurately to the subtle horizontal and vertical modulations of the groove of a disc. Its shape and condition, as well as the cantilever to which it is mounted, all affect this ability.

Tracking A stylus with inherently excellent **tracing** characteristics will not be able to live up to them in performance if the cartridge in which it is mounted is unable to stay firmly in the groove. It is this ability which is known as tracking, and it can be affected, among other things, by either too much or too little tracking force.

Tracking Angle In describing the angle at which the cartridge/ **stylus** assembly meets the record surface there are two distinct relationships to take into consideration. The first is the vertical tracking angle which is the angle between the record surface and the diamond of the stylus. It is widely considered that this angle should ideally be the same as the angle used by the machine which cuts the record master, that is 15 degrees away from a right angle. Given that the cartridge manufacturer has built this 15-degree angle into his product, the user must so adjust his turntable upon installation that the arm is perfectly parallel to the record surface. This is done either by means of an adjustment of height at the pivot, or, where a turntable model has no such adjustment, by the use of shims (thin pieces of hard rubber) to adjust the distance between the cartridge and the headshell. The other angle involved is lateral tracking angle, which is the change in angle of a cartridge vis-à-vis an imaginary line from the central spindle to the stylus. Given that the arm moves in an arc (where it moves in a straight line, in radial tracking models, this is no problem), naturally that angle will change as a record is played. Proper attention to tonearm geometry on the manufacturer's part, and to cartridge alignment on your part, will minimize the effects of this problem, which can be anything from simple channel imbalance to severe audible distortion. Good turntables come with a setup or alignment chart that allows proper positioning of the stylus tip and angling of the cartridge body and stylus.

Transducer Any device that converts one form of energy into another. A solar cell is a transducer because it converts radiant energy from the sun into electrical energy. In the hi-fi world, examples of transducers are cartridges (kinetic to electrical energy), tape heads (electromagnetic to electrical energy), and speakers (electrical to acoustical energy).

Transient A transient is a rapid change, generally upward, in energy. A sudden slam of the cymbals in an otherwise quiet musical passage is a good example of a transient. The ability of a piece of equipment to cope with such unexpected bursts of energy without undue distortion is very important.

Transmission-Line Speaker System Another relative of the **bass-reflex** system. Here, the back wave of the woofer is loaded into a long, tuned duct and the duct's output provides a large proportion of the overall bass output.

Tweeter A **driver** designed for high frequencies.

Vented-Speaker System Any speaker cabinet, such as a **bass-reflex** type, that has a hole through which the back waves of the woofer can escape is considered to be vented. The hole, of course, is the vent.

Voice Coil A precisely wound coil of wire by means of which the electrical signal from the amplifier is converted to mechanical energy with which to move the speaker cone and, hence, the air and, ultimately, your eardrums and emotions.

Weighting A system of audio handicaps. Measurements of various performance parameters are often weighted to compensate for known peaks and dips in the frequency response of the human hearing apparatus or other known factors.

Woofer Once, like tweeter, a much derided term, woofer refers to a **driver** responsible for reproducing low-frequency (bass) information.

Wow Related to, and measured along with, **flutter**, wow is a slow variation in the speed of a turntable or tape transport. Its origin may be in the motor or transmission system of the unit or, in the case of a record, in a badly warped record surface.

RECOMMENDED RECORDINGS

Adler, Larry. *Live at the Ballroom*. Newport Classics. Larry Adler, whose career as a harmonica virtuoso began in 1928, is one of the true legends of old-time show business. In the same way that Segovia single-handedly transformed the image of the guitar, Adler has turned the harmonica into a respectable concert instrument. This disc, which is not a transfer of old material, but a brand new digital recording, features Adler's renditions of 15 great tunes from the "golden age" of American popular music, along with two selections in a more serious vein. The recording, which was made live at New York's Ballroom, is terrific: the combination of ambience and definition is just right. If you've ever huffed and puffed into a Hohner Marine Band you haven't any idea of the more complex chromatic instrument's potential for expression. *Live at the Ballroom* is a revelation, and great fun as well.

Bach, Johann Sebastian. *Mass in B Minor*. Joshua Rifkin, the Bach Ensemble. Nonesuch. Joshua Rifkin's sharply etched performance (combined with the superb recording) lets you hear every vocal and instrumental line with unprecedented clarity, and the result is sensational. If you've already got one of the bigger recordings of this piece, keep it and make this one your first CD version. And if you don't own a copy of the work, or haven't yet even heard it, this is the one to start with.

————. *Toccata and Fugue in D Minor, etc.* Michael Murray, organ. Telarc. One of the very nice things about Telarc is the way they manage to combine demonstration-quality sonics with a uniformly high level of musical content. Take, for instance, this CD of four of Bach's "big" organ pieces. Michael Murray shows himself to be a master of this instrument, extracting from it a dizzying array of timbres. This ability is combined with a great deal of musical sense, resulting in an unusual combination of huge sound and fine detail. This is, then, one of those CD's that should be treated with a great deal of initial respect. When Murray kicks in the 32-foot rank of pipes, watch out! If your amp and speakers are up to the task, the house will shake.

Bartok, Bela. *The Miraculous Mandarin; Music for Strings, Percussion and Celesta.* Antal Dorati, the Detroit Symphony. London. *The Miraculous Mandarin* is very complex music, with textures that are difficult for a conductor to illuminate in the concert hall, much less on disc. Unless everything is just so, it all sounds like noise. But when everything works, it's magic, and in this instance Antal Dorati has wrought some pretty strong sorcery, and London's engineers have captured it intact. This is one of the discs you'll want to keep close at hand. After all, you never know when the need to show off with something truly spectacular will arise.

The Beatles. *Sergeant Pepper's Lonely Hearts Club Band.* Capitol. After more than twenty years there's very little left unsaid about *Sergeant Pepper's Lonely Hearts Club Band.* That being said, let's address the album's transfer to the digital medium. Even a casual audition of the disc reveals a richness of detail that is just hinted at on the LP. This is more than a collection of wonderful songs; it's a studio album whose riches were beyond the reach of 1967 playback technology. That such an obvious effort to make a recording that was better than it had to be is a tribute to the Beatles and their producer, George Martin. *Sergeant Pepper's* is a milestone recording, and one which belongs in the library of anyone who claims to care about contemporary music.

Beethoven, Ludwig van. *Piano Concerto No. 5 ("Emperor").* Rudolf Serkin, piano; Seiji Ozawa, the Boston Symphony. Telarc. Truly a marriage made in heaven, teaming one of the greatest pianists in the world with a first-class orchestra, under the direction of a renowned conductor, and recording it all in Boston's acoustically wonderful Symphony Hall. The magnificent acoustics (preserved by Telarc's minimal miking technique) are transported into your listening room. Once again, CD demonstrates its vast superiority as a medium for capturing the sound of the piano.

Buffett, Jimmy. *Songs You Know by Heart*. MCA. Among the *cognoscenti* this collection of Jimmy Buffett's greatest hits probably lives up to its presumptuous name. In their own way, these songs are classics. From a sonic standpoint, too, *Songs You Know by Heart* leaves little to be desired. Naturally, the original recordings were made on analog equipment, but the remastering has been done with exceptional care and taste and the result is a disc whose sound is exemplary. So if you already know these songs by heart, buy the disc for its sound and convenience. And if you're a newcomer to Jimmy Buffett's world, buy it and you'll soon feel like a life-long resident.

————. *You Had to Be There*. MCA. Jimmy Buffett concerts are as much parties as musical events, so the title of this two-disc recording of 1978 performances in Atlanta and Miami is particularly apt. Buffett and his backup group, the Coral Reefer Band, clearly enjoy their work, a fact that is appreciated by the fans lucky enough to have been there. The 19 songs on *You Had to Be There* include much of Buffett's best material, and the performances are spirited and loads of fun. If you want the closest thing to the real thing, put *You Had to Be There* on the system; it won't be hard to imagine yourself surrounded by throngs of dancing revellers, partying in Margaritaville.

Canteloube, Joseph. *Chants d'Auvergne, Volume 1*. Kiri Te Kanawa, Jeffrey Tate, the English Chamber Orchestra. London. Canteloube transcribed folk songs from all over France, but the five volumes of *Songs of Auvergne* are his best known work, and this recording of Volume One serves as a splendid introduction to them. Kiri Te Kanawa's creamy voice gives these lovely peasant airs a wonderfully rich sound, while Jeffrey Tate's orchestral accompaniment ebbs and swells with the flow of the melody. It's a first-rate performance on all counts, and is well served by the recording.

Choral Masterpieces. Robert Shaw, the Atlanta Symphony and Chorus. Telarc. Nothing shows off a good hi-fi system like a really good recording of big choral music. *Choral Masterpieces* is a compilation of 15 selections, some familiar (like Handel's "Hallelujah" from *Messiah*) and some obscure (like the "Sanctus" from Durufle's *Requiem*). The programming of the disc was done with a superb sense of pace: the true knockout pieces are surrounded by softer, more relaxing selections. You might not think to buy a disc called *Choral Masterpieces*, thinking that you aren't a fan of this type of music. Suppress that thought and trust us. Telarc's *Choral Masterpieces* is itself a masterpiece.

DiMeola, Al, and John McLaughlin, Paco DeLucia. *Friday Night in San Francisco.* Columbia. This disc features duets and trios by three guitar players whose names might not be well-known to the MTV generation but who can play rings around most of the top names on today's charts. Most of *Friday Night in San Francisco* was recorded live, at a concert in San Francisco's Warfield Theater, and the sound is terrific. You get a definite sense of the theater, but there's none of the mud associated with many recordings made in large rooms by small forces. The music on the disc cannot be categorized, for it contains elements of jazz, rock, folk, flamenco, and classical guitar. Labels aside, though, that particular Friday night in San Francisco was one to remember, and we are fortunate that such a fine souvenir has been made available to those of us not lucky enough to have been there.

Dire Straits. *Alchemy*. Warner Brothers. This two-disc set documents Dire Straits' 1983 concert tour, and carries the following apology: "The music on this Compact Disc was originally recorded July, 1983 on analog equipment. We have attempted to preserve, as closely as possible, the sound of the original recording. Because of its high resolution, however, the Compact Disc can reveal limitations of the source tape." Pretty heady stuff, but unnecessary, for in spite of their "humble" origins, these discs provide an excellent sonic stage, and the "limitations" to which they refer are inconsequential. What is more important is the fact that these superb performances, of mostly familiar tunes, are not simply live renditions of the studio cuts. For one thing, the drumming is much more alive and imaginative, and for another, everyone seems to be having a genuinely good time. *Alchemy* is a must-have for Dire Straits' fans, and an excellent "greatest hits" collection.

————. *Brothers in Arms.* Warner. You're likely to be familiar with much of this 1985 album: for quite a while it was the best selling record in the U.S. From a musical standpoint, this is Dire Straits' most adventurous album. Rather than serve as a vehicle for Mark Knopfler's distinctive guitar solo work, it showcases his versatility as a songwriter. Each song is in a different style, and each is remarkable in its own right. What you may not know is that the CD contains more music than the LP, and sounds better to boot.

Glenn Miller Orchestra. *In the Digital Mood.* GRP. There are those music lovers for whom the Swing Era represents the high water mark in Western music. A good big band has a drive, an impact, that's unlike any other type of musical group, and if the Glenn Miller Orchestra doesn't epitomize the improvisational aspects of the genre, it certainly typifies the sound of the era. The original charts used by the Glenn Miller Orchestra have been very active in the four decades since Miller's wartime death. Indeed, there's a touring orchestra that uses the Glenn Miller name, and it is the conductor of that group that led the New York session men who made this recording. You might not know the names of all ten of the songs on this disc, but you'll certainly recognize them: "In the Mood," "Moonlight Serenade," "Tuxedo Junction," and "String of Pearls" are part of this country's musical heritage, and you're not likely to hear them with greater clarity elsewhere. The recording is digital throughout, and the sound is stunning.

The Grateful Dead. *American Beauty.* Warner. This album, originally issued in 1970, is a brilliant collection of songs, performed with consummate skill and recorded with more care than you'd think, given the group's well-known antipathy towards studio work. From the opening chords of "Box of Rain" through the closing of "Trucking" each song is a perfect vignette, evoking strong images that hold up well two decades later.

————. *In the Dark.* Arista. The Grateful Dead has never been totally comfortable with the traditional studio setting, preferring to record live, so when it came time to record 1987's *In the Dark* they decided to split the difference. The basic tracks were laid down in real time, with the band playing in an empty club. The signal was routed to a state-of-the-art sound truck parked outside, allowing for the control (over sound quality) that a studio milieu assures. The result captures much of the Dead's renowned spontaneity while assuring them of a collection of songs that are suitable in every respect for airplay. *In the Dark* is arguably the group's best effort since the classic *American Beauty.* The songs are a delight, and the unusual recording scheme has yielded an album whose sound is, especially on CD, rich and clear.

Holst, Gustav. *Suites 1 and 2.* **George Frideric Handel.** *Music for the Royal Fireworks.* **Johann Sebastian Bach.** *Fantasia in G.* Frederick Fennell, the Cleveland Symphonic Winds. Telarc. This was Telarc's first audiophile release, and it holds up magnificently on the transfer to CD. Fennell's direction is superb — nobody does a better job on serious wind music — and Telarc perfectly captured the Cleveland Symphonic Winds' lush, organ-like sound. The two Holst Suites, based upon English folk songs, are particularly exciting.

The Jefferson Airplane. *2400 Fulton Street*. RCA. Along with the Grateful Dead, the Jefferson Airplane defined the San Francisco sound of the '60's. The group was in its heyday between 1965 and (roughly) 1971, and during that time some pretty sorry material was released along with the gems, but enough of the latter exist to form the basis for a tightly-packed two-disc set. *2400 Fulton Street* is more than a collection of greatest hits. It opens with "It's No Secret" and ends with (of all things) the group's Levi commercials. In between are both classics and a few of the Airplane's lesser-known efforts. Sonically, *2400 Fulton Street* is excellent: RCA has done a fine job of remastering (much better than the original CD release of *Surrealistic Pillow*), and the songs have much more punch than they do on the LPs.

Jongen, Joseph. *Symphonie Concertante*. **Frank**. *Fantasie in A; Pastorale*. Michael Murray, organ; Edo de Waart, the San Francisco Symphony. Telarc. You've probably read speaker reviews that say things like, "The bass will satisfy all but the most rabid pipe organ fans." Well, here's a record for those fans. The Jongen piece is a minor work musically speaking, but right up there in the majors from a sonic standpoint. It is a blockbuster that you should become familiar with, especially as this recording (the first using the new pipe organ in Davies Symphony Hall) will test the mettle of your amp and speakers alike. You think your speakers are "digital ready"? That your amp can really deliver when things get cooking? Maybe. If they can handle this CD, you're in good shape.

Kottke, Leo. *6 and 12 String Guitar*. Takoma/Allegiance. The legendary Leo Kottke has released an impressive collection of discs over the years, but the best of the lot is still his original solo effort for John Fahey's Takoma label. Prepare to be delighted.

Mahler, Gustav. *Symphony No. 2 ("Resurrection")*. Kathleen Battle, Maureen Forrester, Leonard Slatkin, the St. Louis Symphony. Telarc. A respectable performance of Mahler's 2nd symphony should be a highly emotional experience. In the pre-CD era no recording of the work has had that effect on us, regardless of the quality of the performance. The limitations of the pressed vinyl medium simply didn't allow for the total impact. So when Telarc announced the original LP release of this recording we held our editorial breath and waited on tenterhooks for our review copy. How would Slatkin's reading fare against those by Bruno Walter, Leonard Bernstein, and even Claudio Abbado?

We were impressed. While we wouldn't go so far as to discard Walter, Bernstein, or Abbado, Slatkin's performance belongs on every Mahlerphile's shelf. Problem was, the recording didn't leave us physically and emotionally debilitated. It was just another very fine phonograph record. The CD, however, is another story. Nuances that even Telarc's fine LP pressing tended to obscure show up in stark relief thanks to the CD's utter absence of background noise. This Telarc CD is what hi-fi is all about.

Moussorgsky, Modest, and Maurice Ravel. *Pictures at an Exhibition*. Lorin Maazel, the Cleveland Orchestra. Telarc. No one will argue that *Pictures at an Exhibition* is a profound piece of music, but neither is it an empty orchestral showpiece. The truth of this is borne out by Maazel's performance: rather than treat each section independently, he seems to have a sense of the whole, and this cohesion makes *Pictures* work both as a display piece and a serious piece of music. From a sonic standpoint, *Pictures* has tremendous dynamics, and a full palette of orchestral color, both of which are captured with Telarc's usual skill on this CD.

Mozart, Wolfgang Amadeus. *Requiem in D Minor*. Christopher Hogwood, the Academy of Ancient Music, et al. L'Oiseau-Lyre. This splendid performance of Mozart's *Requiem* cannot be faulted in any significant way. The playing, on instruments authentic to the period, displays none of the sloppiness that is often associated with such endeavors, and the singing is fine as well. Hogwood gets a nice big sound out of his smallish forces, which is a far more satisfying approach than simply adding singers or players. The recording, digital from end-to-end, is as clean as can be.

Orff, Carl. *Carmina Burana*. Blegen, Hagegard, Brown, Shaw, the Atlanta Symphony and Chorus. Telarc. When Telarc released the LP version of this performance it was stunning, and the CD just takes it a step further. The ambience of the Symphony Hall of Atlanta's Memorial Arts Center is perfectly preserved, and the background is quiet enough so that the most minute pianissimo is audible above the room noise. The combined vocal and instrumental forces make the dynamic range of this work almost shattering in intensity. By contrast, the frequently-used solo instruments are perfectly defined at their natural volumes. The performance is one of the best available, whether compared solely with other CDs or with the large universe of older recordings.

Pink Floyd. *Dark Side of the Moon.* Harvest. If you've ever bought a pair of speakers in a real hi-fi store, odds are that the salesman used this album as part of the demo process. Musically speaking, *Dark Side of the Moon* is one of the all-time great albums, but it's also a one-disc torture test for your hi-fi system. Want to know if your speakers can put out real bass? See how well they handle the famous heartbeats. Wondering about top end transient response? Check out the sound effects in "Money." *Dark Side of the Moon* is chock full of these little challenges.

————. *The Wall.* CBS. A double album whose length requires two CDs as well, *The Wall* is a work whose pretentious lyrics would disqualify it from serious consideration were it not for the fact that it is a musical and sonic masterpiece. Phil Spector's legendary "wall of sound" pales into insignificance when compared with some of *The Wall* 's textures. But all is not thick and turgid. Solo instruments and small ensembles are presented with great clarity and — equally important — with a good sense of their positions in space. As always with this group, production values are very high; *The Wall* belongs on the "A" side of any prospective CD library's want list.

Pleasures of Their Company. Kathleen Battle, soprano; Christopher Parkening, guitar. EMI. This highly miscellaneous recital begins with a group of songs and instrumental pieces by the Elizabethan lute virtuoso John Dowland. The disc contains Gounod's *Ave Maria*, wonderful lusty Brazilian songs, and Spanish folk songs arranged by Manuel de Falla (then arranged for guitar and voice by Patrick Russ). The disc ends with a half dozen spirituals that range from the exuberant to the heart-rending. Ms. Battle has a beautiful, limpid voice of which she is in total control. In the solo lute pieces (transcribed for the guitar) Christopher Parkening displays dexterity and command of sonority that appear to defy the limits of ten fingers and six strings. The two performers do some serious and very entertaining music-making on this disc.

Prokofiev, Sergei. *Romeo and Juliet (excerpts).* Yoel Levi, the Cleveland Orchestra. Telarc. Prokofiev was a great craftsman, and *Romeo* is one of his masterpieces. This particular recording is a bit more clinical than some of Telarc's other efforts, and lacks some warmth, but is no less satisfying; just different.

Schubert, Franz. *Die Winterreise.* Prey, Bianconi. Denon. *Die Winterreise* is one of the great song cycles, by one of the great songwriters of all time, and Hermann Prey's rich baritone is very well suited to its demands. Schubert's skill at expressing the mood of the text musically makes it possible to appreciate *Die Winterreise* even without benefit of a translation, especially when the performance is as true to the score as this one is. A fine, well-recorded performance.

Stravinsky, Igor. *The Firebird (Suite, 1919).* **Alexander Borodin.** *"Overture"* and *"Polovtzian Dances" from Prince Igor.* Robert Shaw, the Atlanta Symphony and Chorus. Telarc. Nowadays, great sound is the rule. So when I put this CD in the tray my expectation was that it would sound good, but no better than the bulk of the good discs on the shelf. Well, I was right and I was wrong. True, it didn't sound tons better than what I'm used to, but that's OK: it was still thrilling. The original LP, based on a 1978 recording, had astonishing range and clarity. The CD sounds even better.

————. *The Rite of Spring.* Lorin Maazel, the Cleveland Orchestra. Telarc. This performance, available for some time on conventional LP, has already been applauded sufficiently. What's astonishing, though, is how much better the CD is than the already superb pressed-vinyl version. This Telarc CD fulfills the promise of the digital medium by capturing all of the subtleties of this highly complex work and revealing the individual layers that make up its thick texture. If you're a fan of *The Rite of Spring,* this recording alone makes buying a CD player worthwhile.

The Tango Project. Nonesuch. William Schimmel's accordion (accordion!), Michael Sahl's piano, and Stan Kurtis' violin take familiar tunes like "La Cumparsita" and "Jalousie," along with others that you've probably not heard yet, and make you want to dance. These are sensuous, sinewy performances, evoking a time when the tango was considered, if not actually lewd, then highly suggestive. The recording is superb: it places the three instrumentalists right in your living room.

Vangelis. *Opera Sauvage.* Polydor. *Opera Sauvage* was written by Vangelis as background music for the French television series of the same name. It's vaguely New Age, but not enough that you find yourself looking for a reason to hurt something. There's melody, and texture, and even (sometimes) a beat. So put aside any preconceived notions about Vangelis, TV themes, and New Age music, and give *Opera Sauvage* a listen. It's worth the trouble.

Various Artists. *An Evening with Windham Hill, Live.* Windham Hill. The Windham Hill label is known primarily for instrumental recordings of jazz/rock/folk fusion artists, with pianist George Winston being the best known. Word is out that if you like one Windham Hill recording you'll like them all, and this album is ample demonstration of that fact. On it you'll hear Winston, guitarists Michael Hedges, Alex deGrassi, and William Ackerman, along with other members of the Windham Hill stable. All are highly proficient performers, and they play music that can be characterized (in a seemingly contradicting way) as challenging easy-listening. As is typically the case with the label, production values are very high.

Vivaldi, Antonio. *The Four Seasons.* Holloway, Parrott, the Taverner Players. Denon. This is not just another recording of *The Four Seasons*. It is *the* recording of *The Four Seasons*. This performance has muscle; it has depth; it has mystery. Andrew Parrott and the Taverner Players have taken the familiar and made it new, but this is not novelty for its own sake. Rather, it's a long-overdue restoration of a glorious original. This recording — which has stunning sonics, by the way — is a must-have.

Wagner, Richard. *Das Rheingold.* Kirsten Flagstad, George London, Sir Georg Solti, the Vienna Philharmonic. London. For more than three decades the Solti recording of Wagner's *Das Rheingold* has served as a landmark of the recording art. The cohesiveness of Solti's view, the brilliance of the individual artists, and the production by John Culshaw combine to make this one of the all-time great recordings, both from a musical standpoint and for its great sonics. What's more, every advance in playback technology seemed to reveal something new about the recording. Details of texture, nuances of dynamics that the playback technology of 1959 couldn't begin to resolve became apparent as cartridges, amplifiers, and loudspeakers improved. And now, with the digital remastering and transfer to CD, we learn just what was possible in the very earliest days of stereo recording. It's as though Culshaw was able to peer into the future and say "I know it doesn't matter now, but if we get it all on the tape, someday they'll be able to hear what we have in mind." The importance of this three-CD set goes beyond its considerable value as entertainment: it is a historic document whose success will, we hope, inspire the eventual transfer to the digital medium of other great performances.

Weber, Carl. *Der Freischutz*. Hauschild, the Dresden State Opera. Denon. One of the casualties of the World War II destruction in Dresden was the Semper Opera House, completed in 1878 and considered one of the best in Europe. On the fortieth anniversary of its destruction, the Semper Opera House reopened with a performance of the last opera to be performed there before the bombing: Weber's *Der Freischutz*. By all accounts, it was a truly gala event, and Denon was there to record it, live. Denon's engineers devoted a great deal of attention to the problem of providing the same front-to-rear ambience that was heard in the hall (and which is missing in most recordings). They succeeded; this is one of the most convincing recreations of a live performance by large forces we can recall.

Winston, George. *December*. Windham Hill. This is one of the recordings that "made" Windham Hill as a label, and the one that established George Winston as the Yuppie Party's Minister of Music. One of a series of "seasonal" discs, it consists of Winston's interpretations of familiar pieces like Pachelbel's *Canon in D*, Bach's *Jesu, Joy of Man's Desiring*, and *Carol of the Bells*. Winston's music is thoughtful, well-played, and eminently listenable. And if it seems more suitable for background use than serious listening, search your soul: How often do you put on a disc, and then simply sit down and listen? This is, to be sure, a middleweight disc, but it's probably one that you will choose to listen to (or at least, have playing) with some regularity.

LIST OF MANUFACTURERS

Entries in **boldface** are speaker manufacturers.

Acoustic Research
330 Turnpike Street
Canton, MA 02021

Adcom
11 Elkins Road
East Brunswick, NJ 08816

ADS, Inc.
One Progress Way
Wilmington, MA 01887

Advent
25 Tri-State International
Office Center
Lincolnshire, IL 60069

Aiwa America
800 Corporate Drive
Mahwah, NJ 07430

Allison Acoustics, Inc.
1590 Concord Avenue
Framingham, MA 01710

Altec Lansing
Milford, PA 18337

Audio Control
22313 70th Avenue
Mountlake Terrace
WA 98043

Audiosource, Inc.
1327 N. Carolan Avenue
Burlingame, CA 94010

Audio-Technica U.S.
1221 Commerce Drive
Stow, OH 44224

Azden Corporation
147 New Hyde Park Road
Franklin Square, NY 11010

Bang & Olufsen
1150 Feehanville Drive
Mount Prospect, IL 60056

BASF Corporation
Crosby Drive
Bedford, MA 01730

B.I.C. America
895 East Hampshire Road
Stow, OH 44224

Bose Corporation
The Mountain
Framingham, MA 01701

Boston Acoustics
70 Broadway
Lynnfield, MA 01940

Canton
915 Washington Avenue South
Minneapolis, MN 55415

Carver Corporation
P.O. Box 1237
Lynwood, WA 98046

Celestion Industries
89 Doug Brown Way
Holliston, MA 01746

Dahlquist, Inc.
601 Old Willets Path
Hauppauge, NY 11788

Denon America
222 New Road
Parsippany, NJ 07054

ESS Laboratories
11415 Folsom Boulevard
Rancho Cordova, CA 95742

Fisher
21350 Lassen Street
Chatsworth, CA 91311

Fried Products
7616 City Line Avenue
Philadelphia, PA 19151

Hafler
613 South Rockford Drive
Tempe, AZ 85281

Harman Kardon
240 Crossways Park West
Woodbury, NY 11797

Heco
694 Fort Salonga Road
Northport, NY 11768

Infinity Systems
9409 Owensmouth Avenue
Chatsworth, CA 91311

JBL
240 Crossways Park West
Woodbury, NY 11797

Jensen
25 Tri-State International
Office Center
Lincolnshire, IL 60069

JVC
41 Slater Drive
Elmwood Park, NJ 07407

KEF
14120-K Sullyfield Circle
Chantilly, VA 22021

Kenwood
2201 East Dominguez
Long Beach, CA 90801

Koss Corporation
4129 North Port Washington
Avenue
Milwaukee, WI 53212

Luxman
19145 Gramercy Place
Torrance, CA 90501

M & K
10391 Jefferson Boulevard
Culver City, CA 90232

Maxell
22-08 Route 208 South
Fair Lawn, NJ 07410

MB Quart
25 Walpole Park South
Walpole, MA 02081

McIntosh Laboratory
2 Chambers Street
Binghamton, NY 13903

Mirage
3641 McNicoll Avenue
Scarborough, Ontario
Canada M1X 1G5

Mission
2461 Bellevue Avenue
West Vancouver, BC
Canada V7V 1E1

Mordaunt-Short
1225 17th Street
Denver, CO 80202

N.A.P. Consumer Products
I-40 & Straw Plains Pike
Knoxville, TN 37914

NAD (USA)
575 University Avenue
Norwood, MA 02062

Nestorovic Labs
8307 North East 110 Place
Kirkland, WA 98033

Now Hear This
537 Stone Road, Building E
Benicia, CA 94510

Ohm Acoustics
241 Taaffe Place
Brooklyn, NY 11205

Onkyo
200 Williams Drive
Ramsey, NJ 07446

Ortofon
122 Dupont Street
Plainview, NY 11803

Philips
P.O. Box 555
Jefferson City, TN 37760

Pioneer Electronics
2265 East 220 Street
Long Beach, CA 90810

Polk Audio
1915 Annapolis Road
Baltimore, MD 21230

**Precise Acoustic
Laboratories**
200 Williams Drive
Ramsey, NJ 07446

Proton
5630 Cerritos Avenue
Cypress, CA 90630

Revox
1425 Elm Hill Pike
Nashville, TN 37210

Sansui
1290 Wall Street West
Lyndhurst, NJ 07071

Sennheiser
6 Vista Drive
Old Lyme, CT 06371

Signet
4701 Hudson Drive
Stow, OH 44224

Sony Corporation
Sony Drive
Park Ridge, NJ 07656

Soundcraftsmen
2200 South Ritchey Street
Santa Ana, CA 92705

Speakerlab
735 North Northlake Way
Seattle, WA 98103

Stax
20620 South Leapwood
Avenue
Carson, CA 90746

Tannoy
1225 17th Street
Denver, CO 80202

TDK
12 Harbor Park Drive
Port Washington, NY 11050

Technics
1 Panasonic Way
Secaucus, NJ 07094

Thorens
84-03 Cuthbert Road
Kew Gardens, NY 11415

Wharfedale
1230 Calle Suerte
Camarillo, CA 93012

Yamaha
6722 Orangethorpe Avenue
Buena Park, CA 90620

INDEX

A/B repeat, 48-49
A/B test, 162
Acoustic absorption, 114
Acoustic-suspension speakers,
    81-82, 162
Acoustic transmission-line
    speakers, 84-85, 183
Adjacent channel selectivity, 53
Adjacent channel spacing, 53
Air-suspension speakers, 81-82, 162
Alternate channel attenuation, 53
Alternate channel selectivity, 53
Alternate channel spacing, 53
Ambience, 6, 7-8
Ambience replication, 136
Ambience simulators, 133-37,
    162-63
Amplifiers, 9, 61-69
Amplitude modulation (AM), 51,
    57, 59
Analog, 45
Antenna, 163
Anti-skating, 163
Automatic music scan, 49
Automatic reverse, 163
Automatic turntable, 40-41, 163
Auto-reverse decks, 27-28
Auto space, 27, 49
Auxiliary bass radiators (ABRs), 83
Azimuth, 164

Baffle, 78-79
Baffle, infinite, 79-80, 173
Balance, 164
Balance control, 72

Bases, record player, 38-40
Bass-reflex system, 82-85, 164
Bearing friction, 36-37
Belt-drive turntables, 33-34
Bias, 14-15, 164
Budgeting, 138-42

Cabinets, 164-65
Capacitance, 73
Capstan, 165, 169
Capture radio, 53, 54-55, 165
Cartridge matching, 73
Cartridges, phono, 41-44
Cassette decks. See Tape decks
Cassettes
    blank, 29
    caring for, 160
    metal, 175
Catalog houses, purchasing
    equipment from, 144
CD. See Compact disc
Chain stores, purchasing
    equipment from, 143
Clipping, 165
Coloration, 165
Compact disc (CD) players, 45-50
    choosing 48
    features of, 48-50
    setting up, 147-48
    troubleshooting in, 159
Compact discs (CDs), 46, 161,
    165-66
Compander, 166
Compliance, 166
Compressor, 166

Consoles, 9
Convenience features
  of record players, 40-41
  of tape decks, 25-27
Crossover, 77-78, 166
Crosstalk, 166-67

Decibel, 167
Delete mode programming, 49
Department stores, purchasing
  equipment from, 143-44
Digital audio technology, 45-47,
  167
Digital sound, reproducing, 95-97
Digital-to-analog converter, 167
DIN (Deutsche Industrie Norm),
  32-33, 167
Dipole radiator, 90, 167-68
Direct-drive turntables, 34-35
Discount houses, purchasing
  equipment from, 144
Dispersion, speaker, 99-103, 105,
  168
Display features, 49, 168
Distortion, 7, 113-14, 168
Dolby HX Pro, 15
Dolby noise-reduction system,
  19-22, 168
Driver radiating area, 102-3
Drivers, 77, 168
Drone cones, 83
Dropout, 168-69
Dropout, CD, 169
Dynamic headroom, 169
Dynamic loudspeakers, 87-90
Dynamic range, 6, 7, 169-70
Dynamic range enhancers, 133

Efficiency, 170
Electronically equalized speakers
  85
Electrostatic loudspeakers, 86,
  88-90
Enclosures, speaker, 79, 180
  acoustic-suspension, 81-82
  acoustic transmission-line,

  84-85, 183
  alternative box designs for,
    84-85
  bass-reflex, 82-84
  electronically equalized, 85
  horn-loaded, 85
  infinite baffle in, 79-80
  resonance in, 80-81
  vented, 82, 183
Equalization, 16-17, 170
Equalizers, 127-33
Error correction, 170
Expander, 170

Feedback, 113-14
Feedback loop, 39
Filters, 73
Flutter, 18-19, 32-33, 170
Folded-horn speakers, 171
Frequency, 5, 6
Frequency modulation (FM), 51,
  59, 171
Frequency response, 171
Front loading, 171
Full logic, 23
Fundamental vibration, 6

Gap, 171
Graphic equalizers, 129, 171
Ground, 172

Harmonic distortion, 54, 68, 172
Harmonics, 6, 172
Headphones, 123-25
Headroom, 169, 172
Headroom extension (HX), 15
Hertz (Hz), 6, 172
Hi-fi specialty stores, purchasing
  equipment from, 142-43
High blend, 59-60
High-fidelity sound, 3-10
High-fidelity system, elements of,
  8-10
Hiss, 172-73
Horn-loaded speakers, 85
Hum, 173

Idler wheel, 173
Image enhancers, 135-36
Image rejection, 57
Impedance, 173
Index program search, 49
Infinite-baffle speakers, 79-80, 173
Integrated components, 63
Intermediate frequency (IF)
    rejection, 57
Intermodulation (IM) distortion,
    68-69, 173-74
ips (inches per second), 11, 174

Jacks, 174

Keyboard programming, 49

Level, 174
Linear tracking, 38
Load impedance, 64
Logic, 174
Loudness, 5, 7, 174
Loudness compensation, 174-75
Loudness control, 69-70
Loudness control, variable, 71
Loudspeakers. *See* Speakers

Mail order houses, purchasing
    equipment from, 144
Memory functions, 26
Metal tape, 175
Metering systems, 24-25
Microprocessors, 175
Midrange drivers, 76
Mode switch, 72
Modulation, 175
Monaural, 175
Monitoring, 13
Monitors, 175-76
Monophonic systems, 8
Moving-coil cartridge, 43
Multipath distortion, 54-55, 176
Multiplex, 176
Music-search systems, 27
Music standby feature, 49
Muting
    in amplifiers, 73-74
    in tuners, 58-59

Negative feedback, 69
Next/back feature, 49
Noise, 176
Noise reduction, 19-22
Noise-reduction systems, 133

Octave, 176
One-brand systems, 141-42
Oscillators, 34-35
Output-level controls, 26
Overtones, 6-7
Oxide, 176

Parametric equalizers, 129-30, 176
Passive radiators, 83
Pause feature, 177
Peak, 177
Peak hold, 25
Peak level search, 49
Phase, 177
Phase-locked loop (PPL), 177
Phone plug, 177
Phono cartridge, 41-44
Phono cartridge matching, 73
Phono plug, 178
Piezoelectric loudspeakers, 86, 91
Planar-dynamic loudspeakers, 90
Platter drive systems, 33-35
Playback head, 178
P-mount cartridge, 44
Ported enclosure, 82
Power, 178
Power output, 64-65
Power versus current, 67
Preamplifiers, 69-74, 178
Purchasing strategy, 138-44

Quadraphonic sound, 134
Quartz-referenced frequency
    synthesis, 57

Radiation pattern, 113
Random access programming,
    49-50
Real-time counter, 25-26
Real-time spectrum analyzer, 132
Receivers, 10, 63, 137
Record players

automation in, 40-41
bases for, 38-40
convenience features in, 40-41
parts of, 31-33
phono cartridges for, 41-44
platter drive systems in, 33-35
tonearms for, 36-38
troubleshooting in, 156-57
Records, caring for, 159-60
Remote control, 50
Repeat feature, 50, 179
Reproducer, 9
Resonance, 179
    speakers and, 80-81, 114-15
    tonearms and, 37-38
Reverberation, 179
RIAA (Record Industry
    Association of America), 62
Ribbon loudspeakers, 92
Rumble, 32-33, 179

Saturation, 179
Search modes, 50, 179
Selectivity, tuner, 52-53, 179-80
Sensitivity, tuner, 51-52, 180
Separation, 180
Separation ability, tuner, 55-56
Servo control, 34
Setting up equipment. See System
    setup
Signal, 180
Signal processors, 9, 126-37
    equalizers, 127-33
    image enhancers, 135-36
    video processors, 136-37
Signal-to-noise (S/N) ratio, 17-18,
    180
    in amplifiers, 66, 68
    in tuners, 53-54
Skating, 32, 37, 180
Sound
    elements of, 3-10
    problems with, 152-54
    see also Troubleshooting
Speakers
    accuracy, 104-5

acoustic-suspension, 81-82
buying guidelines for, 106-11
choosing, 103-11
design alternatives for, 85-94
design improvements in, 97-98
dispersion in, 99-103, 105
dynamic, 87-88
electrostatic, 88-90
enclosures for, 79-85, 180
hardware for, 105-6
mechanics of, 75-79
one-brand systems and, 141-42
piezoelectric, 91
placement of, 115-21
planar-dynamic, 90
power of, 94-98
ribbon, 92
room types and, 111-15
setting up, 146-47
Walsh, 93-94
wire for, 122-23
Stylus, 43, 181
Subwoofer, 181
System connectors, 122
System setup, 145-46
    of CD players, 147-48
    of equalizers, 132-33
    of speakers, 146-47
    of tape decks, 149-50
    of tuners, 149
    of turntables, 148-49

Tape counter, 25, 26
Tape decks, 11-12
    auto-reverse, 27-28
    bias in, 14-15
    convenience features in, 25-27
    dubbing, 29-30
    equalization in, 16-17
    metering systems in, 24-25
    noise reduction in, 19-22
    setting up, 149-50
    specifications for, 17-19
    tape heads in, 12-14
    transports in, 22-23
    troubleshooting in, 154-56

Tape heads, 12-14
Tape monitor, 72
Tapes
 blank, 29
 caring for, 160
 metal, 175
Tape timing, 50
Timbre, 6
Time-delay circuitry, 134-35
Time display feature, 50, 181
Time programming feature, 50
Timer operation, 26
Tonearms, 32, 36-38
Tone controls, 181-82
Tone defeat, 71
Total harmonic distortion (THD),
 54, 68, 172, 181
Tracing, 182
Tracking angle, 182
Tracking force, 43-44, 182
Transducer, 183
Transient, 183
Transmission-line speaker system,
 84-85, 183
Transport controls, 23
Transport design, 22-23
Troubleshooting, 151-54
 in CD players, 159
 in record players, 156-57
 in tape decks, 154-56
 in tuners, 157-58

Tuners
 capture ratio of, 54
 selectivity of, 52-53
 sensitivity of, 51-52
 separation ability of, 55-56
 setting up, 149
 signal-to-noise ratio of, 53-54
 specifications for, 51-57
 total harmonic distortion of, 54
 troubleshooting in 157-58
Tuning
 high blend, 59-60
 muting, 58-59
 tuning modes, 57-58
Turntables, 31
 automatic, 40-41, 163
 belt-drive, 33-34
 direct-drive, 34-35
 setting up, 148-49
Tweeters, 76, 102, 183

Variable loudness control, 71
Vented enclosures, 82, 183
Video processors, 136-37
Voice coil, 76, 183
Volume Unit (VU) meters, 24

Walsh loudspeakers, 93-94
Weighting, 183
Wire, speaker, 122-23, 146-47
Woofers, 76, 103, 183
Wow, 18-19, 32-33, 183

ABOUT THE AUTHOR

David Drucker has been editor of *The Complete Buyer's Guide to Stereo and Hi-fi Equipment* and *Audio/Video Buyer's Guide*, and has done consulting work for Onkyo, Speakerlab, and other manufacturers of high-fidelity equipment.

More BillboardBooks *for Music Enthusiasts*

THE BIG BEAT
by Max Weinberg. *Foreword by Bruce Springsteen*
Interviews with 14 great rock drummers reveal a compelling view of rock history. Includes Charlie Watts, Ringo Starr, Dave Clark, Levon Helm. 208 pages. 8¾ x 11. 36 B&W photos. Index. 0-8230-7571-0. $18.95 (paper).

THE BILLBOARD BOOK OF GOLD AND PLATINUM RECORDS
by Adam White
Here is the complete guide to all the artists and records to win gold and platinum awards over the past 30 years. 416 pages. 7 x 9¼. 225 B&W photos. 0-8230-7547-8. $19.95 (paper).

THE BILLBOARD BOOK OF NUMBER ONE COUNTRY HITS
by Tom Roland
Here, in one fact-filled volume, are the stories behind the hundreds of number one records on *Billboard's* country charts. A one-of-a-kind reference, blending history, interviews, and chart trivia. 592 pages. 7 x 9¼. 220 B&W photos. Index. 0-8230-7553-2. $19.95 (paper).

THE BILLBOARD BOOK OF NUMBER ONE HITS
2nd Ed., Revised and Enlarged by Fred Bronson
"A treasure trove of pop lore." — New York Times. Drawn from *Billboard's* Hot 100 charts since 1955, this popular volume has been updated to include 95 new songs — 700 entries in all — with anecdotes and chart data. 736 pages. 7 x 9¼. 700 B&W photos. Index. 0-8230-7545-1. $16.95 (paper).

THE BILLBOARD BOOK OF ONE-HIT WONDERS
by Wayne Jancik
Covers 625 one-hit wonders of the rock-and-roll era who rocketed to fame with a single song, then disappeared. Includes biographical details about performers and behind-the-information about the making of the record. 352 pages. 7 x 9¼. 150 B&W photos. Index. 0-8230-7530-3. $19.95 (paper).

THE BILLBOARD BOOK OF TOP 40 ALBUMS
Revised and Enlarged by Joel Whitburn

The ultimate guide to the most popular albums of all time, this compendium lists every album to reach the top 40 since 1955. Hundreds of new titles and 150 new photos have been added to this latest edition. 384 pages. 7 x 9¼. 150 B&W photos. 0-8230-7534-6. $19.95 (paper).

THE BILLBOARD BOOK OF TOP 40 HITS
4th Ed. by Joel Whitburn

"Wonderful browsing fare for music and trivia fans." — Booklist. Here's the latest updated edition of the ultimate reference book on all of the top singles and artists to hit Billboard's top 40 chart since 1955. An absolute must for pop music enthusiasts. 640 pages. 7 x 9¼. 300 B&W photos. Index. 0-8230-7527-3. $19.95 (paper).

THE BILLBOARD GUIDE TO HOME RECORDING
by Ray Baragary

This complete reference on home recording equipment and techniques takes the professional or amateur musician step-by-step through the process of putting together a studio and then making the best possible recordings. 256 pages. 7 x 9¼. 100 B&W illus. Index. 0-8230-7531-1. $18.95 (paper).

BILLBOARD'S HOTTEST HOT 100 HITS
by Fred Bronson

This latest fact-filled compendium combines pop charts with fascinating background information. Here are the most popular records in categories like artists, writers, producers, and record labels. Includes the top 3000 songs since 1955. 416 pages. 7 x 9¼. 200 B&W photos. Index. 0-8230-7570-2. $19.95 (paper).

THE BRAZILIAN SOUND
by Chris McGowan and Ricardo Pessanha

In the only authoritative book on the subject, entertaining text and eye-catching photos cover the music's history, instruments, popular styles, major performers, and international impact. 216 pages. 7 x 10. 150 B&W illus. Index. Discography. 0-8230-7673-3. $18.95 (paper).

BRITISH HIT SINGLES
by Paul Gambaccini, Tim Rice, and Jo Rice

For pop music aficionados, here is a complete listing of all singles — American or British — to hit the U.K. charts since 1952. 408 pages. 8 x 9½. 200 B&W photos. 0-8230-7572-9. $19.95 (paper).

JAZZ GIANTS
Compiled by K. Abé
"Perhaps the best single compilation of jazz photos in print." — Publishers Weekly. 280 pages. 10⅛ x 12⅝. 52 full-color photos, 307 B&W photos. Index. 0-8230-7536-2. $60.00 (cloth).

JAZZ ON RECORD: A HISTORY
by Brian Priestley
Starting with the early 78s and ending with today's compact discs, this absorbing study traces the develoment of jazz through the records themselves, examining the landmark recordings of key jazz artists. 240 pages. 5½ x 8¼. 36 B&W photos. Index. Discography. 0-8230-7562-1. $14.95 (paper).

MUSIC AND TECHNOLOGY
by H.P. Newquist
This much needed guide to the confusing array of revolutionary musical instruments — from guitar synthesizers to computer programs and the MIDI interface — not only explains how they work but gives advice on choosing the right ones and getting the most out of them. 208 pages. 7 x 9¼. 50 diagrams. Index. 0-8230-7578-8. $16.95 (paper).

ROCK MOVERS AND SHAKERS
Revised and Enlarged Edition by Dafyyd Rees and Luke Crampton
This *"exciting and highly recommended new work"* (Los Angeles Herald Examiner) offers 750 career chronologies of the stars of the rock era. Record collectors and trivia fans will welcome it as an entertaining and informative reference. 608 pages. 7⅛ x 9⅜. 125 B&W photos. 0-8230-7609-1. $19.95 (paper).

*You may order any of the Billboard Books
listed above directly from:*

BillboardBooks
P.O. Box 2013
Lakewood, NJ 08701

Please include $2.50 additional for shipping and handling.
(Please add appropriate sales tax in CA, DC, IL, MA, NJ, NY & TN.)